W9-CKA-993

HOOVER WAR LIBRARY PUBLICATIONS — NO. 13

Allied Propaganda and the Collapse of the German Empire in 1918

PUBLISHED UNDER THE AUTHORITY OF THE
DIRECTORS OF THE HOOVER WAR LIBRARY

HOOVER WAR LIBRARY PUBLICATIONS—No. 13

ALLIED PROPAGANDA AND THE COLLAPSE OF THE GERMAN EMPIRE IN 1918

By

GEORGE G. BRUNTZ

1938

STANFORD UNIVERSITY PRESS
STANFORD UNIVERSITY, CALIFORNIA
LONDON: HUMPHREY MILFORD
OXFORD UNIVERSITY PRESS

STANFORD UNIVERSITY PRESS
STANFORD UNIVERSITY, CALIFORNIA

LONDON: HUMPHREY MILFORD
OXFORD UNIVERSITY PRESS

THE BAKER AND TAYLOR COMPANY
55 FIFTH AVENUE, NEW YORK

MARTINUS NIJHOFF
9 LANGE VOORHOUT, THE HAGUE

THE MARUZEN COMPANY
TOKYO, OSAKA, KYOTO, SENDAI

PRINTED AND BOUND IN THE UNITED STATES
OF AMERICA BY STANFORD UNIVERSITY PRESS

FOREWORD

THERE is little exaggeration in saying that the World War led to the discovery of propaganda by both the man in the street and the man in the study. The discovery was far more startling to the former than to the latter, because the man in the study had predecessors who had laid firm foundations for his efforts to understand propaganda. The layman had previously lived in a world where there was no common name for the deliberate forming of attitudes by the manipulation of words (and word substitutes). The scholar had a scientific inheritance which included the recognition of the place of propaganda in society.

If we cannot say that the scholars were taken by surprise, however, we can at least admit that they were not entirely prepared. It is true that they had neglected to give the subject that sustained, comparative, and critical attention which leads to the production of an abundant literature under unified intellectual control. The specialists on abstract words about social processes were cut off from writers who described specific and limited aspects of propaganda. Political scientists and sociologists wrote about propaganda, but they wrote for one another. Students of advertising wrote for students of advertising. Revolutionary tacticians wrote for revolutionary tacticians. Missionaries wrote for missionaries. There was no common body of concepts, propositions, and procedures which unified the disparate efforts of isolated observers.

In the years before the World War there were several factors which combined to retard the candid, comprehensive analysis of the place of propaganda in public life. The study of propaganda (the manipulation of symbols) requires some familiarity with the significance of symbols, and at the beginning of the nineteenth century the intellectuals who were most interested in symbolic factors in social development were impressed by the comparative permanence of "racial" or "national" attitudes. They were prepared to minimize what could be done by the deliberate manipulation of symbols, since they were busy emphasizing the tenacity with which the distinctive "soul" of the people sought and found expression from age to age. They collected the folklore of the common people for the sake of exhibiting the mystic unity of the nation and the permanence of the "soul" which transcended the superficial accidents of a single historical epoch.

These intellectuals of the "conservative reaction" wrote during the early decades of the nineteenth century when an emphasis on predestination could be used to deflate the hopes of those who sought to accomplish revolutionary ends. Those who participated in the French revolutionary epoch relied on premeditation; they had every confidence in the power of the mind to shear through the accumulated error of the ages and to guide men toward happiness and truth. The intellectuals of the conservative reaction discovered predestination, and this they exalted at the expense of premeditation. Hence propaganda, as a form of premeditated activity, came in for scant consideration.

The social revolutionists who rose to challenge the "conservative reaction" turned the weapon of predestinarianism against its formulators. Seeking revolution instead of conservation, they agreed that the social process was determined in advance, but insisted that its predestined path lay toward revolution. New social forms were said to be adumbrating in the inner recesses of the predominating pattern of society. New subjective attitudes were treated as if they were largely predestined by the material forms of production. With so much emphasis upon predestination, the theoreticians of revolution put more emphasis upon "material factors" than upon "propaganda." They relied chiefly upon propaganda; but they deemphasized the role of propaganda in the revolutionary process itself.

We are not surprised to find that the established rulers of society were reluctant to attach very much importance to propaganda. The proponents (propagandists) of the established symbols, like "monarchy," did not have much to offer about the nature of the propaganda which they believed would defend monarchy. The apologists for "democracy" invoked the "will of the people," and were rather loath to describe how it was possible to manipulate the popular will.

The World War drastically changed the relationship of the established order of society to propaganda. The principal governments saw at once that psychological war must accompany economic war and military war. They took seriously the task of psychological mobilization, and they felt the impact of the psychological campaigns of their rivals.

The governments began to talk freely about propaganda. They could impute "propaganda" or "lying propaganda" not to themselves, but to the enemy; and they could refer to their own psychological manipulations as "information" or "truthful propaganda."

When the war came to an end, the Russian, German, and Italian revolutions kept the subject alive before the world public. It became perfectly clear that the practice of propaganda and the practice of talking about propaganda were dominating characteristics of this historical period.

Official emphasis upon propaganda during the postwar years has been connected with the hope of using "propaganda to end propaganda." Rulers cherish the hope of using propaganda to unify national faith; hence the monopolization of propaganda instrumentalities in states like Russia, Italy, and Germany. The ruling groups seek exclusive control of the focus of attention of the young, confident that when attitudes are once thoroughly crystallized around the symbols of the nation such attitudes will transmit themselves spontaneously, thus ending the necessity for relying on propaganda.

In view of the pivotal position of the World War in relation to propaganda, studies of the role of propaganda during the war are especially welcome. Exaggerations of many kinds have grown up around the function of propaganda during the struggle, and there is continual need for critical studies which view the act of propaganda in correct relationship to other political acts. Dr. Bruntz has written a volume which is distinguished alike by diligent research and discriminating judgment. Scholars everywhere will recognize that it is an admirable contribution to the history of the war and the knowledge of propaganda.

This is the book of a disciplined historian who has conducted his studies in the way best calculated to aid the advancement of knowledge. Dr. Bruntz is a specialist on the period; he is saturated in the records of modern history. He is also a specialist in comparative history ("social science"); he has sought to organize his knowledge of the period so clearly that his results would be directly available for comparative purposes. He has used general terms like "propaganda" in an understandable sense, and he has described the phenomena which he calls propaganda in a definitely circumscribed time and place. It is easy to compare what he has so carefully brought together with the work of other students who have described acts of propaganda in the same general setting or in quite different settings.

Dr. Bruntz has written the kind of history which is most helpful in advancing the common intellectual enterprise of all who concern themselves with the understanding of man and his acts.

HAROLD D. LASSWELL

THE UNIVERSITY OF CHICAGO
CHICAGO, ILLINOIS
January 31, 1938

PREFACE

UNTIL the appearance, in 1927, of Harold Dwight Lasswell's *Propaganda Technique in the World War,*[1] writers on the World War period had paid no particular attention to the subject of wartime propaganda. Lasswell's study was the first to describe the general use made of propaganda by belligerent nations in an effort to influence the populace in the country of an enemy.

The present study of the use that the Allied Powers made of propaganda as an instrument for the destruction of German morale was begun in 1928. Since that time Dr. Hans Thimme's *Weltkrieg ohne Waffen*[2] has made its appearance. Much of the research and practically the entire plan of organization of this study were completed before the appearance of Dr. Thimme's work.

To Mr. Philip McLean, the Reference Librarian of the Hoover War Library, and to Dr. Russell Buchanan, the writer is grateful for their willing co-operation in assembling material for this study. Professor Ralph H. Lutz, under whose direction this study was made, and Professor H. H. Fisher gave helpful suggestions of which the writer is deeply appreciative.

Of the illustrations provided, the Chart of German Civilian Morale is from a photostat of the original furnished by the United States War Department General Staff, and the rest are from originals in the Hoover War Library of Stanford University.

GEORGE G. BRUNTZ

LOS GATOS, CALIFORNIA
February 1, 1938

[1] Harold Dwight Lasswell, *Propaganda Technique in the World War* (New York, 1927).

[2] Dr. Hans Thimme, *Weltkrieg ohne Waffen, die Propaganda der Westmächte gegen Deutschland, ihre Wirkung und ihr Aufbau* (Stuttgart and Berlin, 1932).

TABLE OF CONTENTS

LIST OF ILLUSTRATIONS

Allied Propaganda and the Collapse of the German Empire

INTRODUCTION

Ein geistreich aufgeschlossenes Wort wirkt auf die Ewigkeit.—GOETHE

Worte sind heute Schlachten: Richtige Worte gewonnene Schlachten, falsche Worte verlorene Schlachten.—LUDENDORFF

In no other war in history have "words" been so important as in the world conflict of 1914–1918. Along with the development of airplanes, tanks, poison gases, and other marvels of military technique, a propaganda system for purposes of warfare was then set up which for scientific perfection rivaled the military system. Organized on a large scale and supplied with government funds, the propaganda instrumentalities of the warring nations carried on an intensive warfare by word of mouth, in the press, and through leaflets, books, and pamphlets.

This modern emphasis upon words and pictures resulted from the changes in the nature of war in recent times. In time of war today the co-operation of the people with the government is more necessary than it was a century or even half a century ago. In earlier times the result of the combat on the field of battle decided the fate of nations; but conditions of modern warfare have so enormously increased the value of the moral factors that war of late is less a question of armies pitted against armies than of nations against nations. The entire mental and moral forces, as well as the physical forces, of nations are hurled against the enemy. What Lincoln said about public sentiment is particularly true in time of war: "Public opinion is everything. With public sentiment nothing can fail, without it nothing can succeed." And John W. Dafoe quotes Hume as having said:

As force is always on the side of the governed, the governors have nothing to support them but opinion. It is therefore on opinion only that government is founded; and this maxim extends to the most despotic and most military government as well as to the most popular.[1]

Propaganda may be defined as the presentation of a case in such a way as to influence in a desired direction the opinions and actions of others. This is best accomplished by continually repeating expressions of a dominant fact, idea, or principle.

The ultimate objects of propaganda in war are threefold: (1) to overcome opposition to the war within the propagandizing nation and to bolster the spirit of its people; (2) to win favorable action or support from neutral states; and (3) to promote opposition to the conflict within the enemy state and thus to destroy the enemy's will to fight.

Every warring nation set up machinery, soon after it entered the World War, to create a favorable state of mind at home and to kill opposition to the war. Soon a great deal of attention was paid to propaganda in neutral countries, especially Switzerland, Holland, and the United States.[2] In the last years of the war the governments and finally also the military leaders came to the realization that it was necessary to attack the enemy with "word bullets" as well as with steel bullets. The destruction of the enemy morale by the dissemination of defeatist, disheartening, and, finally, revolutionary leaflets, pamphlets, books, etc., was undertaken in a vast and well-organized manner during the war's last years.

Thus to the main business in war of actual physical maiming was added the more subtle business of slaughtering enemy morale. The author of the verse:

> Nicht mit dem Rüstzeug der Barbaren,
> Mit Spiess und Schwert man nicht mehr haut;

[1] Quincy Wright (ed.), *Public Opinion and World Affairs* (Chicago, 1933), p. 4.

[2] England conducted a terrific campaign of propaganda in the United States through Wellington House before we entered the war. For the work of Wellington House, see James Duane Squires, *British Propaganda at Home and in the United States from 1914 to 1917* (Cambridge, 1935).

Nein! Motorbattieren fahren,
Und Bomben wirft der Aeronaut[3]

might well have added a second verse as follows:

Mit Gas Kanonen und Grenaten,
Die siegen am jeden Ort;
Mit Flugblättern für die Kameraden
Tut jetzt man ein schrecklicher Mord.

Although propaganda as an instrument of warfare had been developed on a large scale only in the World War, it had been used as such before. There is a striking parallel between the propaganda of the American Revolution and that of the World War. In the Revolution the Tories pointed out that the Revolution "flew in the face of experience, history, and divine sanction." The spirit of rebellion, argued the Tory propaganda, was stirred up by a few crafty men who had played upon the ignorance and passions of the mob. These conspirators were an "infernal, dark-designing group of men, bankrupt shopkeepers, outlawed smugglers, wretched banditti, the refuse of the dregs of mankind."[4]

When the Hessians came over to fight the Colonists for George the Third, it was proposed to win them over to the side of the Colonists with resolutions of Congress translated into German and floated over into the hands of their sentinels. A little tobacco, it was thought, would increase the allurement of their bait.[5] Occasionally, matters favorable to the American cause were published in the papers. To gain the friendship of the French in Canada the expenses of a French printer were ordered paid to remove his "family and type" to Montreal and there set up a "free press."[6]

[3] Introductory remarks to the Air Post collection of propaganda leaflets, Hoover War Library.

[4] Charles and Mary Beard, *Rise of American Civilization* (New York, 1927), I, 269.

[5] Claude van Tyne, *The War of Independence* (Boston, 1930), II, 318. See also *Letters of Continental Congress* (Burnet, ed.), Vol. I, Nos. 235, 237, 238; Vol. II, Nos. 59 and 63.

[6] Claude van Tyne, *op. cit.*, p. 319.

Nor was that all. Shipwrights in England were tempted with "bags of gold" to demand higher wages or to desert their work and migrate to America where they could be "happy as doves."[7] In order to get the British to desert to the Americans the Colonists circulated handbills among the British troops on Bunker Hill, offering them seven dollars a month, fresh provisions in plenty, health, freedom, ease, and a good farm should they desert and join the American Army. The British on their part gave promises of forgiveness, land, and money to all Americans who would come over to the British side.

But if propaganda was in this elementary stage at the time of the American Revolution, it reached the postgraduate stage in the World War. During the first two years of the war the governments were busy with the task of bringing public opinion at home to a war pitch and with the more strictly military side of the war. But by 1917, when the war had reached the entrenchment stage and fewer military movements were made, the attack of "word bullets" began. Organizations, official and unofficial, were set up in every warring nation to combat the enemy with words. These organizations soon made their efforts felt, and from the beginning of 1918 this battle of words grew more intense each month until it reached its point of greatest activity in September. This *"geistliche Schlacht"* did not cease until the collapse of the German Empire, with its Prussian military system and Junkerism, was complete. Never was it more clearly demonstrated that "Ein geistreiches Wort wirkt auf die Ewigkeit."

Thus, the World War was a struggle of arms and ideas, of words as well as of explosives and steel. When Lord Northcliffe took over the direction of propaganda in enemy countries for England in February 1918, he said that he hoped propaganda would be the means of appreciably shortening the duration of the war.[8] And again, in the spring of the same year, E. E.

[7] Van Tyne, *op. cit.,* p. 161.

[8] *The Times,* London, February 18, 1918.

Slosson said: "The war has resolved itself to a question of morale. Which people will lose heart first?"[9] While Hindenburg is quoted as having prophesied, "He who keeps his nerve the longest wins the war."

Just how the Allies organized this attack upon the morale of Germany, how they bombarded the German lines with leaflets, pamphlets, books, and newspapers, and what success they had in achieving their purpose the pages that follow will narrate.

[9] *Independent Magazine,* March 30, 1918.

CHAPTER I

PROPAGANDA ORGANIZATION

The conditions of modern warfare have now so enormously increased the value of the moral factor that it is less a question of armies being arrayed against armies than of nations against nations—so that the civilian front is scarcely, if any, less important than the fighting front.—T. L. GILMOUR, *Nineteenth Century and After*, LXXXV, 148

FRANCE

Immediately upon the outbreak of the war the civil government of France was overshadowed by the military, which at once gained control of the press and other agencies of public opinion. At the gathering of Paris journalists and the Council of Ministers on August 5, 1914, it was announced that no news concerning mobilization and movements of the army or even of diplomatic operations that would react unfavorably upon the spirit of the army was to be published in the French press.[1]

[1] *Le Petit Journal*, August 6, 1914. Practically the same was true in Germany. The following order from the chief of police in Hamburg is illustrative of the manner in which the military tried to control public opinion there. For a fine collection of documents on German censorship during the war, see R. H. Lutz, *The Fall of the German Empire* (Stanford University, 1932); the following document is from this collection (I, 176):

"FREIE UND HANSESTADT HAMBURG
(Police Department)

"Secret . . . .

HAMBURG, March 20, 1915. J.Nr. 2437/15.IV.M.

"Your attention is called to the order making the publication of all accounts of our military operations subject to the permission of the Chief of Staff of our Field Army. This order applies not only to detailed reports of our operations that are still going on but also to operations that have already been brought to an end.

"The permission of the Chief of the General Staff may be obtained by applying to the Intelligence Bureau of the General Staff, Berlin.

"DR. ROSCHER, Chief of Police."

Only the news sent out by the War Department was to be published.[2] The General Headquarters of the French Army set up an information section under the Military Intelligence Division, which issued bulletins and stories to the press. At first this bureau was under the leadership of Colonel Carence. M. André Tardieu also took a great interest in it and assumed the task of editing the daily *communiqués* and the official reports.[3]

No one at that time believed that the war would last long; hence a psychological attack upon the enemy was not considered at the outset of the war. The immediate need was a concentration upon the military phase, for an invading enemy had to be checked. The French government was consequently late in entering the field of propaganda activity against the enemy. To be sure, three days after the outbreak of the war the Foreign Minister, Viviani, had received an appropriation of 25 million francs for propaganda purposes.[4] But it was not until Briand came into power in 1916 that steps were taken by the Foreign Office to make use of this original appropriation. The War Department seemed equally neglectful of the psychological side of the war. Early in the war, however, a group of men in the Military Intelligence Section of the General Headquarters conducted unorganized and spasmodic attacks upon the enemy with leaflets. Out of the efforts of these men there gradually evolved the "Service de propagande," which became the propaganda agency of the General Headquarters. Under the direction of Etienne Fournol it remained the only official agency for the attack upon the enemy morale until 1916, when the French government established the "Maison de la presse" in Paris.

[2] France, Assemblée Nationale, *Annales de la Chambre des Députés,* Sessions ordinaires et extraordinaires de 1914. Tome II (Paris, 1915), p. 915.

[3] Jean de Pierrefeu, *French Headquarters 1915–1918,* tr. from the French by Major C. J. C. Street, O.B.E., M.C. (London, 1927), p. 85.

[4] France, Assemblée Nationale, *Annales de la Chambre des Députés, Documents parlementaires,* Tome LXXXXI, Session ordinaire de 1917, Deuxième partie (Paris, 1918), p. 1712, Annexe 3982, and p. 2030, Annexe 4084.

However, despite the fact that an official organization was slow in developing, propaganda was not entirely neglected. France was in a fortunate position at the outbreak of the war in that she had many existing organizations all over Europe designed to spread French culture. These could easily be converted into agencies for the dissemination of war propaganda. The most outstanding of these was the Alliance Française which had been founded in July 1883 by Pierre Foncin.[5] Three years later it had received the official approbation of the French government. Until the outbreak of the war it had steadily increased its membership, and by 1914 it comprised over 60,000 members.[6] During the war its chief efforts were devoted to war propaganda. Among its members were almost all of the high French officials, ministers, and generals. Jules Gautier, a member of the Cabinet Council, was its president during the war period.

The Alliance Française published a *Bulletin* regularly on the first and the fifteenth of each month, the first appearing in November 1914.[7] This was a news sheet intended to give war information to people all over Europe. Published first in Spanish and French, it came out in seven different languages in March 1915, and by April 1916 it appeared in French, German, English, Danish, Dutch, Swedish, Spanish, Portuguese, Italian, and Greek.[8] With agents in all of the neutral countries, the Alliance was in a position to get information of all kinds and to use it to good advantage in its *Bulletin*. It published many atrocity stories, and in some numbers the propaganda is directed

[5] Edgar Stern-Rubarth, "Methods of Political Propaganda," in Quincy Wright (ed.), *Public Opinion and World Politics* (Chicago, 1933), p. 102.

[6] Dr. George Huber, *Die französische Propaganda im Weltkrieg gegen Deutschland 1914 bis 1918* (Munich, 1928), p. 35. Dr. Huber has made the most thorough study of all phases of French wartime propaganda that has appeared thus far. Hereafter cited *Französische Propaganda.*

[7] *Bulletin de L'Alliance française,* No. 1, November 1, 1914.

[8] A fairly complete file of the *Bulletin* can be found in the Hoover War Library at Stanford University.

at the Alsatians and Lorrainers in the German Army, calling on them to desert to the French and thus help free their provinces from the yoke of the Prussian militarists.

As the war progressed, the organization of the Alliance Française expanded into a number of different bureaus or departments. There were eight of these, of which only one concerns us in this study. This was the one for the dissemination of propaganda among various religious groups. The Roman Catholics, for instance, were organized to propagandize among the Catholics in neutral and enemy countries, the Protestants among Protestants, and the Jews among Jews. Each of these three religious faiths had an active propaganda committee.[9]

The most active and the largest of these three committees was that of the Catholic faith, the "Comité catholique de propagande française à l'étranger." Organized in 1915, the Comité catholique soon had over 50 members, including the Archbishops of Rheims and of Paris and Denys Cochin, member of the French Academy and Minister of State. The head of this committee was M. A. Baudrillart, rector of the Catholic Institute of Paris.[10]

The Comité catholique entered into a publication agreement with Bloud et Gay in Paris. The most notable publication of this committee was *La Guerre allemande et le catholicisme.* This collection of essays by persons of high estate appeared in six different languages — French, Spanish, Portuguese, Italian, English, and German. Over 65,000 copies of it were distributed *gratis* by April 1916. Many of the essays were published singly in pamphlet form also and given wide circulation.

Branches of the Comité catholique were organized in most of the neutral countries, and on March 7, 1917, a general organization, "L'union sacrée de la propaganda," was effected, which had charge of all propaganda work of the committee. The principal duties of the central committee were to edit and

[9] Huber, *op. cit.,* p. 40.

[10] M. Baudrillart tells the story of his campaign in his *Une campagne française* (Paris, 1917).

distribute propaganda, send missions to foreign countries, and take action through the press.[11] The burden of the propaganda was that the war was a religious war, a war by Prussia against Catholicism; and an appeal was made not only to Catholics generally but specifically to Catholics in southern Germany.

Similar activities were carried on by the "Comité protestant de la propagande française à l'étranger," which sprang up in September 1915. Less is known of this body, since it was almost completely eclipsed by the very active Catholic organization. It sought especially to influence the Protestants in neutral countries by acquainting them with the cause of the conflict and with Germany's imperialist designs.[12] It tried also to show that Germany's struggle was not only against Catholicism but against religion in general. Examples of this type of propaganda are Doumergue's *L'Allemagne religieuse,* and Monnier's *Le Dieu allemand et la réforme.*[13]

André Weiss, professor of the faculty of law at Paris, was the head of this committee. At first the Comité protestant française worked in co-operation with the Protestant publication, *Foi et vie;* but by December 1915 it had its own monthly publication, the *Bulletin protestant française.*[14]

The last of this trio of religious propaganda committees was the "Comité d'action auprés des juifs des pays neutres," more commonly known as Comité Israélite. M. Leygues was the president of this group, and M. Sylvain Levi the vice-president.[15] The Jews of Switzerland, Holland, the Scandinavian and the Balkan countries were especially friendly with France, and this fact made it easy to propagandize there. The aim of the propaganda of the Jewish committee was to declare that, whereas Germany was the land of anti-Semitism, the

[11] Jean Vic, *La Littérature de guerre, manuel méthodique et critique des publications de langue française* (5 vols, Paris, 1923), III, 344; also *Almanack catholique pour 1920,* p. 431.

[12] Huber, *op. cit.,* p. 41.

[13] Baudrillart, *Une campagne française,* p. 37.

[14] *Ibid.,* p. 38.

[15] *Ibid.,* p. 39; also Huber, *op. cit.,* p. 43.

Jews in France and England had nothing to fear; further, that, not only had the Jews nothing to fear from the Allied countries but they could actually expect protection there, and hence a victory for the Allies meant a victory for the Jews.[16]

During the first two years of the war, French unofficial propaganda organizations seemed to spring up spontaneously. However, since their work for the most part was to arouse enthusiasm among the French people and to destroy opposition to the war at home, we need not go into detail regarding them. Suffice it to say that on March 7, 1917, some 30,000 societies, with more than eleven million members, banded themselves together in a "Union des grandes associations contre la propagande ennemie."[17] At the head of this vast organization were Paul Deschanel and the historian, Ernest Lavisse.[18]

The French government, though depending a great deal upon private organizations to carry on the psychological warfare, likewise set up in 1914 a propaganda agency known as the "Bureau de la presse et de l'information," under the direction of the Minister of Foreign Affairs. During the first two years of the war, however, no systematic plan of organization or attack was adopted by the government. Propaganda agencies in this or that official bureau also sprang up, the largest of which was the "Service de propaganda" under Etienne Fournol.[19] When Briand, who of all the French statesmen was most convinced of the value of propaganda, became Prime Minister of Foreign Affairs in October 1915, he laid plans for a central propaganda organization and in January 1916 set up the

[16] Other propaganda organizations in France were the Comité Franco-Amérique, the Bibliothèque France-Amérique, and the Ligue Française de propagande (working in South America).

[17] Jean Vic, *La Littérature de guerre,* III, 344.

[18] *Ibid.;* also G. Demartial, *La Guerre de 1914: comment on mobilisa les consciences* (Rome, Paris, etc., 1922), p. 186 n.

[19] Hans Thimme, *Weltkrieg ohne Waffen* (Stuttgart and Berlin, 1932), p. 7. Dr. Thimme's study is one of the most authoritative works yet to appear on the subject. He had access to the official archives in Germany while preparing his work.

Maison de la presse in a six-story building of some two hundred rooms in Rue François Premier in Paris.[20] Under the direct control of the Minister of Foreign Affairs, as it was, this became the official French agency for the conduct of propaganda. Gradually all of the propaganda agencies were merged with the Maison de la presse. The Paris Chamber of Commerce bulletins, the *Bulletin de l'Alliance française,* the *Bulletin de l'Asie,* the *Bulletin de l'Afrique française,* as well as the productions of the Comité catholique, Comité protestant, and the Comité Israélite, were issued by the Maison de la presse.[21]

Beginning its activities under the leadership of M. Berthelot, this official organization was at first divided into four main sections. The first was the Section diplomatique, which had four subdivisions: (*a*) an agency for the receipt of French and foreign journals; (*b*) an agency which conducted a daily two-hour telephone service with Switzerland, England, Italy, and Spain and which had telegraphic connections with the United States, Russia, Roumania, Greece, Denmark, and Holland; (*c*) the Bureau d'études, which supplied information, with proper comments, on the happenings of the day; and (*d*) the radio division, which sent out dispatches eight times daily from the Eiffel Tower, from Lyons, and from Carnarvon, Wales.

The second main division was the Section militaire, which was directly connected with General Headquarters. This section had the same duties in the military field which the diplomatic section had in the diplomatic field. It kept the French and foreign journals informed concerning the war situation. It also gave to the press diaries and letters which were found on German soldiers, and other materials having propaganda value.

The Section de traduction et d'analyse de presse étrangère

[20] Baudrillart, *op. cit.,* p. 35. It was on the top floor of this building that Belgium atrocity pictures were made from wooden or wax figures.

[21] Baudrillart, *op. cit.,* p. 36; also Huber, *op. cit.,* p. 32.

was the third main division. It concerned itself with the translation and analysis of reports from the most representative papers of Europe. This section was subdivided according to countries and languages, and counted among its workers university professors and specialists. Each of the divisions—for German, English, Spanish, Portuguese, Italian, Greek, Roumanian, Scandinavian, Slavic, etc. — gave weekly or fortnightly reviews of the press of the country with which it was concerned.

Finally, there was a section of the Maison de la presse called the Service de propagande, which was connected with the Military Intelligence Division of the General Staff. This section followed the trend of opinions in the most important countries. It contained a section for the neutral countries bordering on Germany or Austria, so that information could be secured from the enemy countries as well as from the neutrals.[22] It took charge of the distribution of propaganda leaflets, books, photographs, and films in the neutral and enemy countries. It had agents in all the neutral countries, receiving instructions and information from headquarters in Paris.

For its financing the Maison de la presse was dependent upon government appropriations. It had at its disposal the major portion of the twenty-five million francs which, three days after war was declared in 1914, had been voted for propaganda purposes by the Chamber and the Senate.[23]

Despite this organization there was still no unity in the propaganda activity of France, for the various ministries—Foreign Affairs, Commerce, and War—were still doing independent work. When Clemenceau came into power in Octo-

[22] Huber, *op. cit.*, pp. 30 ff.; also *Hinter der Kulissen des französischen Journalismus, von einem Pariser Chefredakteur* (Berlin, 1925), pp. 266 ff. It is regrettable that one has to rely so much on German sources for information on the Maison de la presse. Though many French writers refer to it, there is no official report of its work available.

[23] *Vide supra*, p. 9.

ber 1917 the Section militaire was handed over to the Minister of War. The remaining sections were put under M. Haguenin, who was later replaced by M. Klobukowski.[24]

Within the War Ministry there grew up the propaganda agency which was to become the center of the moral offensive against Germany—the Service de la propagande aérienne, often cited as "Service aérienne," established by agreement between the General Headquarters and the War Ministry in August 1915.[25] Its duties were to get leaflets into the hands of the Germans.

At first it was under the direction of M. Tonnelat, an assistant interpreting officer. In November 1915 Hansi was attached to the service. Hansi, or Jean Jacques Waitz, his real name, was an Alsatian who had fled to France in the summer of 1914 to escape punishment at the hands of the German authorities for seditious propaganda. He was as enthusiastic a propagandist as Lord Northcliffe and had an advantage over the English journalist in that he wrote very beautiful and highly idiomatic German. His work as an interpreter at Epinal gave him opportunities for conversations with German war prisoners and thus he gained a thorough understanding of the psychology of the German soldier.[26]

It was while he was engaged in the work as interpreter at war prison camps that he became convinced that something should be done to shatter the belief among the Germans that the Fatherland was on the defensive. When the book, *J'accuse,* by Grelling, came into his hands, the idea occurred to him to distribute the contents of this book over the German lines.[27] This part of his technique Hansi had learned from the Ger-

[24] Vira B. Whitehouse, *A Year as Government Agent* (New York and London, 1920), p. 65.

[25] Hansi et Tonnelat, *À Travers les lignes ennemies, Trois années d'offensive contre le moral allemand* (Paris, 1922), p. 13. The entire story of the work of the Service aérienne is well described here.

[26] Huber, *op. cit.,* p. 57.

[27] Hansi et Tonnelat, *À Travers les lignes ennemies,* p. 10.

mans themselves, who, in September 1914, had dropped leaflets over Nancy in an effort to overawe its civilian population.

The difficulty of presenting the material of a 400-page book to the Germans seemed almost too great for even Hansi's enthusiastic mind. But he invented a letter, supposedly found in the diary of a prisoner of war; in this letter the German soldier, writing to a friend, marvels at the good treatment he is receiving and tells about the book, *J'accuse,* which he had found and in which the German war guilt is clearly shown.[28] These letters were distributed along the entire Western Front. When the Propaganda Bureau was set up under the control of the War Ministry, all leaflets had to be approved by that ministry; and in this way Hansi's *Briefe eines Kriegsgefangenen* was brought to the War Ministry, where his talent was recognized. It was then—in August 1915—that he was appointed to assist Tonnelat in the organization of the Service de la propagande aérienne.[29]

This propaganda bureau was a small but enthusiastic organization, never having more than ten people on its staff at one time. A committee composed of Dupuis, the Abbé Wetterle, and Fournol met once a week to decide upon policies, and the Imprimerie nationale (the national printing office) was at the disposal of the Bureau.

This was the situation of the French propaganda activities when Lord Northcliffe became the head of the British propaganda organization in 1918. The English and French until then had been working independently. Realizing the need for greater co-operation between the French and the English propagandists, Northcliffe called a conference at London in March 1918. The French delegate, appointed by the Minister of Foreign Affairs, was M. Moysset.[30] But the Service de la propagande aérienne[31] was under, not the Ministry of

[28] *Ibid.,* p. 11. [29] *Ibid.*

[30] Hansi et Tonnelat, *op. cit.,* p. 160.

[31] Hereafter referred to as *Service aérienne.*

Foreign Affairs, but the War Ministry; hence no representative from this division was present at the conference at first. However, when the matter of air propaganda came up, a delegate from the Service aérienne was requested. Tonnelat was now sent to London, where Hansi's work was openly praised.[32]

The result of the conference was the reorganization of the propaganda agencies in France and the creation of the Centre d'action de propagande contre l'ennemie, which enveloped Hansi's organization. Thus, to the end of the war France had two official propaganda organizations: the Maison de la presse, which concerned itself particularly with atrocity propaganda, propaganda in neutral countries, and propaganda among the Catholics, Jews, and Protestants in all Europe, Germany included; and the Centre d'action de propagande contre l'ennemie, which concerned itself with the tasks of tearing down the morale of the enemy, inducing German soldiers to desert, and weakening the power of resistance both at the front and among the German people behind the lines.[33]

ENGLAND

The British were not so quick to recognize the value of propaganda as an instrument of warfare as were the French. This was perhaps due to the geographical location of the British Isles, for it must be remembered that no enemy territory bordered upon England. Hence, for her the immediate task was not so much the dissemination of offensive propaganda abroad as the distribution of patriotic propaganda within England. Opposition to the war at home had to be conquered before propaganda against the enemy could be attempted. The chief agency for carrying on a patriotic campaign in England was the Central Committee for National Patriotic Associations, which was formed in the latter part of August 1914. This or-

[32] Hansi et Tonnelat, *op. cit.*, p. 161.

[33] *Ibid.*, p. 170.

ganization induced certain people to lecture and write upon the causes of the war and to "justify both historically and morally, England's position in the struggle." It also took steps to inform the neutral countries of the reasons which "inevitably compelled this country to intervene swiftly and with all her strength."[34] The honorary president of the Central Committee was Prime Minister Asquith, the vice-presidents were the Earl of Rosebery and the Rt. Honorable Arthur Balfour, and the headquarters were at 8 Carlton House Terrace.[35]

By organizing lectures, patriotic clubs, and rallies in the cities and in country districts throughout the Empire the Central Committee did everything possible to overcome opposition to the war among the subjects of the British king. Subcommittees for each of the different parts of the Empire were formed. There was also a Neutral Countries Subcommittee, which, though begun on a private basis in August 1914, was taken over by the Central Committee the following month.[36] The method of this subcommittee was as far as possible one of direct personal approach. Material was sent out, not in the name of the committee, but in the name of various distinguished Britishers, whose acquaintances, colleagues, fellow workers, or business associates in neutral lands received—oftentimes unwillingly—propaganda material prepared and sent by the Neutral Countries Subcommittee. By this means every possible variety of interests in the neutral countries—philosophical, educational, religious, scientific, philanthropic, artistic, legal, medical, agricultural, mining, banking, and commercial—was reached.[37] Some 250,000 pamphlets, booklets, and other publications were thus distributed between August 1914 and January 1, 1916.[38]

The Central Committee was also in close connection with

[34] *Report of the Central Committee for National Patriotic Organizations* (London, 1916), p. 3; hereafter cited as *C.C.N.P.O.*

[35] *C.C.N.P.O.*, p. 26.

[36] *Ibid.*, p. 17.

[37] *C.C.N.P.O.*, p. 18.

[38] *Ibid.*, p. 22.

English universities, which helped to produce literature. Oxford, for instance, printed the "Oxford Leaflets."[39] However, the most influential piece of literature published by the committee was *J'accuse,* which was distributed in the original German as well as in the French and English translations.[40]

Another organization which devoted its energies to arousing the patriotic spirit of the British people was the War Aims Committee, founded in June 1917. Lloyd George, the Prime Minister at that time, and Asquith were the heads of this committee. It sought especially to combat pacifism.[41] Late in 1917 it was taken over by the War Cabinet, and subsequently it worked in close connection with the Ministry of Information.[42] From March 1918, when the final co-ordination of the various phases of British propaganda was completed, to the end of the war, this committee had charge of all propaganda within Great Britain.[43]

The first official propaganda organization in England for activity elsewhere was the War Propaganda Bureau, established by the Foreign Office in the latter part of 1914. It concerned itself with the distribution of leaflets, pamphlets, and other material in Allied and neutral countries. The director of this bureau was the Rt. Hon. C. F. Masterman, and its headquarters were at Wellington House, the office of the National Health Insurance Company. The existence of this committee was unknown to the general public, as it was thought best

[39] This was a collection of essays including eighty-seven titles, most of which gave a strong patriotic tinge to their otherwise authentic information. The complete list of titles is given in G. W. Prothero, *A Select List of Books Concerning the Great War* (London, 1923), pp. 344–48.

[40] *C.C.N.P.O.*, p. 24.

[41] It was this committee that published Lichnowsky's *Memoirs* in England, over a million copies of which were distributed by May 1918 (*The Times* [London], May 9, 1918).

[42] Dearle, *Dictionary of Official War-Time Organizations* (London, 1928), p. 128.

[43] *The War Cabinet Report of the Year 1918,* found in *Reports: Commissions . . . .,* XXX (1919), 35.

to attach as little publicity as possible to its operations at home and in Allied and neutral countries.[44]

Although Wellington House directed most of its efforts toward winning the sympathy of the neutrals, especially Holland, Switzerland, and the United States, it also concerned itself somewhat with the task of sending propaganda into Germany. This it did by delivering material to people in Holland who were known to be sympathetic with the Allied cause. These people relayed the propaganda to their friends in Germany. Dr. Hans Thimme tells how a letter from Wellington House to the British Consul-General in Holland fell into German hands in October 1917. The letter stated in part:

> We have prepared lists of all protestant clerics in Holland, so that the examples can be sent directly from here. We have printed 15,000 pieces. About 4,000 will be needed here for our list and the other 11,000 we are sending you. We should be very happy if you could pass them on to people who are interested in them.[45]

Although the German postal inspection agencies did all they could to prevent the influx of propaganda from Holland into Germany, leaflets and pamphlets addressed to private individuals in Germany continued to cross the border. A Freiburg University professor, Dr. Krebs, complained in November 1917 that one of his overindustrious Dutch friends had sent him another heavy packet of British anti-German propaganda.[46] Then, too, smuggling of leaflets into Germany was an active business. S. A. Guest, who was connected with Wellington House, undertook on his own initiative to establish smuggling agencies in Holland, Switzerland, and the Scandinavian countries.[47]

[44] Rear-Admiral Sir Douglas Brownrigg, Bt., *Indiscretions of a Naval Censor* (New York, 1920), p. 52 n.; also *Times History of the War* (London, 1920), XXI, 328.

[45] Hans Thimme, *Weltkrieg ohne Waffen,* p. 16.

[46] *Ibid.,* p. 16.

[47] *Times History of the War,* XXI, 330; also *Northcliffe, die Geschichte des Englische propaganda Feldzuges,* p. 10.

Although Wellington House was very active in its particular field, the need for an expansion of the work was soon realized. With the elevation of Lloyd George to the Prime Ministry in December 1916 there came a reorganization of official British propaganda activity. A Department of Information was created[48] which gathered together the various organizations which had sprung up in England since the beginning of the war. This department was first under the direction of Mr. C. H. Montgomery, of the Foreign Office, who was responsible for getting facilities for government guests and for Allied journalists who were invited to visit places of interest in England. Working with Mr. Montgomery was Mr. G. H. Mair, who had especially to do with the visits of Allied and neutral journalists to the fleet which he arranged with the Naval Censors.[49] Presently the whole department was placed under Colonel John Buchan and was organized into four subdivisions as follows: (1) Wellington House, which was now to continue producing and distributing material for neutral and domestic consumption; (2) the Cinema Division, under the direction of Mr. Mair, who, as stated above, also concerned himself with the entertainment of foreign visitors; (3) the Political Intelligence Division, which

[48] It is difficult to say exactly when this was founded. No two authorities agree. N. B. Dearle, *Dictionary of Official War-Time Organizations,* p. 128, gives February 1917, while on the floor of the House of Commons on August 5, 1918, it was stated that the Department was begun in January 1917. In the *Reports from the Select Committee on National Expenditure,* H.C., No. 132, 1918, pp. 36–37, the date is given as December 1916. The exact date is not important. It is sufficient to say that at the beginning of 1917 the English government officially entered the field of propaganda against the German morale.

[49] Rear-Admiral Brownrigg, *Indiscretions of a Naval Censor,* p. 94. One member of Parliament, Mr. Lief Jones, speaks with sarcasm about the loose way in which the work was organized and the money spent by the department. He characterized the department as "the imaginative department, the fiction department, the body which dresses up the facts for presentment to the public, a most important function and one leaving scope for individual imagination." Hansard, *Parliamentary Debates,* 5th ser., CIX, 949, August 5, 1918.

was to gather information on the state of public opinion throughout the world; and (4) the News Division, which gave war news to the general public.[50]

To assist Colonel Buchan an Advisory Committee consisting of Lord Northcliffe, Lord Burnham, Mr. Robert Donald, and Mr. C. P. Scott was appointed. When Lord Northcliffe went on his mission to America, Lord Beaverbrook was appointed to the committee, and later Sir George Riddell was added to it. Shortly afterward the committee and the department were placed under the supervision of Sir Edward Carson.[51]

This plan of organization was never satisfactory for there was a great deal of friction between the committee and Colonel Buchan. Northcliffe attacked in his editorials the whole plan of organization in general and Buchan in particular. Commenting on the need for a more efficient publicity bureau he said:

> There are too many governmental departments dealing with "publicity," but there is no central authority with full responsibility. The first essential is to call such an authority into being. We were in high hopes when Mr. Buchan was created "Director of Information," a sufficiently comprehensive title. But Mr. Buchan turns out to be virtually a subordinate of the Foreign Office where he works. . . . . His work, we are sure, is of greatest national importance. The point is that it is merely that of an addition to the existing "publicity" departments, not that of a supreme co-ordinating agency. . . . . What is needed is some authority, working for choice as head of a reconstructed Press Bureau which will supervise and control the activities of all the various departments, including Mr. Buchan's present office, which deals with the Press at home and abroad.[52]

These differences between the department and the Advisory Committee resulted in another attempt at reorganization. On

[50] *Ibid.*, CIX, 951, August 5, 1918.

[51] Hansard, *Parliamentary Debates*, 5th ser., CIII, 917; also *Reports from Committees*, Vol. IV, 1918, Sixth Report of the Select Committee on National Expenditure.

[52] *The Times* (London), August 7, 1917.

February 13, 1918, the Foreign Office asked certain members of the Advisory Committee of the Department of Information to undertake the direction of the various branches of the department. Lord Northcliffe was now made Director of Propaganda in Enemy Countries, Mr. Robert Donald was made Director of Propaganda in Neutral Countries, Mr. John Buchan became Director of Intelligence, General A. D. MacRae became Director of Administration, Sir William Jury was put in charge of Cinematograph Propaganda, and Sir Roderick Jones was made Deputy Director of Allied and Foreign Propaganda.[53] Thus the Department of Information as such was abolished, and in March 1918 the branches named were brought under one head with the creation of the Ministry of Information under the direction of Lord Beaverbrook. This new Ministry concerned itself entirely with publicity in Allied, neutral, and enemy countries, and was responsible not to the Foreign Office but directly to the War Cabinet.[54]

Thus England had, from March 1918 to the end of the war, two chief propaganda agencies: the Ministry of Information, which dealt with publicity in countries outside of England; and the National War Aims Committee, which concerned itself with patriotic propaganda within England and was independent of the Ministry of Information.[55]

One division only of the Ministry of Information concerns us in this study, Lord Northcliffe's Division of Propaganda in Enemy Countries. That genius of propaganda took over his duties as Director of Propaganda in Enemy Countries immediately and gathered around him a staff of able journalists and political writers. Sir Campbell Stuart was made deputy director of the department and deputy chairman of the Advisory Committee. The other members of the committee were: Colonel the Earl of Denbigh, C.V.O.; Mr. Rob-

[53] Hansard, *Parliamentary Debates,* 5th ser., CIII, 917.

[54] *The Times* (London), March 19, 1918.

[55] *The War Cabinet Report of the Year 1918,* in *Reports: Commissions,* . . . ., XXX (1919), p. 35.

ert Donald (then editor of the *Daily Chronicle*); Sir Roderick Jones, K.B.E. (managing director of Reuter's agency); Sir Sidney Low; Sir Charles Nicholson, Bt., M.P.; Mr. James O'Grady, M.P.; Mr. H. Wickham Steed; Mr. H. G. Wells; Mr. H. K. Hudson, C.B.E., who acted as secretary; and Mr. C. S. Kent, who acted as financial controller and accounting officer.[56]

The headquarters of the department, first established at Adastral House, after July was at Crewe House, the town mansion of the Marquis of Crewe, who had placed it at the disposal of the government for war purposes.[57]

The department was divided into two main branches, one for the production and the other for the distribution of propaganda materials. The production branch was subdivided into German, Austro-Hungarian, and Bulgarian sections.[58] Mr. Wickham Steed and Mr. R. W. Seton-Watson, who knew the history and psychology of the people of Austria-Hungary, were made co-directors of that subdivision, while Mr. H. G. Wells became the first chairman of the German section. The propaganda in the Near East was left to the Near East section of the Ministry of Information.

These men immediately set up a program of attack. It was decided that since Austria-Hungary was the weakest, the propaganda campaign should start there. H. Wickham Steed aimed to convince the different races of the Hapsburg monarchy that the Allies were determined to secure democratic freedom for them. The subject nationalities were to be encouraged to break away from the Hapsburg empire. Such statements as "self-government" and "autonomous development" were to be avoided because they had unpleasant associations in Austria-Hungary and tended to discourage the friends

[56] Sir Campbell Stuart, *Secrets of Crewe House* (London and New York, 1920), p. 10. The story of Northcliffe's propaganda campaign is graphically told in this book.

[57] *Ibid.*, p. 11; also *Times History of the War,* XXI, 344.

[58] *Ibid.*

of the Allies. Instead, the expression "government by consent of the governed" was to be used extensively.[59]

Wickham Steed and Seton-Watson went to Italy, where they helped to organize the Rome Congress of the Subject Nationalities of Austria-Hungary. This congress itself was a propaganda move, for Wickham Steed not only worked among the delegates while the congress was in session but also delivered a speech to the congress in which he outlined the plan of the Allies to free the subject races from the Hapsburg yoke.[60] In addition, a Central Inter-Allied Commission was set up at Italian Headquarters, from which the campaign among the Austro-Hungarian troops against the Hapsburgs was launched in the field.

Concerning the attack upon the German morale, about which he was getting anxious, Lloyd George wrote to Northcliffe in May 1918:

> It seems to me that you have organized admirable work in your Austrian propaganda. . . . . I trust that you will soon turn your attention towards German propaganda along the British and French fronts. I feel sure that much can be done to disintegrate the morale of the German Army along the same lines as we appear to have adopted with great success in the Austro-Hungarian Army.[61]

The problem of influencing the minds of the German soldiers, however, was quite different from that so easily solved on the Austrian front. While the Austrian armies contained large numbers of men who were already disloyal, who were anxious for the war to end, and who hoped to see the Hapsburg monarchy collapse, the German troops were practically all of the same nationality and the same racial stock and were proud to be Germans.[62] Northcliffe realized that an entirely different appeal would have to be framed for the Germans. "Our biggest asset," he said, "is the fact that the American

[59] H. Wickham Steed, *Through Thirty Years* (Garden City, New York, 1924), II, 188–89. [60] *Ibid.*, p. 210.

[61] Hamilton Fyfe, *Northcliffe, An Intimate Biography* (London, 1930), p. 241. [62] *Ibid.*, p. 242.

troops are arriving. 'You are almost at the end of your resources in man-power. The Allies have only just begun to pump men out of an enormous new reservoir of inexhaustible depth.' That is what we shall tell the German soldiers."[63]

Thus, the German soldiers were to be bombarded with propaganda intended to make them feel that their task was hopeless. Leaflets were sent out to show the advance the English manufacturers had made in lines such as lenses, scientific instruments, dyes, etc., in which Germany had been supreme before the war. Wells's aim, as outlined by his famous "Memorandum," which he submitted to Northcliffe, was to set up an organization of free nations against Germany and then bring home to the German people the fact that a world organization existed which was pledged to seek the overthrow of the German militarists. He proposed that this organization should control the raw materials and the shipping, and that it should have power to exclude for an indefinite period the enemy, or even neutrals, until they should subscribe to and give pledges of their acceptance of the principles of the "League of Nations." He aimed further to emphasize: "that nothing stands between the enemy peoples and lasting peace except the predatory designs of their ruling dynasties and military and economic castes; that the design of the Allies is not to crush any people but to assure them the freedom of all on the basis of self-determination."[64] Though he did not mention the overthrow of the German government as one of his aims, he implied as much. "The fact has to be faced," he said, "that while the present German Government remains, no such economic resumption is possible."[65] And further:

And since it is impossible to hope for any such help or cooperation from the Germany of the Belgian outrage, the Brest-Litovsk Treaty,

[63] Hamilton Fyfe, *op. cit.*, p. 242.

[64] Sir Campbell Stuart, *Secrets of Crewe House*, pp. 65–86, gives a complete text of the Wells Memorandum.

[65] *Ibid.*, p. 78.

the betrayal of Ukrania, THE CHANGING OF GERMANY[66] becomes a primary aim, the primary war aim for the Allies.[67]

Mr. Wells, however, severed his relations with Crewe House before he could put his ideas into practice. Differences arose between him and Northcliffe over the discrepancy between the views which the Director of Propaganda was supposed to hold as to the right method of making the Germans dissatisfied and the tone adopted toward them by the Northcliffe press. The Northcliffe newspapers were full of threatenings. Nothing would serve but the extermination of the German race. These denunciations formed a great contrast with the lofty reasoned arguments of the propagandists, who told the German people that the Allies were fighting not against the people of Germany but only against the militarists and the Junkers, and that the Allies would make a friendly peace with the German people after the fall of the Hohenzollern dynasty. Mr. Wells, feeling that this supposed propaganda policy and the actual policy of the Northcliffe press were too contradictory, resigned on July 17, 1918.[68] On the 23d of July his place was taken by Mr. Hamilton Fyfe.[69]

At the same time that Mr. Fyfe took over the work of Mr. Wells the organization moved into its large headquarters at Crewe House. At this time also, Captain Chalmers Mitchell and the enthusiastic Mr. S. A. Guest, who had carried on a propaganda campaign of his own in the early part of the war, became attached to Crewe House. Furthermore, closer cooperation between Crewe House and the Military Intelligence

[66] Mr. Wells's capitals.

[67] Stuart, *op. cit.*, p. 79.

[68] Because of Northcliffe's activities in stirring up hatred against the Germans some people considered him the wrong person for the propaganda against the German morale. Mr. Denman said in the House of Commons on May 16, 1918, that Northcliffe was despised by the Germans as much as Reventlow was despised by the English. "Northcliffe is unsuited for this peculiar form of activity," said the speaker.

[69] Fyfe, *op. cit.*, p. 243; also *Times History of the War,* XXI, 344.

was now established by the appointment of Major the Earl of Kerry as liaison officer between Crewe House and the Military Intelligence, which had been doing effective work since the early part of 1916.

Thus we have an outline of the organization set up by the civil government of England to combat the enemy with words. But it must not be supposed that the military leaders neglected the "war of words" entirely. The War Office began an independent propaganda campaign in the early part of 1916 when Major General Sir George MacDonogh was made Director of Military Intelligence. As a result of his efforts and those of Brigadier General G. R. Cockerill, a special branch of the Military Intelligence Department for propaganda purposes was created. This was known as M.I.7b.[70] An army order was issued inviting those officers and men who had had previous literary experience to communicate with the new organization. As a result there was enrolled a more or less regular staff of some thousands of writers who consented to contribute "the produce of their pens during such times as they could spare from their more active military duties."[71] From these were selected two or three who were unfit for service overseas—a number subsequently raised to twenty. They were attached to the staff of M.I.7b and gave their whole time to the production of propaganda.

One of the early functions of M.I.7b was the establishment of *Le Courier de l'air*.[72] The purpose of this paper—some eight inches by six in size—was to keep up the morale of the French and Belgian peoples in the enemy-occupied territory.[73] In the spring of 1916, subsections of this branch of the War Office began the preparation of leaflets for distribution among the enemy troops.[74] During 1917 reports obtained

[70] Stuart, *op. cit.*, p. 52.

[71] Major C. J. C. Street, "Behind the Enemy Lines," *Cornhill Magazine*, XLVII (1919), p. 490. [72] *Ibid.*

[73] This little newspaper, except for one short break, was distributed regularly by air until November 1918. [74] Stuart, *op. cit.*

by the examination of prisoners, and information derived from secret sources, convinced the officials that results were being achieved by this propaganda. The Directory of Military Intelligence, in co-operation with the G.H.Q. in France, made arrangements for the work to be extended, so that by spring of 1918 about a million leaflets were being issued monthly.[75]

When Northcliffe's organization moved into Crewe House it took over part of the work of M.I.7b. Crewe House was now responsible for the preparation of propaganda material and M.I.7b concerned itself entirely with its distribution.[76]

Thus Northcliffe's propaganda machinery was at last complete and active. His office might have been called the "Ministry for the Destruction of German Confidence." It continued its activities until the Armistice, when Northcliffe, feeling that his task had been accomplished, handed Lloyd George his resignation. This was accepted in a letter in which the Prime Minister expressed his gratitude for the "great services you have rendered to the Allied cause while holding this important post."[77]

The details of Northcliffe's "great services" will be described in another chapter.

THE UNITED STATES

Shortly after the outbreak of the World War, America became the focal point of European propaganda. Both the Central and the Entente Powers competed for American friendship. In this competition it is now generally conceded that because of Britain's control of the cables and news agencies the Entente Powers had the advantage. As a result of this propaganda there had developed, long before we broke diplomatic relations with Germany, a pro-Entente and anti-German feeling in America.

German militarism, German Junkerism, and the Hohenzollern dynasty were hated as much in certain circles in America as they were in France or England. Those who felt

[75] Stuart, *op. cit.*, p. 54. [76] *Ibid.*, p. 16. [77] *Ibid.*, p. 235.

this way believed that England and France were fighting in the defense of democracy and that unless the Kaiser and his militarists were checked American democracy would be endangered. Hence from the very day of our declaration of war we had a definite war aim—to crush German militarism and to defend democratic institutions.

President Wilson's War Message of April 2, 1917, described our war aims in such statements as: "It is a war against all nations. . . . . The challenge is to all mankind"; and "our object now, as then, is to vindicate the principle of peace and justice in the life of the world as against selfish and autocratic power, and to set up amongst really free and self-governed peoples of the world such a concert of purpose and action as will henceforth ensure the observance of those principles." And, finally: "we have no quarrel with the German people. We have no feeling towards them but one of sympathy and friendship. It was not upon their impulse that their government acted in entering this war."[78]

The American war aims became the material for the American propagandists at home and on the fighting front. Always it was a war for the liberation of humanity—German humanity included—from the clutches of unprincipaled autocracy. The end of the war was to see the establishment of a democratic government in Germany, and with this democratic government the Allies would make a just and lasting peace. These were Wilson's ideals; and his speeches, expressing these ideals, were considered by the Allied propagandists the most effective material for propaganda purposes.

From the outset President Wilson recognized the necessity for a central propaganda agency in this country. On April 14, 1917, just eight days after war was declared, he created, by executive order, the Committee on Public Information.[79] The members of the Committee were the Secretary of War, the Secretary of the Navy, and Mr. George Creel, civilian

[78] *Woodrow Wilson's State Papers and Addresses* (New York, 1918), pp. 273 ff.

[79] Hereafter referred to as the C.P.I.

chairman.[80] Mr. Creel gathered around him a large staff of writers, and enlisted the help of thousands of other people in America. Not only did the C.P.I. reach into every community in the United States, but it carried to other lands the aims and objects of America in the war. Said Mr. Creel:

> There was no part of the great war machinery we did not touch, no medium of appeal that we did not employ. The printed word, the spoken word, the signboard—all these were used in our campaign to make our people and all other people understand the cause that compelled America to take arms in defense of its liberties and free institutions.[81]

In order to advertise America with the greatest possible efficiency, the C.P.I. had to disseminate news abroad by other means than through the foreign press. In close co-operation with the Navy a wireless news service went out from Tuckerton to Eiffel Tower for use in France. From here it was relayed to Switzerland, Italy, Spain, and Portugal. News was also flashed from Tuckerton to England, from where it was relayed to Holland and the Scandinavian countries.[82] Thus the C.P.I. made a fight for public opinion in neutral and Allied countries, and "by balloons, mortars, and aeroplanes we carried the truth across the firing line into the Central Powers."[83]

Foreign commissioners of the C.P.I. were stationed in every foreign neutral and friendly belligerent nation of the world. Mrs. Vira B. Whitehouse was the Commissioner in Switzerland.[84] Here she organized her work into several departments. The daily news service was under the direction of Mr. George B. Fife. This department dealt with the problem of getting news into the Swiss press. As the news arrived each morning it was translated into French and German and delivered to the (official) Agence Télégraphique Suisse, which

[80] *Complete Report of the Chairman of the Committee on Public Information* (Washington, D.C., Government Printing Office, 1920), p. 1; hereafter cited as *Report,* C.P.I.

[81] *Report,* C.P.I., p. 1. [82] *Ibid.,* p. 5. [83] *Ibid.*

[84] Mrs. Whitehouse tells the story of her work in Switzerland in her book, *A Year as Government Agent* (New York and London, 1920).

distributed it to the Swiss press.[85] By August 1917 Mr. Fife was able to report to Washington that an estimated minimum of 20,000 paragraphs of news of American origin was being published weekly in the Swiss papers.[86]

There was also a motion-picture-films department in Switzerland which was under the direction of Mr. Valentine. In order to get propaganda films into Switzerland the C.P.I. induced the American distributors to agree not to send any pictures to Switzerland unless the Swiss theaters agreed to use a certain amount of American propaganda film.[87] Since the war made it impossible for the European producers to supply the demands of the Swiss picture houses, the Swiss had to agree to the American terms.

The work in Denmark, under the direction of Mr. Edward V. Riis, followed the same principles as that of Mrs. Whitehouse in Switzerland. In Holland Mr. Henry Suydam not only strove to place American news with the Dutch press but he also aimed to use Holland, as far as possible without violating her neutrality, as a means of approach to the Germans.[88]

Mr. James Kerney was the C.P.I. Commissioner for France. In addition to employing all possible agencies for sustaining the morale of the French people, the headquarters of Mr. Kerney in Paris was the clearing house for the diffusion of full information on American naval and military preparations. In June 1918 this Commission was given offices in the Maison de la presse.[89] It co-operated with the French Bureau which had charge of distributing, in Germany and among the German troops, facts regarding American preparations. The Intelligence Section of the A.E.F. assigned Lieutenant Harry A. Franck, the famous author and traveler, who was familiar with the German language and conditions,

[85] Vira B. Whitehouse, *op. cit.*, p. 125.

[86] *Ibid.*, p. 152; also *Report*, C.P.I., p. 185.

[87] This same method was used to get propaganda films into other countries.

[88] *Report*, C.P.I., p. 175.

[89] *Ibid.*, p. 166.

to the service of the Kerney Commission. Lieutenant Franck kept in close touch with the enemy propaganda section of the Maison de la presse.[90]

This French Commission saw to it that full and complete reports of President Wilson's speeches were printed in the neutral press, and that accurate, if not complete, summaries of them were printed in the enemy press. Whenever the commission found that the German newspapers misrepresented Wilson's speeches, tracts and pamphlets correcting these misrepresentations were sent over the German lines by airplanes and balloons and dropped over the cities. Usually these leaflets gave in parallel columns the German version and the correct version. Emphasis was given to those portions that had been left out.[91]

When, early in July 1918, some of the German papers began to publish stories which gave indications of war-weariness, this material was immediately put into pamphlet or leaflet form and distributed among the German troops.

Certain changes in the organization of the French division of the C.P.I. were effected at the Inter-Allied Conference of Propaganda Agencies which met on July 18, 1918. General Dennis E. Nolan, Major Henry James, and Captain Mark Watson of the Intelligence Section A.E.F. attended the conference. Soon after that a group of experts, under the immediate direction of Major James, took over the American phase of the propaganda work.[92]

The C.P.I. also had various nationality bureaus working among the different racial groups in America. There were, for instance, a Lithuanian bureau, a Czechoslovak bureau, a Polish bureau, and an Italian bureau. Each of these had a director who was responsible for keeping his particular racial group informed concerning the war activities of the United States and of keeping them loyal to America. The foreign-language press helped greatly in this "loyalty drive."

[90] *Report,* C.P.I., p. 173. [91] *Ibid.* [92] *Ibid.,* p. 174.

Of the various nationality groups in America working for the maintenance of loyalty among the foreign-language elements, the most active was the Friends of German Democracy. This was organized by a group of loyal German-born Americans in October 1917, and because of its activity among the German-Americans the C.P.I. asked it to function as the German bureau.[93] Mr. Julius Koettgen, executive secretary of the Friends of German Democracy from the first, also acted as manager of the German Bureau of the C.P.I. There were twelve branches of the Friends of German Democracy in as many German-American centers in the United States. Four organizers were in the field continually until 1919, visiting German-American colonies and arranging and addressing public patriotic meetings.

This organization did not, however, limit its activities to the United States. As its name implies, its purpose was to encourage and aid as much as possible the establishment of a democracy in Germany. The members sent letters and appeals to certain groups in Switzerland, who saw to it that these letters got into Germany. It also helped to support the *Freie Zeitung,* a German newspaper in Berne working for a German Republic.[94]

At the beginning of 1918, when the American troops came to the Western Front, the Friends of German Democracy started their front propaganda. The Intelligence Division of the A.E.F., as well as the French Service aérienne, distributed the material produced by this group. Many little cards were dropped over the German lines which contained graphs and

[93] *Ibid.,* p. 89.

[94] *Report,* C.P.I., p. 90; see also *Werk des Untersuchungsausschusses der Deutsche verfassungsgebenden Nationalversammlung und des deutschen Reichstages 1919–1928; Die Ursachen des deutschen Zusammenbruchs im Jahre 1918,* Series 4, edited by Dr. Albrecht Philipp, Deutsche Verlagsgesellschaft, für Politik und Geschichte (Berlin, 1925–1928), 8 vols. The entire fourth series of this report deals with the collapse of the morale of Germany. Hereafter the work will be cited as *U.D.Z.* and, unless otherwise stated, the fourth series will be meant.

statistics to show the rapid increase in the number of American soldiers coming to the aid of the Allies. For example:

> More than one million Americans are on the West front. . . . . One million five hundred thousand American troops are now in France. More than twice this number are being trained in America.[95]

Others of these pointed out that the Americans were fighting not the German people, but the German rulers, militarists, and Junkers who had brought on the war. Leaflets called upon the German soldiers to desert to the Americans and assured them of good treatment and plenty of food. All of this propaganda stated that the Friends of German Democracy wanted to help Germany, that they were working for the best interests of Germany—the overthrow of the German militarists.[96] One of their appeals ran as follows:

> BROTHERS!
>
> The world is in great need. You and you alone can end this need rapidly. We are American citizens of German descent. We know you and trust you. We beg you to trust us.
>
> The great German nation is the barbarian and the breaker of trust in the eyes of the world. You can recover your good reputation only if you overthrow this government, which has made German intelligence and German industry a danger to the world. Take the determination of your destiny into your own hands. . . . .
>
> If you will do this the world war will end. In the name of America we give you our word, that the new Germany will be taken up as an honorable member of the society of nations. Your intelligence and industry will again be a blessing to humanity, instead of a curse. . . . .
>
> Arise for a struggle for a free Germany!
>
> In the name of Americans of German descent.
>
> UNION OF FRIENDS OF GERMAN DEMOCRACY.
>
> NEW YORK, March 1918[97]

[95] Friedrich Felger, ed., *Was wir vom Weltkrieg nicht wissen* (Berlin and Leipzig, 1929), p. 510.

[96] *Ibid.;* see also any of their propaganda material.

[97] Miscellaneous leaflet collection, propaganda material (*Fliegerabwurf-Schriften*), in the Hoover War Library. For want of a better name the leaflets in this collection will hereafter be cited as *Fliegerabwurf-Schriften.*

These German-Americans were very active. They issued a weekly bulletin, and sent articles to the 200 most important German-language newspapers in America and to 400 American newspapers that were read by persons of German descent.[98] They sent out over one million copies of twenty different pamphlets. Among these were: *German Militarism and Its German Accusers; The Spirit of America; The German Poison Growth of Prussianism;* Lichnowsky's *Memoirs;* and editions of the *Freie Zeitung* of Berne.[99]

Thus did the Americans of German descent aid the C.P.I. in fighting "indifference and disaffection in the United States," and militarism, Prussianism, and Junkerism in Germany.

The United States Army recognized the value of propaganda and set up a propaganda subsection of the Military Intelligence Division. The purpose of this subdivision was to study enemy propaganda and to take steps for the dissemination among the enemy of positive American propaganda.[100] From the very first this military agency co-operated with the C.P.I.[101] Memoranda concerning the foreign situation, to-

[98] The Germans repeatedly accused Otto H. Kahn, the New York financier of German birth, of having contributed large sums of money and articles to the Friends of German Democracy and the *Freie Zeitung.* In the discussion before the *Untersuchungsausschusses* on Otto H. Kahn's connection with the Friends of German Democracy, Dr. Herz says that, in response to his inquiry, Mr. Kahn replied: "I never financed means nor established means of getting propaganda leaflets or propaganda material into Germany." He also denied having heard of the propaganda leaflet, *Amerika und der Weltkrieg,* which appeared under his name. As for the Friends of German Democracy, his connection with it, he insisted, was never an active one and he never took it seriously. He again denied any connection with the *Freie Zeitung.* On the other hand, the *Freie Zeitung* itself insisted that Mr. Kahn was definitely connected with the Friends of German Democracy. *U.D.Z.,* V, 64.

[99] *Report,* C.P.I., p. 90. In a personal letter to the writer Mr. Otto H. Kahn, shortly before his death, again denied any connection with the *Freie Zeitung* or that he had given money to the Friends of German Democracy.

[100] Major E. Alexander Powell, *The Army Behind the Army* (New York, 1919), p. 347.

[101] The military people state, however, that Creel's organization did not co-operate fully with the Military Intelligence (Powell, *op. cit.,* p. 348).

gether with comments and suggestions, were sent almost daily to the C.P.I., thus giving that civilian organization the military point of view and bringing to the attention of the committee urgent calls for American propaganda.

In February 1918, Major Charles H. Mason, of the General Staff at Washington, strongly recommended the "utilization of the psychological factor of the strategic situation," and entrusted to Heber Blankenhorn the task of organizing a psychological subdivision of the Military Intelligence.[102] This subsection took over the work of the former propaganda subsection and became known as the Psychological Subsection of the Military Intelligence Division. It established liaisons with the State Department, the C.P.I., and the "Inquiry," the body of experts under Colonel House which was preparing America's data for the peace conference.[103]

When Blankenhorn and his staff[104] reported to General Dennis E. Nolan, G2, of the G.H.Q. on July 18, 1918, he ordered them to study Allied propaganda methods before attempting to commence work. At the end of August there was set up at General Headquarters, A.E.F., in France, an organization within the General Staff for propaganda against the enemy.[105]

The center of this intensive propaganda activity was Room 65 on the floor above General Pershing's offices in Damremont Caserne, the seat of the G.H.Q. at Chaumont, Haute-Marne. This room was connected by telephone with editors and printers in Paris and Langres, with propaganda field units at Barle-duc and Toul, with army and corps headquarters from the Argonne to Vosges, and with aviation fields toward Verdun.[106]

[102] Heber Blankenhorn, "War on Morale," *Harper's Magazine,* CXXXIX (1919), p. 512.

[103] *Ibid.*

[104] His staff consisted of Lieutenants Ludlow, Griscom, and Ifft of the M.I.D., also Captain Walter Lippmann and Lieutenants Charles Merz, William F. Miltengerger, and E. M. Wooley (*ibid.*).

[105] *Ibid.,* p. 510.

[106] *Ibid.,* p. 510.

In order to keep a close check on the advance of the "propaganda campaign" Blankenhorn put "propaganda maps" on the walls of his room at headquarters with little flags pinned to them. These little flags were moved forward as the truckloads of leaflets reached the front and penetrated into Germany by means of balloons and airplanes.

With such close observation of conditions at the front and with such a systematic organization, it is no wonder that the M.I. alone had sent more than three million leaflets over the German lines when the Armistice was signed.[107]

ATTEMPTS AT CO-ORDINATION

The Allies found that it was just as necessary to co-ordinate their various propaganda activities as it was to centralize their economic and military forces. A preliminary inter-Allied propaganda conference was held in London in March 1918 to consider ways and means. The French government delegated M. Franklin-Bouillon; Italy sent Gallenga-Stuart, the head of her propaganda department; and the United States was represented by Mr. Robinette, an American commissioner for propaganda in Northern Europe. Upon the insistence of Mr. Wickham Steed the French government allowed M. Henri Moysset, chief secretary to the French Minister of Marine, who knew Germans and German psychology well, to attend the conference. He brought Tonnelat of the Service aérienne with him.[108]

On July 18, 1918, another conference of heads of the British, Belgian, French, and American services was held in the Paris office of the American C.P.I.[109] Here it was decided to concentrate the work upon the American lines, which were shortly to be greatly extended. Mr. James Keeley, editor of the *Chicago Herald,* was the American representative at

[107] *Ibid.,* p. 523.

[108] H. Wickham Steed, *Through Thirty Years,* II, 191.

[109] George Creel, *How We Advertised America* (New York and London, 1920), p. 287.

those conferences, which were attended by all the Allied Powers.[110] Before the end of August there was created an Inter-Allied Board for Propaganda against the Enemy. This met at regular intervals at Crewe House in London, under the presidency of Lord Northcliffe.[111]

We now have the propaganda machinery set up. Each of the Allied countries has a working organization and their efforts are, to some extent at least, co-ordinated by the Inter-Allied Board. Let us now consider the methods and tactics used by the propagandists in their effort to tear down the morale of the enemy peoples.

[110] Creel, *op. cit.*, p. 284.

[111] Blankenhorn, *op. cit.*, p. 513.

CHAPTER II

PROPAGANDA METHODS AND TACTICS

> It may be said that, while the artillery was pounding the German troops with shells and the infantry was shooting and slashing at closer range, the unsung propaganda section was silently bombarding them with arguments; busily unsettling them by suggestions.
>
> —*Stars and Stripes,* A.E.F. official newspaper, January 3, 1919

FRANCE

The tactics of the propagandists and the methods of distribution were practically the same in all of the Allied countries. As has been shown in the previous chapter, the governments built up special departments composed of individuals who were acquainted with the political and psychological conditions of the various countries in which the propaganda was to be made. Every government issued a regular wireless service; and large sums of money were spent on cables, the press agencies, and neutral newspapers.[1] However, there are certain features by which one can distinguish the technique of the various countries.

The French themselves were not effective producers of the type of propaganda needed for an attack upon the morale of the enemy. It was difficult for them to get away from

[1] The anonymous booklet, *Hinter den Kulissen des Französischen Journalismus von einem Pariser Chefredakteur* states (page 234) that the French set aside 20 million francs for use in gaining the favor of the neutral press. The *Journal de Genève,* it says, was given 30,000 francs and the *Gazette de Lausanne* 25,000 francs to carry stories of a propaganda nature. No substantiation of these accusations has been found by the present writer.

the propaganda of hate—the atrocity-story type of material. Hence they made great use of the German émigrés in Switzerland.[2]

There were many people in Germany who felt that the war had been planned by the German militarists and that it was being waged for imperialistic ends. Many of these people desired the overthrow of the monarchy and the establishment of a German republic. Because of their convictions many of them emigrated to Switzerland. Here they formed an organization known as the German Democrats in Switzerland with the purpose of working for the overthrow of the existing German government. They founded the *Freie Zeitung* in Berne, and with this, which appeared every Wednesday and Saturday, they made known in many lands, Germany included, their hopes for a free and democratic Germany.[3]

Among the most prominent German Democrats in Switzerland were Richard Grelling, Hermann Fernau-Latt, Hermann Rösemeier, Hans Huber, and Dr. Hans Schlieben.[4] These men were willing to co-operate with the Allies to accomplish the democratization of Germany. Some of them wrote propaganda pamphlets which were bought by the French propaganda bureau. Siegfried Balder wrote many poems and a number of pamphlets which were distributed by the French among the German troops at the front. One of his contributions to this cause pictured the food situation in Germany—and the concern which the Kaiser is supposed to have felt over it—in the following manner:

[2] Friedrich Felger, ed., *Was wir vom Weltkrieg nicht wissen* (Berlin and Leipzig, 1929), p. 504.

[3] Dr. Hans Thimme, *Weltkrieg ohne Waffen,* devotes an excellent chapter to the part played by the German émigrés in the propaganda against their Fatherland.

[4] See Dr. George Huber, *Die Französische Propaganda im Weltkrieg,* p. 69; also Dr. Julius Wernsdorff, *Dies Buch gehört dem Bundesrat: eine Studie die "Deutschen Republikaner in der Schweiz" während des Weltkrieges* (Zürich, 1918), in which the author devotes a chapter to each of these men.

Die Kinder darben, frieren, jammern
Nicht Milch, nicht Mehl, nicht Brot noch Brei!
Die Schwindsucht schleicht sich in die Kammern,
Die Mutter reisst das Herz entzwei.

Kein Kaiser frägt nach euren Tränen
Kein General nach eurer Not.
Doch wird man loben es erwähnen,
Stirbt euer man den Heldentod.[5]

Another German émigré in the service of France was Hermann Rösemeier. This propagandist had written two pamphlets in 1916, *Die Schuld am Weltkrieg* and *Deutsches Volk wach auf,* which the French publishers, Payot & Co., printed. More than 100,000 copies of the Rösemeier pamphlets were used by the French propagandists. Dr. Rösemeier was considered so valuable to the French that he was called to Paris, where he wrote a great many leaflets and pamphlets.[6] Returning to Switzerland in April 1917, he became associated with the *Freie Zeitung.*

A third German in the service of the French was Hermann Fernau-Latt. In Paris he contributed to the *Zeitung für die deutschen Kriegsgefangenen* (No. 8, Vol. 20, III, 1915). In May 1915 he was in Switzerland again, providing the Allies with welcome propaganda materials. Among these contributions were *Gerade weil ich ein Deutscher bin, Durch zur Demokratie!* and *Das Königtum ist der Krieg.*[7]

The Germans realized the effectiveness of the propaganda written by the émigrés in Switzerland. Walter Nicolai, chief of the German secret service, states, regarding the activities of Grelling, Balder, Rösemeier, etc.:

It is one of the most melancholy sides of the enemy propaganda

[5] Liste I, propaganda collection, Hoover War Library.

[6] Dr. Julius Wernsdorff, *Dies Buch gehört dem Bundesrat,* p. 18; also Wilhelm Ernst, *Die antideutsche Propaganda durch das Schweizer Gebiet im Weltkrieg, speziell die Propaganda in Bayern* (Munich, 1933), p. 5.

[7] Wilhelm Ernst, *Die antideutsche Propaganda durch das Schweizer Gebiet,* p. 6.

that the Germans worked for it or at least provided material for it. It increased the effectiveness of the propaganda when it could quote German sources and point to the support of representatives of Germany.[8]

The French also used, for propaganda purposes, the letters and declarations from German prisoners, describing the conditions in the French prison camps. Many examples of such propaganda can be found among the materials sent out by the Service aérienne. The most interesting of these examples is the group called *Grüsse an die Heimat, Briefe deutscher Kriegsgefangener*. These letters were not issued regularly, but eleven of them had appeared by May 1918. They were eight-page papers, profusely illustrated, and containing facsimiles of the letters written by the prisoners telling of the fine food and wonderful treatment they were receiving from the French. The pictures usually showed the prisoners at play, at work in the gardens, in the social hall opening packages from home, or at meals, with plenty of food on the tables.[9]

Another effective piece of propaganda literature emanating from Hansi's Service aérienne was *Die Feldpost*. This was a newspaper modeled after the English "trench newspaper." The chief purpose of *Die Feldpost* was to intensify the war-weariness of the German soldiers. The joys of home life, the quiet peace of the country, and the busy prosperous existence of the city during times of peace were played up. As early as Christmas 1915 the editors celebrated the Christmas season by recalling all of the simple pleasures of Christmas at home with one's family.[10] The amusements of civilian life

[8] Walter Nicolai, *The German Secret Service,* translated with an additional chapter by George Renwick (London, 1924), p. 163.

[9] *Grüsse an die Heimat* propaganda collection, Hoover War Library. Nicolai (*op cit.,* p. 161) believes these letters to be forged: "Forged letters from German war prisoners in France and England and illustrations of the alleged enviable treatment of German prisoners . . . . were designed to persuade the German soldiers to desert or to depress their spirit."

[10] Hansi et Tonnelat, *À Travers les lignes ennemies;* Figure 4, opposite page 24, is an illustration of *Die Feldpost*. A few of these are in the Hoover War Library.

were especially featured and those pleasures which the Germans love most were invitingly portrayed in word and picture.[11]

Perhaps the most individualistic French method of getting propaganda to the Germans was the "sausage method." The much-ridiculed German sausage was made to play an important part in disintegrating the Kaiser's army. The French message to the German troops, stating that they would do well to surrender and give the password, "Camarade Republique," was carried to them in "sausage meat." Small vials, containing the message on oil paper, were prepared so that they looked like a German sausage, and these were dropped behind the lines.[12] The French hoped that the families of the soldiers, once having discovered that the messages were meant for their sons or husbands at the front, would send these "sausages" to the troops. To make certain that the messages would be put into the hands of the German soldiers, the French promised safety, food, and comfort to all who would desert to France.[13]

The methods of delivering French propaganda to the Germans varied. At first the hand grenade was used extensively. Instead of being dangerously explosive, these hand grenades were stuffed with propaganda leaflets which would fly out when the grenade landed. This method was not satisfactory, however, since it was dangerous work to throw "paper grenades" at the enemy from the trenches only to receive bullets in return.

The next method of delivering the leaflets to the enemy was by airplanes. Although the French and Germans had on several occasions dropped leaflets from the air in 1914, it

[11] After No. 13 the name was changed to *Kriegsblätter für das deutsche Volk.* Later it became known as *Das freie deutsche Wort;* in this last stage it is more revolutionary in tone. See Hansi et Tonnelat, *op. cit.,* p. 18.

[12] At one time the French, wishing to taunt the Germans because of the food shortage in Germany, dropped actual loaves of bread into the trenches of the Germans; the Germans sliced these, buttered them, and sent them back to the French (incident told to the writer by a former German soldier).

[13] *New York Times,* February 16, 1918.

was not until the beginning of 1915 that the airplane came into general use for propaganda purposes.[14] So important did the French consider the matter of leaflet delivery that, after the G.Q.G. had established its "Bureau of Enemy Psychology" the crack Lafayette Flying Squadron was used for the purpose.[15] J. Norman Hall gives a graphic account of this work when he says:

> Then they started to swamp us with clever ideas. Pamphlets began to arrive, bundles at a time; paper ammunition intended to be rained down upon the heads of the benighted Boche until he broke beneath the weight, and they were weighty too. I could read a bit of German and I appreciated their appeal more than did my French Comrades. There was, for example, a fake news-sheet purporting to emanate from Berne. This gave all the latest news of the Allied victories, coupled with the most pessimistic statements of certain German Socialists.[16]

Other material among the propaganda cargo included a "dainty little card printed in tri-colors that touched the heart by its human appeal." This was a friendly letter, written by one soldier to the rest of his comrades under arms. The soldier was a prisoner in France so kindly treated by his captors that he wanted to pass the word along: If there were any

[14] The French in August 1914 had dropped leaflets in Alsace-Lorraine telling the people that France was fighting for the liberation of these "lost provinces" from the German yoke. The Germans, in September of the same year, had used airplanes to drop leaflets over Nancy (Hansi et Tonnelat, *op. cit.*, p. 10).

[15] J. Norman Hall and Charles B. Nordhoff, *The Lafayette Flying Corps* (Boston and New York, 1920), 2 vols. In the chapter on propaganda these two Americans describe in a most interesting manner how they delivered propaganda leaflets to the Germans.

[16] Hall and Nordhoff, *op. cit.*, II, 138. At first the members of the Lafayette Flying Corps considered the propaganda a joke. Whenever the big guns made unusual noises at night the boys would say, "That's the propaganda; you've got the Boches aroused to their danger." And when the nights were quiet they would remark: "They scarcely resist at all these days, since Wilson's speech got among them." And then Mr. Hall concludes, "Perhaps this bit of propaganda did as much to bring about the happy ending as I myself did to bring down my plane safely in the middle of the woods. In any case, it's a good story for a man's grandchildren."

who found themselves ground down under the heel of the German oppressors, they could easily come over to the land of liberty and democracy. "The charming picture," says Mr. Hall, "of the deserter's reception in France, made me feel like deserting to France myself."[17] On another occasion Mr. Hall carried with him "40 pounds of eloquence printed in German." The leaflets were all done up in half-pound rolls.

> It was warfare in the ultimate degree. Instead of killing our enemy with sudden dismemberment, we rained down upon him the power of the printed word, to unjoint his moral strength and dislocate his will to resist. It was a triumph of reason over matter.[18]

The Escadrilles des Armées was another famous flying unit used for the delivery of propaganda. Twice a week this corps delivered faked German newspapers to the enemy.[19] These had been produced, for the most part, by the Friends of German Democracy and were intended to carry the gospel of democracy to the German troops. Of this work Mr. B. A. Molter says:

> Literally, the French fliers are the paper carriers for the Boche. . . . . Each plane takes about 1,000 "tracts" aboard and goes sailing off on its missionary errand. The objective of each is some barracks where it is known that considerable number of soldiers are quartered. The tracts give the news of the conditions in America, the nations that have severed diplomatic relations with Germany, and the aims of the Allies. The entry of America into the war on the side of the Allies with the promise of active support, the news of the great war preparations in this country—all were told in tracts which we showered on the Huns.[20]

The French airmen also were engaged in delivering Wilson's messages. The American President's message of Febru-

[17] Hall and Nordhoff, *op. cit.*, II, 138.

[18] *Ibid.*

[19] These newspapers were supposedly the *Neue Deutscher Freie Zeitung* and the *Frankfurter Zeitung* of July 31, 1917. Actually they were editions of the *Freie Zeitung*.

[20] Bennet A. Molter, *Knights of the Air* (New York and London, 1918), p. 190.

ary 8, 1918, to Congress, was considered of special importance, and the delivery of it to the Germans was regarded as a "special task." On February 11, 1918, two American airmen in the French service, W. A. Wellman and "Tommy" Hitchcock, were ordered by their captain to deliver this speech to the Germans. "It was really a message addressed to the German people," said the captain, "and today, Americans from the different Escadrilles along the front are to have the unique privilege of flying over the enemy's country and dropping copies of it, printed in German."[21] Of the actual delivery of these packets of leaflets Mr. Wellman says:

> My delivery route took me twenty-five miles into German territory over the towns of Saarburg and Mittersheim. . . . .
>
> It was great sport. When it came to delivering the mail, however, I found out very shortly that it was quite a trick to get my notes off successfully and intact. Simply tossed overboard when I was going 130 miles an hour, they developed a habit of getting mixed up with my wings, or caught in the *fuselage;* but I finally found a solution to the problem. It was by doing a vertical *virage,* tossing the bundles over when I was flying perpendicularly, and at the same instant kicking my machine around violently so that the tail would not strike them.[22]

And then, perhaps a little too enthusiastically, Mr. Wellman completes his picture with: "It was amusing to look back and see the men below and behind us dropping their rifles and scrambling for such of our messages as fell square in the trenches."[23]

Before the close of the war the whole French Army believed in the campaign of ideas, and company commanders regarded the spread of propaganda as part of their day's work.[24] New means of distribution were being discovered continually. When the British perfected the free balloon, this was used extensively by the French. In 1918 the French developed a plan

[21] W. A. Wellman, *Go Get 'Em* (Boston, 1918), p. 191.

[22] *Ibid.,* p. 192. [23] *Ibid.,* p. 195.

[24] Heber Blankenhorn, "War of Morale," *Harper's Magazine,* CXXXIX (1919), p. 513.

DAS FREIE DEUTSCHE WORT

Die Zahl der deutschen Republikaner, Demokraten und Sozialdemokraten, die vor der drohenden Schutzhaft in das neutrale Ausland flüchten mussten, mehrt sich täglich. Andere, die wegen ihrer politischen Überzeugung trotz Alter und Gebrechen in die feldgraue Uniform gesteckt wurden, sind zum Feinde übergegangen; sie haben dort eine gute Aufnahme und die Freiheit gefunden. Sie alle haben nur einen Wunsch : dem deutschen Volke die Wahrheit zu verkünden, ihm die Binde von den Augen zu reissen, ihm den Abgrund zu zeigen, in den es von seiner Regierung, von seinen Ausbeutern geführt wird. Diese Deutschen haben uns gebeten, auf dem einzigen noch möglichen Wege ihre Worte unter dem deutschen Volke zu verbreiten.

Preussischer Militarismus und preussisches Junkertum (*).

Vom Verfasser des Buches « J'accuse ».

Wie Kinder lasst Ihr Euch betrügen,
Bis Ihr zu spät erkannt, o weh,
Die Wacht am Rhein wird nicht genügen.
Der wahre Feind steht an der Spree.
Georg Herwegh.

Europa — und die Welt — haben ganz richtig erkannt, wo der Sitz des Kriegsübels, welches der Bazillus ist, der die Kriegsseuche erzeugt hat. In der Tat, die Diagnose ist nicht allzuschwer. Jener Preussengeist, der Kriegsgeist heisst, ist ein ganz spezielles Gewächs preussischen Bodens. Er ist ein Rest mittelalterlichfeudaler Anschauungen, der sich nur in den östlichen, etwas abseits von der Kulturentwicklung liegenden Provinzen Preussens konserviert hat und unter der sorgsamen Pflege der Hohenzollern, unter dem machtvollen Aufstieg des preussischen Königtums zur deutschen Kaiserwürde, zu neuer Blüte und Entfaltung gelangt ist. Dieses militärisch-preussisch-hohenzollernsche Draufgängertum findet seine vollkommenste und «sympatischste» Verkörperung heute in dem Erben des preussischen Königs- und deutschen Kaiserthrones. Seine Schriften, seine Reden, seine Handlungen, seine Armeeaufrufe, ja seine in allen illustrierten Blättern prangenden Kriegsphotographien mit dem strahlend-befriedigten Antlitz, beweisen, dass er in dem jetzigen «Immer feste druff!» sich so recht in seinem Elemente fühlt, dass für ihn der Krieg nicht die schlimmste Geissel der Menschheit, sondern die erhabenste Betätigung menschlicher Schöpferkraft, die edelste Aufgabe gottbegnadeter Herrscher ist.

* * *

Wie man einem Fremden, das heisst einem Nichtdeutschen oder auch nur einem Nichtpreussen, niemals wird beibringen können, was ein preussischer Junker sei, so wird man ihm auch niemals einen deutlichen Begriff von dem Wesen des preussischen Militarismus geben können. Junker und Militarismus sind so speziell preussische, ja innerhalb Preussens noch so speziell ostelbische Begriffe, dass nur der, der diese Menschen und ihre Geitesverfassung von Jugend an gesehen, gefühlt, unter ihnen gelebt und gelitten hat, sich einen klaren Begriff von ihrem Wesen machen kann. Nirgends in der Welt findet sich diese eigenartige Mischung von Standeshochmut, Profitgier, Herrschsucht, Borniertheit, brutalem Draufgängertum gegen oben und gegen unten, wenn es sich um die eigenen Interessen und Vorteile handelt, — von raffiniertem Intrigenspiel gegen missliebige Regierungsmänner, die nicht ganz nach der Pfeife der Junker tanzen wollen, — von brutalem Missbrauch der Zoll-, Steuer- und Finanzgesetzgebung zu dem Zwecke, sich selbst möglichst zu entlasten und alle anderen Klassen, sogar die ärmsten, möglichst zu belasten, — von rücksichtsloser Ausnutzung der Corps- und Familienbeziehungen zur Beherrschung der Staatsverwaltung, zur Erlangung der fettesten Posten, zur Vorwärtsschiebung der Vettern und Gesinnungsgenossen. Dabei verstehen diese Leute es meisterhaft — und haben es stets verstanden —, ihren Klassen Egoismus hinter den tönenden Phrasen von Thron und Altar, von Zucht und Sitte, von Gott, König und Vaterland zu verstecken.

So lange die Junker in Preussen und durch Vermittlung Preussens im deutschen Reiche die herrschende Klasse bilden, ist jeder Gedanke an eine Besserung der preussisch-deutschen Zustände und damit an eine dauernde Friedensorganisation Europas ausgeschlossen. Der preussische

(*) Aus No. 1 der von Grumbach herausgegebenen «Republikanischen Bibliothek». Diese Studie wird in dem zweiten, demnächst erscheinenden Band des Werkes : «Das Verbrechen» enthalten sein, das der Verfasser von *J'accuse* als weitausgreifende und tiefschürfende Fortsetzung seines ersten Buches herausgibt.

German Émigrés Attack the Fatherland

The writings of German émigrés in Switzerland and Allied countries were used extensively for propaganda purposes. Here the author of *J'accuse* attacks Prussian militarism and junkerism. This leaflet was distributed by the Service de propagande aérienne.

of mass distribution of leaflets at short range. They constructed "propaganda bullets" of tinfoil similar to the "defense" grenades, which could be shot to a distance of 200 meters. They exploded in the air and could be counted on to float another 100 meters before they reached the ground. Each *portetract,* as the French called these, carried about 150 leaflets, or from five to ten newspapers.[25] The first use made of these was in the battle of Champagne in the night of May 12–13, 1918. It was estimated that between one and two million leaflets were shot over to the Germans in one quarter of an hour. That many of these reached the hands of the enemy troops is shown by the fact that in the First Army alone over 14,000 leaflets were turned in.[26]

The one handicap of this propaganda bullet was that it would not go far enough. Hence by March 1918 the French perfected a propaganda shell for use in the 75 mm. field guns. These had a range of from 4 to 5 kilometers.[27] The burst of these could be regulated and enemy positions could be flooded with leaflets with great accuracy.[28]

ENGLAND

As has been stated, the British from the very beginning put the distribution of their propaganda into the hands of the military authorities. In order to get the right kind of leaflets

[25] Blankenhorn, *op. cit.,* p. 513; also Hansi et Tonnelat, *op. cit.,* p. 155.

[26] Hans Thimme, *op. cit.,* p. 47. Dr. Thimme's source for this is *Akten der O.H.L.,* abt. III *b.*

[27] Blankenhorn, *op. cit.;* also George Creel, "America's Fight for World Opinion," *Everybody's Magazine,* XL, 10.

[28] Walter Nicolai gives some further information on the supposed tactics of the Allies in general. He tells about discovering countless secret printing plants that "were concealed in the cleverest ways. These establishments," he states, "concerned themselves, too, with the production of false passes and leave papers for German soldiers. With the help of these, efforts were made to persuade them to desert and to make desertions easy" (Nicolai, *op. cit.,* p. 167). The present writer has been unable to find verification of Mr. Nicolai's statements.

to the front at the proper psychological moment, the British divided their propaganda material into two classes: "priority" leaflets and "stock" leaflets.[29] The priority leaflets were those of a news character with which the English proposed to "educate" the Germans; the stock leaflets were those with matter of a less urgent nature.

For the priority leaflets a time table was prepared in which the time allotted for the different processes of composition, translation, printing, transport to France, and distribution was cut down to the absolute minimum. In this way the British were able to put new bulletins into the hands of the Germans within 48 hours after being written in England. Three times a week a consignment of not less than 100,000 leaflets of the priority type was rushed over to France for immediate delivery to the Germans.[30]

As the spring and summer of 1918 came on, these priority leaflets became more and more important. One of Northcliffe's aims was to inform the German people of the great odds against them. The American troops were arriving in greater and greater numbers; the submarine warfare of Germany had failed; the Allied industries were increasing their output, while the German industries were almost at a standstill because of the lack of raw materials and men. All of these facts were good material for propaganda, and many a pamphlet of "education," with its statistics of American troops in France and its picture of the vast industrial activities of the Allies, found its way across the lines and into the hands of the weary German soldiers. These pamphlets stressed British progress in those fields of industry in which Germany had excelled before the war. The British propagandists also took advantage of the Scientific Exhibition which was held in London to get certain facts before the enemy. Catalogues of the Exhibition were printed in great numbers and smuggled into Germany. Scientific articles were written and sent to the

[29] Sir Campbell Stuart, *Secrets of Crewe House*, p. 92. [30] *Ibid.*, p. 93.

Dutch and Swiss press with the hope that they would somehow find their way into Germany.[31]

Another British propaganda enterprise was the publication of the "Trench Newspaper."[32] This was written especially for the German soldiers, the general make-up of the paper resembling that of a German publication.[33] In order that it might appear to be genuinely German, the head of the Kaiser decorated the title page. The propagandists filled this "newspaper" with stories and articles that were interesting to read. Here and there harmless-looking paragraphs gave the German soldier information which he received from no other source. In the middle of an article otherwise highly patriotic would be "slipped a sentence or two intended to startle the reader and to make him reflect."[34] As many as 250,000 copies of this propaganda sheet were distributed to the Germans each week.[35] Says one of the co-workers of Northcliffe:

> We worked on, editing our trench paper, making our leaflets more and more pointed, sending "London Correspondence" to neutral newspapers [Swedish, Dutch, Swiss] which sent copies into Germany; putting slips into books which were going to German buyers through neutral lands; announcing daily the figures of the American divisions which were taking the field.[36]

The British tried also to take advantage of the religious strain in the German character. Leaflets were printed in which it was pointed out that the German military defeats were a just retribution for the crimes of the German government. Various sermons were sent out which had in them a touch of propaganda. The text of one of these sermons was: "Be sure, your sins will find you out."[37]

Another ingenious method was the publication of the *War Pictorial*. This was a monthly picture album which contained pictures of the wonderful factories in the Allied countries, the thousands of American troops that were coming to France,

[31] Stuart, *op. cit.*, p. 98. [32] Hamilton Fyfe, *Northcliffe*, p. 248.

[33] Stuart, *op. cit.*, p. 100. [34] Hamilton Fyfe, *op. cit.*, p. 249.

[35] Stuart, *op. cit.* [36] Fyfe, *op. cit.*, p. 250. [37] Stuart, *op. cit.*, p. 100.

and the great food supplies and the immense war activities of the Allies at home and at the front. Copies of this album were smuggled into Germany in great numbers.[38]

Later, when the people at home wrote to the soldiers about their troubles, the English made use of these letters by publishing them with some letters of English mothers to their sons, to show the contrast in conditions in the two countries.[39] Another type of "comparative" leaflets was the "comparative menu" group. The English, who were ever alert for new methods, got their idea when certain German newspapers complained of the high cost of living in Germany. The *Vossische Zeitung* for November 18, 1915, had published a price list of the various articles of food.[40] And later the propagandists obtained information as to the food rations in Germany and the cost of foodstuffs in Berlin restaurants. Immediately leaflets were sent out which compared the food rations in England with those in Germany[41] and which contrasted the prices of food in London and Berlin restaurants.[42]

Like the French, the British also made use of the writings of Germans of note. Over a million copies of Prince Lichnowsky's *My London Mission, 1912–1914* were distributed by the War Aims Committee.[43] Muehlon's *Vandal of Europe*

[38] Generalleutnant Altrock, *Deutschlands Niederbruch* (Berlin, 1919), p. 19.

[39] Eugene Neter, *Der Seelische Zusammenbruch der Kampffront, Betrachtungen eines Frontarztes* (Munich, 1925), p. 10. Reprint from *Süddeutsche Monatshefte,* 22 Jahrgang, Hefte 10, München, 1925.

[40] *Vossische Zeitung,* November 18, 1915.

[41] Great Britain, *Department of Propaganda in Enemy Countries,* A.P. [Air Post] 75, Hoover War Library collection, gives the comparison of food rations in England and Germany. The "Air Post" leaflets will be cited hereafter as *A.P.* with the proper number. Those cited are all in the Hoover War Library.

[42] *Leaflet A.P. 80* gives a comparison of the cost of food in the London and Berlin restaurants.

[43] *The Times* (London), May 9, 1918. Lichnowsky's memorandum was one of the most popular bits of propaganda of the Allies. It was never intended for publication. It was written in 1916 for private circulation and

was also given wide circulation in the Allied and enemy countries.[44] In order that these propaganda materials by German writers could be thrust into Germany more readily, the covers were decorated in the manner of German publications and in many cases the names of revered German authors appeared on the covers, thus making sale on the German market more probable.[45]

Keeping in close touch with the military events at the fronts, the propagandists aimed to inform the Germans promptly of those happenings which would have propaganda value. After the downfall of Bulgaria the British succeeded in getting published in German newspapers reports of the occurrence, together with reports of the kindly way the Allies intended to treat the fallen foe. On October 5, 1918, for instance, we find a dispatch in the *Kölnische Zeitung,* printed on the front page, quoting the *London Daily Mail* as follows:

> The Associated Powers intend neither to disturb nor overthrow Bulgaria. They merely desire to bring justice between the individual races. They cannot forget the past deeds of the king; but that is a question which concerns the Bulgarian peoples themselves. If they take

---

intended only for the family archives. Prince Lichnowsky showed these to a few political friends, in whom he had the utmost confidence. Without his knowledge one of these men gave the memorandum to an officer in the political department of the General Staff. This officer made copies of the memorandum and sent them to persons unknown to Prince Lichnowsky. "When I heard of the mischief done," says the Prince, in a letter to the German Chancellor in March 1918, "it was unfortunately too late to be able to call in all the copies sent out. I therefore placed myself at the disposal of the then Imperial Chancellor, Dr. Michaelis, and intimated to him my most sincere regrets for the whole painful affair. I have since endeavored to prevent the further publication of my opinions, unfortunately without the desired effects" (*Norddeutsche Allgemeine Zeitung,* March 19, 1918); also cited by R. H. Lutz, *The Fall of the German Empire, 1914–1918* (Stanford University, 1932), I, 58.

[44] Muehlon was a former director of the Krupp Works and he, like Lichnowsky, was convinced that Germany was guilty of starting the war. Both men blamed the blundering, underhanded diplomacy and the selfishness of the pan-Germans.

[45] Stuart, *op. cit.,* p. 104.

steps to keep the ruler that brought them to misfortune it is their own business.[46]

The English also made use of the German prisoners by encouraging them to write home describing conditions in the English prison camps.[47] In those war prisons from which the English needed propaganda, the German prisoners were especially well fed. The Germans, grateful for their fine food and good treatment, would write home describing in glowing terms their life in British camps. These letters were reproduced with great accuracy and sent over to the German trenches.[48] Postcards from German soldiers in prison labor camps were used in a like manner. These prisoners were asked if they would like to send a postcard home to say they were in good health and well treated. The prisoners would write their postcards and address them, after which multiple copies were made from a jelly pad. These were then sorted into bundles of a dozen selected cards and each bundle was wrapped in a fly-sheet with a notice in German printed on it in bold type. This notice, which was stereotyped, read:

Soldaten! In dem Schützengraben erfriert man. Heraus aus dem Schützengraben! Hinein ins warme Bett! Täglich drei Mahlzeiten! Wo? Warme Kleidung! Wo? bezahlte Arbeit! Wo? Bei den Engländern! Darum ergebt Euch ihnen. Die Engländer töten keine Gefangenen. In Lager der Engländer durft Ihr Euren Civilberuf aufnehmen. Für Eure Arbeit werdet Ihr gut bezalt. Im Lager der Engländer

[46] *Kölnische Zeitung,* October 5, 1918, Morgen Ausgabe; see also *London Daily Mail* (editorial), October 1, 1918.

[47] Toward the end of 1916 the German prisoners upon arriving at the British camps were handed letter sheets, with instructions on them, for their use. *Deutsche Kriegsgefangene in Feindesland, Amtliches Material, England* (Berlin, 1919), p. 66.

[48] Another way the English worked on the German troops in prison camps was to tell them that after they were exchanged for English prisoners and returned to Germany they dare not go to the front and fight against the English again, for if recaptured they would be shot by the English. "As a result," says von Stein, "it was difficult to persuade them to go back to the front." General der Artillerie z.D. von Stein, *Erlebnisse und Betrachtungen aus der Zeit des Weltkrieges* (Berlin und Leipzig, 1919), p. 153.

dürft Ihr an eure Freunde und Verwandte schreiben und Ihr erhaltet sämmtliche Briefe und Postpackete welche sie Euch zusenden. Es ist nicht unpatriotisch Sich ehrenhaft dem Feinde zu ergeben um später in die Heimat zurückkehren zu können. Darum ergebt Euch und erfriert nicht in dem Schützengraben.[49]

The speeches of leading British and American statesmen were considered valuable for propaganda purposes, and were promptly put into leaflet form and dropped over the lines. Another way of getting these speeches to the enemy was to arrange for interviews on important subjects between neutral newspapermen and British public men.[50] In these the altruism of the Allies was always stressed. The British war aims—especially the destruction of German militarism and autocracy, which were enslaving the German people and threatening the entire world—were points which the British statesmen and high public officials emphasized. Reports of these were printed in the neutral press and often quoted by the enemy newspapers.

Reaching the German people with propaganda through the neutral press was not such a difficult task. The big problem came in finding means of delivering the thousands of leaflets to the German troops and to the German people behind the lines. The method of delivery went through different stages of development, and it was not until the summer of 1918 that a suitable method was developed.

The first method employed the trench mortar. The idea was to construct a sort of a bomb with a small bursting charge which would, upon its arrival over the opposing lines, release a shower of leaflets upon the enemy. This, however, proved ineffective; it was poor psychology to hurl a shower of leaflets at a German in so direct a manner, for "even the most susceptible of the enemy troops might resent it."[51]

[49] F. M. Cutlack, *The Australian Flying Corps in the Western and Eastern Theatres of War, 1914–1918* (Sydney, 1923), p. 208.

[50] Stuart, *Secrets of Crewe House,* p. 98.

[51] Major C. J. C. Street, "Behind the Enemy Lines," *Cornhill Magazine,* XLVII (1919), p. 494.

It was not long, therefore, before the trench mortar gave way to the airplane. This plan seemed well chosen, for the planes would scatter leaflets from a convenient height. Furthermore, owing to the length of time taken by the leaflets in falling, their arrival would have no apparent connection with the flight of the airplane. It was known to the propagandists that greater effect could be produced by a leaflet blowing into the trenches apparently from nowhere in particular than by one obviously hurled directly at the enemy. The airplanes could penetrate deeply into the enemy territory and scatter leaflets over rest billets as well as over trenches, permitting the Germans behind the lines, who had more leisure, to ponder the contents of the leaflets.[52]

However, opposition to the use of the airplane developed. It was pointed out by the military leaders that while fliers were risking their lives dropping leaflets of unknown value over the trenches they could very profitably be dropping bombs instead.

New devices were experimented with, and soon the observation balloon was put to use. This proved unsatisfactory, since the occupants of the balloons were too busy with their regular observations work to be bothered with leaflets.[53] Late in 1916 the free balloon was considered a possible vehicle of propaganda.[54] This seemed a very simple method, and easy to put into practice. All that was necessary was to fill the balloons with hydrogen, tie the leaflets to them, send them up with a favorable wind, and let the wind and the balloons do the rest. The difficulty, however, was in predicting within miles where the balloons would come down. The science of meteorology helped out the propagandists in this matter. The meteorologists were able to gauge the velocity and the direction of the wind at practically any height in any given locality.[55] Now the work of the propagandist was simple:

[52] *Ibid.*, p. 494.
[53] Street, *op. cit.*, p. 494.
[54] *Ibid.*, p. 495.
[55] *Ibid.*, also Stuart, *op. cit.*, p. 55.

You took your balloon to a given spot, say ten miles behind the lines:[56] you knew your balloon would rise say six thousand feet and travel at that height until its burden was released. The "meteor" gave the velocity of the wind at twenty-five miles an hour southwest at that height and place. Forty miles from the balloon position, and bearing northeast was an enemy camp. Load balloon with propaganda, set release to act in rather less than two hours to allow for drift of the leaflets, and there you are.[57]

The Air Inventions Committee, the Munitions Inventions Department, the Inspectorate of H. M. Stores, and the Army Intelligence Officers experienced in the use of silk balloons for other military purposes all assisted the War Office in overcoming the various difficulties. Designs and apparatus were tested in workshops and laboratories and at experimental stations near London and on Salisbury Plain. They were then taken to France and tried out under actual conditions of war, and gradually each difficulty was overcome.[58]

Once perfected, this balloon was manufactured at the rate of nearly 2,000 per week.[59] It was made of paper, cut in ten longitudinal panels, with a neck of oiled silk about twelve inches long. The circumference was about twenty feet, and the height, when inflated, over eight feet. Inflated with ninety or ninety-five cubic feet of hydrogen, the lifting power of each balloon was about five and one-half pounds.[60] The weight of

[56] The British had various "balloon release" stations at the front. One of these was near Lozingham, about midway between Bethune and Choques, a convenient point in a bold salient of the British lines. Street, *op. cit.*, p. 487.

[57] *Ibid.* Nature worked in favor of the Allies in this matter, for "above an altitude of 10,000 feet 95 per cent of the winds over Western Europe blow from west to east." Robert Mearns Yerkes, ed., *The New World of Science; Its Development during the War* (New York, 1920), p. 55.

[58] *The Times* (London), January 2, 1919; also Stuart, *op. cit.*

[59] *The Times* (London), January 2, 1932; also Stuart, *op. cit.*

[60] Filling the balloons with hydrogen presented another problem. Since hydrogen readily passes through paper, some suitable varnish had to be found to make the paper gas-tight. After many disappointments a formula was arrived at, the application of which prevented the evaporation of the gas for two hours or more (Stuart, *op. cit.*, p. 55).

the balloon itself was a little over one pound. The head of the German secret service gives a picture of these propaganda distributors as they appeared to the Germans:

". . . . and were made of tissue paper of light-bluish color difficult to see in the air. They could be filled with an ordinary gas-jet. The packets which were thrown down contained one, two or three balloons, folded and with complete instructions how to make use of them. Often chemicals were included in the packets, so that the finder could make gas on the spot to fill the balloon.[61]

For releasing the leaflets several devices were tried. One method was to affix a fuse of suitable length set to burn five minutes to the inch. The leaflets were attached on a wire neck of the balloon, the fuse wrapped around the wire. Each packet of leaflets was released in turn by the burning fuse, thus dropping propaganda packet by packet. Another method was to attach a time-clock combination to the release.[62] Thus, without risking a man, and without much effort, the British propagandist could flood the German lines and the hinterland with propaganda of every sort.

THE UNITED STATES

"Make the world safe for democracy," was the cry that aroused the American people to war against Germany. The psychology of this was so successful at home that the American propagandists made use of it in their attack upon Germany. The American pamphlet, "Number 5," for instance, which was distributed over the German lines in November

[61] Walter Nicolai, *The German Secret Service*, p. 159. Colonel Nicolai also tells how the Allies fitted out the German population behind the lines with wireless telegraphic apparatuses. "These were senders of the newest construction from the Marconi Works, with four accumulators, 400-volt dry batteries and 30-meter antennae; by means of them message could be sent about 50 kilometers. The packet with these apparatuses contained, in addition to the usual material, instructions for ciphering. . . . . Though a number of wireless sets were found, we never discovered one at work" (*Ibid.*, p. 159).

[62] Street, *op. cit.;* also Stuart, *op. cit.*, p. 58.

1917, pointed out that America was fighting the German autocrats and not the German people.[63] "America wishes merely to protect democracy and the people against the Kaiser and his militarists," ran the appeal. "The only hindrance to peace is the autocratic government of Germany. Once that government is removed then peace will come."[64] Another appeal ran as follows:

German Soldiers!

As you know the United States of America has entered the war. Not against the German people, has this Republic declared war, but against your Junkers. The United States has declared itself prepared to throw its entire force against military powers; it is giving the Allies her navy, her unlimited number of troops, her incalculable riches. Do you still believe that your government can bring the world to her feet? . . . . Do you want to continue to offer yourselves up for the warmongers and the exploiters?[65]

The most important producer of propaganda for America and the Allies was President Wilson. He had a knack of timing his speeches properly and of saying just the right thing. One American propagandist comments thus upon a speech of the President:

No words could have been better timed, better put, than the speech of September 27, to vitalize German despair. It meant action; that there could be no peace with the German government. It meant peace: "The League of Nations must be . . . . the most essential part of the peace settlement. . . . . No discrimination between those to whom we wish to be just and those to whom we do not wish to be just." Stronger than a call from Lenin, this speech would really stir the hardened soldier of the Western Front. For him the essential part went into a leaflet entitled *"The Way to Peace and Justice."*[66]

[63] See also Wilson's War Message of April 2, 1917, and Charles Seymour, *The Intimate Papers of Colonel House,* III, 127.

[64] Leaflet No. 5, Hoover War Library collection.

[65] *Fliegerabwurf-Schriften* (no number), Hoover War Library.

[66] Heber Blankenhorn, "War of Morale," *Harper's Magazine,* CXXXIX (1919), p. 520. Wilson's persistent distinction between the German people and the German government was possibly inspired by Colonel House. On June 3, 1915, in the midst of the "Lusitania" affair, House wrote to Wilson that, in case of war with Germany, Wilson might well, in his speeches, "exonerate

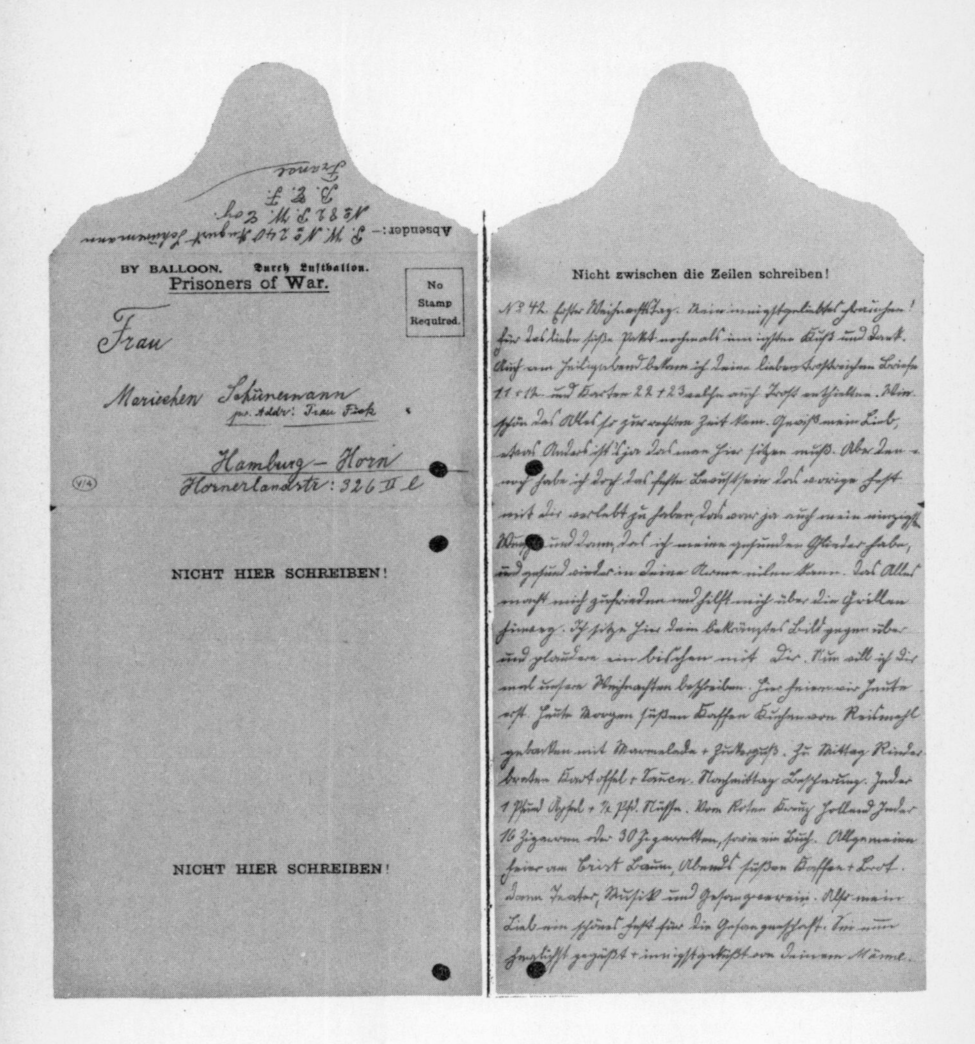

Absender:—

BY BALLOON. Durch Luftballon.
Prisoners of War.

No
Stamp
Required.

Frau
Mariechen Schünemann
pr. Addr: Frau Fick
Hamburg-Horn
Hornerlandstr: 326 II l

NICHT HIER SCHREIBEN!

NICHT HIER SCHREIBEN!

Nicht zwischen die Zeilen schreiben!

LETTER OF A GERMAN PRISONER

Here are two views of one of the letters that the German prisoners in English prison camps are supposed to have written home. Written on printed forms, they were distributed to the German troops via free balloon.

And in the *New York Times* for November 9, 1918, we find another tribute to Wilson's propaganda value: "Our propaganda outfit," says the report, "claims Wilson as its favorite author; his speeches and notes are included extensively."[67]

To facilitate speedy delivery of these speeches and other propaganda materials to the Germans, the Americans had a large printing establishment in Paris under the command of Captain Arthur Page of Doubleday, Page & Co. The editorial work was under the direction of Captain Walter Lippmann, while Colonel House acted as an unofficial adviser because of his knowledge of German psychology.[68]

It was Colonel House who, after reading a letter from Bernard Ridder, suggested that the American propaganda should advertise American war-preparation and play up the inexhaustible resources of this country. On August 9, 1917, the Colonel wrote to President Wilson:

> The letter from Bernard Ridder is interesting. I believe he is right when he says, "There is no adequate realization in Germany today of the enormous preparations being made in our country."
>
> I believe furthermore, that where the Allies have fallen down is in their lack of publicity work in neutral countries and in the Central Powers.[69]

---

the great body of German citizenship, stating that we were fighting for their deliverance as well as the deliverance of Europe" (Seymour, *The Intimate Papers of Colonel House,* II, 466).

House and Northcliffe had talked over this strategy when the English propagandist was in America with the British War Mission. It was then that Northcliffe decided that American preparations, resources, etc., should be played up by the British propagandists.

[67] *New York Times,* November 9, 1918. The *New York World,* in a front-page article on April 15, 1917, told how Wilson's War Message was to be delivered to the Germans: "The ignorance of the German people as to why the United States entered the World's War against them is to be dispelled by *The World,* acting in conjunction with the French authorities, through the medium of the French Aviation Corps. Swarms of aeroplanes will drop hundreds of thousands of copies of President Wilson's address to Congress, printed in Paris in the German language by *The World* under the direction of its correspondent."

[68] *New York Times,* November 9, 1918.

[69] Seymour, *The Intimate Papers of Colonel House,* III, 140.

To this "educative program" the C.P.I. and the Military Intelligence set themselves with great vigor.

> Unemotional diagrams of the ever mounting American troop shipments; the unsentimental war map; a few plain questions: "Will you ever be as strong again as you were in July 1918? Will your opponents grow stronger or weaker?" Ahead of the boys, in the picture and type went our snow-storm of icy meaning.[70]

They hammered at the fact that the odds were against Germany, that American resources were unlimited,[71] and that the Germans could never hope for victory. They also emphasized the German casualties and tonnage losses and the shortage of food in the Fatherland.

One of the ways by which the C.P.I. hoped to advertise America was by entertaining foreign journalists in America. Mrs. Vira B. Whitehouse, head of the Swiss Commission of the C.P.I., tells how she succeeded in getting six distinguished Swiss journalists to go on a tour of the United States.[72] These

[70] *Stars and Stripes,* January 3, 1919. This was the official newspaper of the A.E.F. in France. See also Blankenhorn, *op. cit.,* p. 519.

[71] This campaign got Mr. Creel and his C.P.I into a little difficulty. His enthusiasm carried him away from the truth at times. The *Daily Bulletin* of March 28, 1918, had four photographs illustrating the building and shipment of airplanes to France. Said the *Bulletin:* "These aeroplane bodies, the acme of engineering art, are ready for shipment to France. Though hundreds have already been shipped, our factories have reached quantity production and thousands and thousands will soon follow." The truth of the matter was that these pictures had been taken in the airplane factories, the parts not yet ready for shipment, and that only one airplane had been shipped to France at that time. Mr. Rubel, head of the division of pictures of the C.P.I., was brought before the Senate Military Affairs Committee, and, together with George Creel, was severely criticized for making these false statements after the committee had warned them not to (*Congressional Record,* Vol. 56, pt. 5, 65th Congress, 2d Session, March 29, 1918, pp. 4253–55).

[72] Since neither Mrs. Vira B. Whitehouse in her book *A Year as Government Agent,* nor George Creel in his official report of the work of the C.P.I. gave the names of the Swiss journalists—though both mention that they came—the present writer wrote to Mr. Creel asking if those names were available. Mr. Creel replied that he could not give me the information, since he did not have it, but referred me to Mrs. Whitehouse. A letter to

visitors were taken to the New York Shipbuilding Company in New Jersey, the Squantum & Quincy plants of the Fore River Shipbuilding Company outside of Boston, the Brooklyn Navy Yard, and the Newark plant of the Submarine Boat Corporation.[73] The correspondents were allowed to write anything that they desired, the only restriction being that certain secrets of construction were not to be discussed. These men wrote home a number of enthusiastic articles concerning America's war preparations.[74] However, the Armistice came before they had returned to Switzerland and their stories had no significant part in hastening the end of the war.

In the matter of direct propaganda the Americans, though late in the field, soon became proficient. At first, they too, like the British and the French, used airplanes for the purpose of delivering leaflets. The 104th Squadron of the 5th Army was especially active in this work. This squadron made twelve trips over the German lines in the Argonne district and north of Verdun.[75] The 99th Aero Squadron was also used exten-

---

Mrs. Whitehouse elicited the reply that she had forgotten the names and that the records were destroyed. She mentioned, however, M. Martin, of the *Journal de Genève,* and Herr Oeuri, of the *Basler Nachrichten,* who could perhaps enlighten me. Finding that M. Martin was dead and that the other name was Oeri and not Oeuri, I proceeded to write to Herr Oeri. He replied very promptly with a most courteous letter, in which he gave me the names of the six journalists, told which are still living, and promised to send me copies of the articles written by these men. The journalists were: Dr. Ed. Fuster, *Neue Züricher Zeitung;* Dr. William Martin, *Journal de Genève* (both are now dead); J. Elie David, *Gazette de Lausanne;* Ernst Schürch, *Bund* of Berne; Dr. Edwin Strub, *National-Zeitung,* Basel; and Dr. Albert Oeri, *Basler Nachrichten.* The four pamphlets Dr. Oeri sent me are the collected articles written by Dr. Oeri, Dr. Edwin Strub, and Ernst Schürch. These have been placed in the Hoover War Library.

[73] For the rest of the itinerary of these journalists, see *Report,* C.P.I., pp. 106 ff.

[74] See Dr. Albert Oeri, *Aus Amerika* (Basel, 1919); Ernst Schürch, *Aus der Neuen Welt, mit der Schweizerischen Presssemission in Amerika* (Berne, 1919); and Dr. Edwin Strub, *Im Weltkriege nach Amerika* (Basel, 1919) for reprints of articles these journalists wrote.

[75] *New York Times,* July 20, 1919, Section 7, p. 4.

sively. Lieutenant C. H. Ball, who was attached to the 104th Aero Squadron of the 5th Army Observation group, says:

> We carried large packets of circulars and folders written in German, which had been prepared at a printing press behind our lines.
>
> The first of these folders distributed among the Germans was a map of the St. Mihiel salient, which showed the great gains of the Allies during a short period of time.[76]

This same folder gave the figures of the number of German prisoners taken during that and previous offensives. This was to correct the misinformation that had been given the German troops by their commanders. Other pamphlets distributed contained photographs showing the large body of American troops concentrated on the French and British fronts. "These pictures," says Lieutenant Ball, "in hundreds of thousands of instances, gave the German soldiers their first correct information as to the odds against them, and were more potent than H.E. shells."

Another of the methods of the American propagandists was to distribute thousands of postcards along the German trenches. Each had blanks for the finder to fill out in case he was taken prisoner and could then be mailed to his relatives. They were an invitation not only to stop fighting and surrender but also to send a like request to the folks behind the lines.[77]

In order to distribute propaganda with the greatest possible effectiveness the Military Intelligence ascertained the actual state of the enemy morale. This was done, for the most part, by questioning the prisoners. The officer in charge of this would first study the daily intelligence reports at General Headquarters, then visit the prison camps near Toul and Souilly and hold long interviews with prisoners of all ranks and from all parts of the Empire. Arguments which had suggested themselves as suitable for propaganda use were tried out on the prisoners and their effects noted. Specimens of Allied propaganda were discussed with these prisoners and

[76] *Ibid.* [77] *Ibid.*

they were asked to give their opinions on them. A sufficient knowledge was thus gained of the German mental process to give the officers of the Propaganda Subsection a fairly accurate idea of the sort of arguments which would make the strongest appeal.[78] The text of the proposed propaganda was then prepared, and after being approved by G.H.Q. was printed in Paris. The leaflets were then sent to the field stations which the Propaganda Subsection had established at Bar-le-Duc and Toul. A close liaison was maintained with the Air Service and leaflets were sent to the various flying fields for distribution by airplanes.[79]

In addition to the airplanes many varieties of balloons were used for spreading American ideas among the German soldiers. The largest rubber company in the United States, for instance, made 12,000 small rubber balloons at the order of the Army and Navy authorities. These balloons could be inflated to a diameter of 3½ feet and could carry 1½ pounds. At first used as targets in airplane practice, these little balloons were soon used to deliver propaganda.[80]

The advantage of these was that they could travel several hundred miles with their "eloquence," thus penetrating deeper into the enemy territory than was possible for the airplanes.[81]

The Americans also used a larger balloon with a tin container that would hold ten thousand leaflets. The balloon had a sailing range of from 600 to 800 miles. Its climb was governed by a clock attachment, and a rather ingenious mechanism allowed the leaflets to drop all together or packet by packet at regular intervals. After the last printed "bullet" had broken loose, the balloon would blow up.[82]

[78] Major E. Alexander Powell, *The Army Behind the Army,* p. 350.

[79] *Ibid.* [80] *New York Times,* July 20, 1919, Section 7, p. 4.

[81] It was found that one of these actually traveled 740 miles from the place where it was let loose (*ibid.*).

[82] George Creel, "America's Fight for World Opinion," *Everybody's Magazine,* XL, 10. The Americans also put a chemical on the leaflets so that they would not spoil if they lay out in the rain.

Our propagandists also attempted to fly kites over the trenches and to drop leaflets from traveling containers that were run up the kite wire. But this method could be used only on the fronts where airplanes were not active, since the kite wires were a menace to the planes.[83]

Thus the problem of penetrating the enemy's lines and the enemy's country with propaganda material was solved by devices and schemes of various kinds. No one method was used all the time. Nor was it always possible to distinguish between the propaganda tactics of the various countries. After July 1918, when the Allies had worked out a system of coordination, it is almost impossible to say that a certain piece of propaganda emanated from this or that country. All produced propaganda as the need arose, and those methods of delivery were used that would best meet the needs of a particular campaign at a particular time or place. The significant fact is that the Allies seemed as busy discovering new ways to send paper "bullets" over the lines as they were at inventing new implements of warfare with which to fire bullets of steel at the enemy. Bullets are important, but so is a strong morale—a will to victory.

[83] *Ibid.*

CHAPTER III

NEUTRAL COUNTRIES AS BASES OF ATTACK

> The important thing was to get the propaganda into Germany to the German people. . . . . Its publication and dissemination through the neutral papers was especially sought, since from these it went into the German newspapers.—NORTHCLIFFE, *Die Geschichte Englischen Propaganda Feldzuges* (p. 17).

No stone was left unturned by any of the warring nations in their effort to win the sympathy or the favor of the neutral countries: The press was influenced. Films of a propaganda nature competed with each other in the neutral countries' theaters. In those nations still at peace, agents and commissioners were established to devise ways and means of winning favorable sentiment for the Allies or for the Central Powers, as the case might be. No neutral country was slighted. As much attention was paid to Mexico and the South American countries as to Norway, Sweden, or Denmark. One has only to read the report of the activities of the American Committee on Public Information to grasp the importance attached to this influencing of world opinion. Mr. Robertson summed it up well when he said in the British House of Commons on August 5, 1918:

> It has been a battle of propaganda. In the neutral nations the Germans put their case and we put ours, and if, as I believe, in Europe as a whole the balance of that battle of propaganda has gone to the side of the Allies it is because they put forward the best literature, the best arguments, the most truthful and dispassionate statements.[1]

But the warring nations did not feel that it was enough to win favorable public opinion in the neutral countries; they

[1] Hansard, *Parliamentary Debates,* 5th Series, CIX, 778.

sought to make, through certain of these states, a direct attack upon their enemy. Switzerland and Holland, two neutrals which bordered upon Germany, and where many German émigrés resided, formed the logical bases for this attack.[2]

SWITZERLAND

Because of its geographical position, bordering upon France, Italy, and Germany, Switzerland was an important center for the attack upon the German home front, especially in the period from 1914 to 1917. Here the German émigrés in Switzerland attacked the German government with their newspaper, the *Freie Zeitung*. The aims of this publication were stated in the issue of September 1, 1917:

> We will be friendly to the Entente as long as it offers us a better guarantee of achieving the democratic ideals than the Central Powers. . . . . Our struggle against the regime of the Hohenzollerns and Junkers is not a struggle against the German people. On the contrary it is a struggle for the liberation of the German people from an unworthy situation.[3]

The chief editor of this newspaper was Dr. Hans Schlieben, and associated with him were Richard Grelling, Hermann Fernau-Latt, Hermann Rösemeier, Hans Suttner, Claire Studer, Jacob Feldner, Solomon Grumbach, Edward Stilgehauer, Hugo Ball, and Dr. Friedrich Wilhelm Foerster.[4] All of these were men whose value as propagandists was recognized by the Allies. They maintained close relations with the

[2] From Sweden the attack was made through a new telegraph bureau, "Dordiska Presszentralen." However, because of its geographical location Sweden was never an important center for attacks upon the enemy morale.

[3] *Almanach der Freien Zeitung 1917–1918,* herausgegeben und eingeleiten von Hugo Ball (Berne, 1918).

[4] Wilhelm Ernst, *Die antideutsche Propaganda durch das Schweizer Gebiet im Weltkrieg, speziell die Propaganda in Bayern* (Munich, 1933) p. 8. Dr. Ernst based his study on the materials in the Archives in Munich and cites the original sources for his material. Since extensive use was made of Dr. Ernst's work in this study, the writer had certain citations verified by Dr. Riedner, chief of the Bavarian Archives at Munich. Dr. Riedner's letter to the present writer is given in the appendix.

French propagandists in particular. British and American writers also were given space in the columns of the paper.[5]

The *Freie Zeitung* first made its appearance in April 1917 as a semiweekly. This four-page publication was not a newspaper in the true sense of the word. It was for the most part a collection of articles hostile to Germany.[6] When the editors wanted to expand the paper they found that they were unable to do so because they were already using their quota of paper. Hence they purchased, in May 1918, the *Tessiner Zeitung,* which was to be discontinued, so that its allotment of paper could be taken over by the *Freie Zeitung.* The latter was then made a daily instead of a semiweekly publication.[7]

The center of the French propaganda in Switzerland was at Berne under the direction of the French attaché, Frouville.

[5] According to Thimme (*Weltkrieg ohne Waffen,* p. 83), money was received by the *Freie Zeitung* from the American pacifist Herron, and from Tobler, a director in the Swiss Chocolate Factory. The articles that appeared in the *Freie Zeitung* were varied. George D. Herron, American "traveling diplomat" and close friend of Woodrow Wilson, wrote a series of articles entitled "Woodrow Wilson und der Frieden," which appeared in issues from August 15 to September 5, 1917. Otto H. Kahn, despite his denial of any connection with the *Freie Zeitung,* wrote an article "Ein Amerikaner deutscher Geburt und der Krieg," which appeared in the issue of March 2, 1918. *Almanach der Freien Zeitung 1917–1918, passim.*

[6] Examples of these are: extracts from *J'accuse* which appeared in the issues of September 8 to 12, 1917; Muehlon's *Die Verheerung Europas* ("*The Vandal of Europe*"), which appeared in part in the May 1918 issues; and Fernau's *Die Junker,* appearing in the issues of April 14 to 16, 1917. The July 1917 issues advocated the surrender of Alsace-Lorraine by Germany, stating that these provinces never were happy under Prussian rule. *Almanach der Freien Zeitung 1917–1918* has many other examples.

[7] Wilhelm Ernst, *op. cit.,* p. 8. In the summer of 1918 the Swiss authorities took legal measures against the publication for violating the act restricting the use of paper. It had used more paper during the first seven months of 1918 than it was allowed for the entire year. However, undaunted by restrictions placed upon their publication, the editors of the *Freie Zeitung* printed only a few copies of each edition in Switzerland and sent these to various foreign countries, where many copies were printed and distributed. Ernst, *op. cit.,* giving as his source *Bayer. Kriegsarchiv,* "Akten des stellv. Generalkommandos," Ib. AK, Bund 343; "Einfuhr von Druckschriften—*Freie Zeitung.*"

He kept in close touch with the central agency in Paris and also with the English Legation in Berne.[8] The French worked hand in hand with their Military Intelligence and their Secret Service. The military attaché in Berne and the consul-general at Geneva acted as intermediaries between the agents actually in Germany and the intelligence bureaus which had been established along the Swiss frontier at Annemasse, Evian, and Pontarlier.[9] Between the propaganda headquarters and the agents in Germany, there was a regular information service. The extent of this propaganda in Switzerland and the importance it had in the eyes of the participants is clearly shown in a report of the military attaché of the German Legation in Berne. According to this report, 31 XI 1917, the French attaché, Frouville, brought from Paris money and signed agreements with certain publishers in Berne to help in a campaign of propaganda against the Hohenzollern dynasty. The French also proposed to send into Germany about four hundred persons of all walks of life to form a net over Germany and to pour out propaganda against the ruling house. Their efforts were to be directed, not against the Hohenzollern dynasty alone, but against all ruling houses in the German principalities. The report states:

> The center of this movement is in Stuttgart. There four or five bureaus have already been erected by private individuals where the propagandists appear for instructions and where they are given leaflets, pamphlets, etc., to disseminate.[10]

Then the report lists the instructions which were given to the propagandists and which tell how best to avoid the suspicion

[8] Ernst, *op. cit.*, p. 4.

[9] *Ibid.*, p. 5; also Walter Nicolai, *The German Secret Service*, p. 88. Foreign agents in Switzerland became so numerous that the Swiss government was moved to warn them of the fact that Switzerland was a neutral country. *Neue Zuricher Zeitung*, August 16, 1918.

[10] *U.D.Z.*, Band 10, I, p. 267; see also Ernst, *op. cit.*, p. 26; Ewald Beckmann, *Der Dolchstoss Prozess in München vom 19 Oktober bis 20 November 1925* (Munich, 1925), p. 208.

of the police and how to do the work in the most effective manner. It continues:

The pay—plus certain expense allowances—is according to the following scale:

	Francs per month
Writers, journalists, editors	4000
Architects, language teachers	3000
Technicians, engineers	2000
Banktellers, commercial men and Department heads	1500
Merchants, bureau chiefs	1000
Waiters, cooks and porters	800
Factory workers of all sorts	500
Agricultural laborers	500

Each person designated to go to Germany was to establish affiliate groups so that all of Germany would be covered with anti-Hohenzollern groups. The affiliates were to be supplied with the necessary printed matter from Stuttgart and Berlin. The individual propagandists were to give their reports to the affiliates, and from these they were to receive their instructions, new assignments, their pay, and, when necessary, new personal papers.

For the most part the printed matter was produced in Berne. Before a publisher was given a contract to print this matter he had to attest before a notary that he had no relations with Germany, had no German capital invested in his business, employed no deserters of the Allies, and would bind himself to work for the Allies for a period of three years.[11]

Instructions on how to disseminate propaganda, for the use of German women, were also given out. In the spring of 1918 during the search of a house in Zürich an invitation to spread *Flugblätter* was found. Among other things the finder of the leaflet was told:

1. To use the leaflets as wrapping paper for bread and other foodstuffs which were sent to the soldiers.

[11] Ernst, *op. cit.*, p. 27; facts verified by Dr. Riedner, head of the Archives in Munich.

2. To look up the addresses of workers in different towns, friends, and acquaintances, and send the leaflets to them through the mail.
3. To learn the whereabouts of widows of fallen workers and give them printed matter. [Such women were thought a great help in the spread of propaganda material.]
4. To find out the attitude of the workers in the war industries toward the war. If there were any who were of an opposition mind, leaflets were to be given them for study and distribution.
5. To give to soldiers home on furlough gifts of cigars, tobacco, paper, etc. These were to be wrapped in propaganda leaflets.
6. To leave leaflets in the restaurants and in all places where workers and soldiers congregated.[12]

Evidence that the Allied propagandists were working with the liberals in Germany is found in Instruction Number 7, which asked the individual to keep in close touch with the German confidants (*Vertrauensmänner*) of the Allies and to talk things over with them first. "If there is no confidante, go to the confidante of the U.S.P.D."

The Allies had numerous agents in Germany who were working for the overthrow of the German government,[13] or who were assisting the Independent Socialists in stirring up labor troubles, especially in the munitions plants. Major General Wrisberg, Director of the National War Department, records in his book that incoming reports to the War Ministry stated:

> It is almost certain that there is in Germany a secret committee of central activity, which works under English authority and unlimited English financial aid in conjunction with the radical elements of the Social Democrats for a revolution among the German working class.[14]

[12] Germany, Reichstag, *Verhandlungen des Reichstags,* Band 313, 173 Sitzung, June 12, 1918, p. 5447; also Ernst, *op. cit.*, p. 28, quoting from *Bayer Kriegsarchiv,* "Akten des Kriegsministeriums," "Verbreitung revolutionärer Propagandaschriften—Abwehr," Vol. J, 1917 mit 1918.

[13] Colonel House wrote in his diary, May 19, 1917: "My thought is to give the German liberals every possible encouragement" (Charles Seymour, *The Intimate Papers of Colonel House* [New York, 1926–1928], III, 125).

[14] Ernst Wrisberg, *Der Weg zur Revolution 1914–1918* (Leipzig, 1921), p. 50.

In regard to the labor disturbances in the early part of 1918 the *Norddeutsche Zeitung* for February 8, 1918, reported from Munich:

> The Civil Court has issued an order for the arrest of a mechanic named Lorenz Winkler for participation in the strike. Before the war Winkler was abroad, and after his return to Germany kept up his relations with foreign countries. That foreign influences were at work during the strike may also be shown by the fact that on each of the men arrested a pamphlet was found which was certainly written by a foreigner. In this pamphlet an endeavor is made to prevent the people from subscribing to the Eighth War Loan, and stir up the German people.[15]

The methods used to smuggle propaganda into Germany were numerous. One method was to give the leaflets to Germans who worked in Switzerland and crossed the border every morning and every evening. The same method was employed among school children who had to cross the border to go to school. One of the most interesting methods was to fill leather sacks with propaganda leaflets, put cork on the ends of them, and throw them into the Rhine to be carried into Germany.[16] Sailboats which had balls of propaganda literature attached to them under water often floated on Lake Constance across to Germany.[17]

The English, though more active in Holland, had propaganda headquarters in Switzerland also. The British Consulate in Zürich was the center of propaganda activity in Switzerland. In the service of the English was a Swiss by the name of Wolfsohn, alias Mendelbaum, born in Prussia. He had under him a staff of subagents and *Vertrauensleuten*. His chief agent was Fräulein Claire von der Mühle, in Basle. An American, John F. Kern, in Zürich, was also in the British propaganda service. When, in June 1917, the British prepared to get 60,000 copies of a leaflet entitled *Bayern! Landesleute* from Rorschach to

[15] *Norddeutsche Zeitung,* February 8, 1918; also *British Daily Review of the Foreign Press,* Vol. 6, p. 972.

[16] Huber, *op. cit.,* p. 65.

[17] *Ibid.*

Germany by way of Lake Constance,[18] Kern expressed this opinion:

> It is right that the authors of the printed materials should be mostly Germans who are seeking to democratize their country. In Germany we possess many confidantes (*Vertrauensleute*), namely, under the Socialists and among the working class, who are working hand in hand with us. The circle is getting larger. We hope for success soon and then for peace![19]

False editions of German newspapers also were published and sent into Germany. The Service aérienne sent an "edition" of the *Frankfurter Zeitung* of July 31, 1917, and two false editions of the *Strassburger Post* into Germany.[20] Hansi also bought up the entire edition of the *Berner Tageblatt* of March 29, 1917, which contained good propaganda material, and sent it across the border to Germany.[21] Hiding propaganda among freight shipments from Switzerland to Germany became so prevalent that the General Staff complained to the War Ministry that a more careful inspection system should be established. But, despite closer inspection, leaflets and books continued to cross the Swiss border into Germany.[22] In Lindau, for instance, a crate of books, supposedly coming from the firm of Heheber of Geneva, was taken by the German authorities. This contained, besides a few harmless works, more than 8,000 pieces of propaganda material.[23]

Revolutionary material began to find its way into Germany from Switzerland during the latter part of the war.[24] In July 1917 the following leaflet crossed the German-Swiss border.

[18] The delivery was made on the night of June 2–3, 1917. For his part of the work Kern received 1,000 francs, while a Swiss, a Mr. Fischer, who had been engaged by Kern for translating purposes, got 600 francs. Thimme, *op. cit.*, p. 60.

[19] Wilhelm Ernst, *op. cit.*, p. 3.

[20] Hansi et Tonnelat, *À Travers les lignes ennemies*, p. 65.

[21] *Ibid.*, p. 144.

[22] Thimme, *op. cit.*, p. 59.

[23] Thimme, *Weltkrieg ohne Waffen*, p. 59. Hansi admits that these were not sent by the Geneva firm but by Raymond Schule, Hansi's arch-smuggler. Hansi et Tonnelat, *op. cit.*, p. 145.

[24] Generalleutnant W. F. K. Altrock, *Deutschlands Niederbruch*, p. 24.

Germany Awake and send away those who are most responsible for this whole madness.

All princes and diplomats who are responsible for this world-disrupting war have to sink before one can think of peace!

Who needs a Kaiser and King? Man is born free and does not need a Divine Right master, who can be, by the Grace of God, the greatest criminal and dumbhead.

We have preached for four years already, a Republic as the only form of state and the only thing that will guarantee the peace. . . . .

No one should reign, for Lordship means Lords, servants, freemen and slaves. . . . . But man is free and if the situation will not allow it, we are here to change the situation. . . . .

We are the state! Each one of us![25]

By January 1918 the smuggling of revolutionary propaganda into Germany from Switzerland began in earnest. Berne was the center of the Zimmerwald propaganda from 1915 on. The Swiss Left Social Democrats took part in this propaganda and they also helped the Allies in their campaign against the Hohenzollerns. With this help and that of the German exiles in Switzerland, the Allied propagandists were able to flood Germany with well-written propaganda literature of a revolutionary character.

HOLLAND

Holland offered a convenient field for the propagandists because of its long frontier bordering upon Germany over which propaganda could be smuggled easily, and because the sympathies of the Dutch were from the first favorable to the Allies. A glance at the map will show that the whole of the Netherlands eastern frontier, from Groningen on the north to the southern extremity of Limburg in the south, lies open to Germany. As soon as Belgium was invaded by the Germans, the Dutch viewed their situation with consternation.[26] If Ger-

[25] Ernst, *op. cit.*, p. 13.

[26] It was part of the Schlieffen plan to violate the neutrality of Holland; but Moltke, Schlieffen's successor, did not want to make an enemy of Holland: "If we make Holland our enemy we shall stop the last air-hole through which we can breathe" (C. R. M. F. Cruttwell, *A History of the Great War 1914–1918* [Oxford, 1934], p. 8).

many went so far as to invade Belgium, what would prevent her from invading Holland should she feel the need of such action? By August 5 some parts of Holland had already been placed in a "state of war," and on August 10, when the Germans made progress in Belgium, mobilization was rushed in the southern provinces of Limburg, North Brabant, and Zeeland, as well as in part of Gelderland. On August 29 various frontier communities near Belgium were placed in a "state of siege," and on September 8 the mouths of rivers were declared to be in a "state of siege."[27]

Thus the Allies had one great advantage from the very beginning. We have already seen how the Entente propagandists worked through the neutral press; how news dispatches of Allied origin were sent to the neutral papers; and how, through these, Allied news leaked into Germany. From Holland, however, the great attack upon Germany was not through the press. In the Netherlands there existed a revolutionary agitation, quietly encouraged by the Allies and at times openly assisted by them. Besides deserters from the German Army there were in Holland political refugees, people who desired the overthrow of the German government. Chief among the refugees was Carl Minster, who had spent fourteen years in America as a journalist. While in America he had edited the *Neu Yorker Volkszeitung* and had acted as correspondent for various German Social Democratic newspapers. Returning to Germany in 1912 he became editor of the *Bergischen Arbeiterstimme* and later managing editor of the *Niederrheinischen Arbeiterzeitung* in Duisburg.[28] He was expelled from the Social Democratic party early in 1916, and in July he founded his own radical weekly, *Der Kampf,* which was published at Duisburg. To avoid military service he fled to Holland on March 31, 1917.

[27] *Times History of the War,* XIII, 182. Various naval measures were also adopted. The channels between Wadden Eslands, north of the Zuider Zee, were barred by mines; mines were placed also in the Scheldt.

[28] *U.D.Z.,* Band 10, I, p. 236; also Thimme, *op. cit.,* p. 107.

From Holland, Minster corresponded regularly with members of the Independent Socialist party in Germany such as Hugo Haase, Rosi Wolfstein, and Else Beck. His relations were not limited to the U.S.P.D., however, for he was in close touch with the Left radicals and the Spartacists.[29] In Holland, also, Minster found friends among the Socialists—the Dutch Social Democratic party—who supported him in the establishment of *Der Kampf* in Amsterdam.[30] This weekly had as its purpose the overthrow of the German government and its slogan was, "Our enemy is Germany."

To make his work more effective Minster enlisted the help of the various deserters' organizations in Holland. He soon converted Der Freie Arbeiter and Arbeiter Verbildungsverein Deutscher Zunge—two of the deserters' organizations in Holland—into political associations, with the overthrow of the Hohenzollerns as their aim.[31] Besides these, the followers of Minster founded Die Freien Leser des Kampfes, which spread to nearly all cities in Holland. He also founded a German section of the Dutch Social Democratic party.[32] Thus Minster, through these various organizations and through *Der Kampf,* was in a position to attack the German government very effectively.

Minster directed his attention especially to the radicals and to the young workers in Germany. He called on these people to refuse military service and to desert from the trenches. Helped by like-minded friends in Germany, Minster was able to get large numbers of leaflets over the German borders each week.[33] One of his co-workers summed up their activities when he said, in a speech before the Social Democratic party in Rotterdam,

[29] Thimme, *op. cit.,* p. 237; also *Süddeutsche Monatshefte,* April 1924, p. 9.

[30] This was not necessarily a continuation of *Der Kampf* of Duisburg. He merely called it by the same name.

[31] *U.D.Z.,* Band 10, I, p. 238.

[32] *Ibid.*

[33] "Die Vermittlungsstellen im neutralen Ausland," "Auf Grund unveröffentlichter Akten" (*Süddeutsche Monatshefte,* April 1924, p. 10).

We went to the borders daily to bring our leaflets to Germany. . . . . We went secretly through the brush, so that no one could see us, to the border, and there we were met by friends who took our material from us. Not only we, but various Social Revolutionary Parties in Holland sent their people to the borders to distribute their leaflets.[34]

Minster also obtained the services of a tailor, Grohmann, in Hamborn[35] and two deserters, Rohbach and Simon, for smuggling *Der Kampf* into Germany. Dutch workers also took copies of this publication across the border.

The Allied propagandists made use of this Minster organization to get propaganda into Germany.[36] Although it cannot be definitely established that the British provided Minster with money, as charged by the Germans, it has been established that the English worked with Minster in getting leaflets and pamphlets into Germany. Captain Tinsley, one of the British agents in Holland, was especially close to Minster and his organization. Minster's list of people who were pledged to distribute propaganda material in Germany was at the disposal of Tinsley.[37] Furthermore, according to Minster, the English subscribed for 9,000 copies of *Der Kampf,* after it was established in Amsterdam.[38]

In the use of the German deserters for propaganda purposes Minster was a great help to the Allies. When the deserters into Holland became too numerous,[39] the Dutch government

[34] *U.D.Z., op. cit.,* p. 239.

[35] As a reward for his services he was to get rubber to smuggle into Germany. *Ibid.*

[36] Rohbach himself stated that he had been engaged by the French agent in Holland, de Corte, to distribute *Der Kampf. Ibid.,* p. 240.

[37] *Ibid.*

[38] *Ibid.*

[39] An estimate of the number of deserters who went to Holland is given in a letter of April 2, 1917, from Antwerp to Sheffield. It states in part: "Holland is full of Boches, and there are now 90,000 Boche deserters. The exact number has been discovered from their bread cards, for which they have to enter their names" (*Confidential Supplement to the Daily Review of the Foreign Press,* No. 142, April 28, 1917).

established institutions for them.[40] These deserters were accessible to the Allied propagandists, and especially to Minster. He examined them regarding their place of service, the spirit of the troops and the people, the facts regarding the food situation, and other matters. This information was given to the anti-German paper, *De Telegraaf,* in Amsterdam, from which it went directly to Mr. Brain, the correspondent of *The Times* (London).[41] Furthermore, through his many associates and confidants in Germany, Minster was able to supply the Allies with news regarding the economic and political situation behind the front, facts of particular interest to the propagandists.[42]

Besides this work with Minster, the Allies had organizations of their own in Holland. The French had established, through their Intelligence Service, nine sections located at The Hague, Amsterdam, Rotterdam, Arnheim, S'Hertogenbosch, Maastricht, Zwolle, Assen, and Groningen.[43] From these sections propaganda literature was sent into Germany. A fairly active organization was also set up under the French agent, Javaux. Under him were such men as DeJong and Blens, who sought means for getting propaganda into the enemy country.[44] These men enlisted the support of longshoremen at Deljzyl, who smuggled leaflets into boats destined for Germany. They also got the help of railroad-station agents, who put leaflets into cars headed for Germany, while German deserters got material into the Fatherland through their friends. One of these deserters in Holland, Herr Ruhr, gives the following account of this activity:

[40] *Times History of the War,* XIII, 198.

[41] *Süddeutsche Monatshefte,* May 1924, p. 81.

[42] In December 1917, Minster himself crossed the Dutch border at Limburg to receive the mail brought from Cologne.

[43] *U.D.Z.,* Band 10, I, p. 261. The French had Joseph Crozier on a special mission in Holland, and he penetrated into Germany as an agent. Mr. Crozier gives a rather melodramatic account of his activities in Holland and Germany in his book, *In the Enemy's Country,* translated from the French by Forest Wilson (New York, 1931).

[44] *U.D.Z.,* Band 10, I, p. 263.

I discovered in the meantime, that two deserters came over to Germany with propaganda books which called on the soldiers to desert. . . . . In Arnheim I gave one of these away myself. In the first page it said in the book, *Kaiser—Republik, Krieg und Frieden.* On the back side is the call to desert. It says there, "He who calls out *Deutschland—Republik* will not be treated as an enemy." . . . . These books were brought in packages, across the border in great numbers. The chief aim is to cause discontent at the front. The organization is in the hands of Asselt. The leaflets are brought to the border by Dutch confidantes and from here they are taken over the border by German deserters.

The names of the two deserters who went to Germany with the propaganda books were Friedrich Grasshoff and Gerhart Breuer. Both returned to Holland.[45]

In the latter part of the war the Northcliffe organization became active in Holland also. In June 1918 the Intelligence Section of the German Foreign Office sent out the following communication:

FOREIGN OFFICE
INTELLIGENCE SECTION A.N.
Secret 667

BERLIN, June 25
1918.

To the Military Representative at the Foreign Office.

According to a report received here, the newly established propaganda bureau of Lord Northcliffe in Holland, which is in close connection with the English Legation at The Hague, is henceforth to direct political propaganda against the Central Powers. This Bureau plans to purchase various restaurants and hotels on the Dutch-German border, particularly on the line from Nijmegen to Maastricht, in order to be able to expedite their propaganda literature from these points to Germany without hindrances. According to one estimate, this Bureau has

[45] *U.D.Z.,* Band 10, I, p. 263. A German ship captain relates how he almost helped the English get propaganda into Germany from Sweden: "During my stay at Gothenburg an unknown man came aboard my ship and asked me if I could take a box of glass with me to Germany. I told him I could, and the man left me his telephone number. He spoke Swedish rather brokenly and it is my opinion that he was a Britisher. It became known to me in Gothenburg that the British attempted to smuggle leaflets into Germany in glass boxes. Glass was chosen because there was no restriction on its exportation from Sweden" (*ibid.,* p. 266).

been organized with a fund of about two million dollars which will be exclusively used for political propaganda.[46]

Whether or not the English purchased or even planned to purchase hotels and restaurants along the Dutch-German border it is impossible to prove. But they did use these places for depositing propaganda material which could be picked up and read, and if the leaflets themselves were not taken across the border, at least their contents might make an impression upon those people who went over the border into Germany.

Of the use made of the Dutch workers, Northcliffe's chief colleague says:

There crossed the Dutch frontier every morning a large number of Dutch workers who were employed on German soil. Every evening they returned to their homes in Holland. An envoy from Crewe House mixed with them, won over a certain trustworthy few and these found means of disseminating either by word of mouth or by printed matter, information designed to prove to German minds that their interests were being betrayed.[47]

The American Committee on Public Information also was active in Holland. Mr. Henry Suydam was the commissioner for Holland. Realizing the value of "personal tours," he escorted, on June 5, 1918, Dr. Peter Geyl, of the *Nieuwe Rotterdamsche Courant* and Mr. E. W. DeJong, of the *Handelsblad* (Amsterdam), to Queenstown for an inspection of the American destroyer base. Upon returning from Queenstown the correspondents had a long interview with Admiral Sims. Arriving in Paris on June 14, they proceeded to the French coast at St. Nazaire and followed the American communication lines to the front in Lorraine.

Thus, the two representatives of the two most important Dutch newspapers had followed the course of an American soldier from the moment his transport was picked up by the convoys until he had arrived in a front line trench. From this trip, which was one of the first excur-

[46] R. H. Lutz, *The Fall of the German Empire, 1914–1918* (Stanford University, 1932), I, 161.

[47] Hamilton Fyfe, *Northcliffe,* p. 243.

sions of neutral editors to the American front, there resulted 19 long telegrams and 9 mail stories in the Dutch press, all of which were copied extensively by the German press, and provided good neutral testimony of the size of the American effort.[48]

Great pains were taken by the American propagandists to get Wilson's speeches to the German people. Mr. Suydam and the American Minister, John W. Garrett, at The Hague, both insisted that these speeches be given directly to the Dutch and German news agencies. In several instances, therefore, the addresses were telegraphed directly to the Committee on Public Information headquarters and from there they were distributed to a Dutch news agency, which either telegraphed the texts directly to the German press, or handed them to German correspondents, who telegraphed them to their newspapers.[49]

Suydam also had a list of people in Germany to whom material could be sent directly through the mail. Wilson's pronouncements concerning the League of Nations, comprising excerpts from his speeches from February 1, 1916, to September 27, 1918, were put in pamphlet form. Efforts were made to send these pamphlets to the German people on this list. Many of them were also placed in Dutch libraries, schools, and universities and distributed to editors and Dutch governmental officials.[50]

Thus did the Allies use Switzerland and Holland as centers of attack upon the morale of the enemy. The methods used for this attack were many and varied. The aim was always to win over the neutral press and through it to disseminate stories in Germany, and to send propaganda leaflets directly into Germany by whatever means possible. As Sir Campbell Stuart states:

> Some of the methods can never be revealed, but it is permissible to hint that, for instance, among foreign workmen of a certain nationality

[48] C.I.P., *Report*, p. 177. Arrangements were made also to take the leading Dutch editors in Paris on similar trips.

[49] *Ibid.*, p. 176; Creel, *How We Advertised America*, p. 328.

[50] *Ibid.*, p. 332.

who went into Germany each morning and returned each evening, there might be some to whom propagandist work was not uncongenial. And of course, all secret agents were not necessarily Allies or neutrals. Somehow, huge masses of literature were posted in Germany to select addresses from which the German Postal revenues derived no benefit. . . . . No avenue of approach into enemy countries was considered too insignificant, for each had its particular use.[51]

[51] Sir Campbell Stuart, *Secrets of Crewe House,* p. 103.

CHAPTER IV

ANALYSIS OF PROPAGANDA

> When in 1917, the Supreme Command was quartered at Kreuznach, there was already a vast amount of material. A collection of it, consisting of extraordinary brochures, pamphlets, and of single leaflets and pictures, covered several layers thick, a table in my bureau large enough for twelve people to sit at, although there was only one specimen of each document.—WALTER NICOLAI, *The German Secret Service* (p. 162).

A study of the leaflets, books, and pamphlets issued by the Allies against the enemy reveals that the propaganda material went through five fairly well-defined stages. Each of these stages had a definite aim, and all led up to the final aim: the destruction of the German Empire. Although it is impossible to state exactly when one stage left off and the other began, the five types of propaganda material are quite clearly distinguishable in the following order: (1) propaganda of enlightenment; (2) propaganda of despair; (3) propaganda of hope; (4) particularistic propaganda; and (5) revolutionary propaganda. Since it would be an endless task to give all of the points of view of the messages, or all of the insinuations that the many leaflets and pamphlets contained, we shall give examples of only the more or less typical, and through these see just how the paper war was carried on. Only the first four types will be discussed now, the revolutionary propaganda being left for another chapter.

PROPAGANDA OF ENLIGHTENMENT

In time of war no nation gives out information regarding the military or political situation which would be detrimental to the fighting power of the country or disheartening or depressing to its population. France, by the law of August 5, 1914, forbade the publication of any news of a military or diplomatic nature that might have the effect of weakening the morale of the people. Only such military or diplomatic news could be printed as came from the War Department.[1] In England the Defense of the Realm Act regulated the printing and distribution of pamphlets and leaflets. This act made it an offense for any person by word of mouth or by writing or by means of any printed book, pamphlet, or document to spread reports or make statements "calculated to cause disaffection to His Majesty or prejudice His Majesty's relations with foreign powers."[2] In the United States the Committee on Public Information persuaded the press to accept a "voluntary censorship," and only such war news was printed as emanated from the C.P.I. or the War Department.

The press of Germany was no less restricted than that of the Allies. The German General Staff set up the "Kriegspresseamt," which supplied the press with war news.[3] In all of the warring nations, therefore, there were restrictions on the type of news that could be printed, and war news emanated from official sources only.

This restriction meant that facts of a military nature were withheld from the public. If the Germans failed to tell their people of their military defeats, the English failed to report all of the ships lost in the submarine campaign.[4] If the Ger-

[1] *Vide supra,* chapter i.

[2] See *Supplement to the London Gazette,* August 13, 1914, pp. 6380–81, for complete provisions of the act. *The Times* (London) for February 4, 1918, tells of the arrest of one Samuel H. Street for distributing leaflets outside of Central Hall, Westminster. On August 21, 1917, Arnold Lupton, a former M.P., was charged with distributing leaflets to prisoners of war.

[3] For a full discussion of German censorship during the war, see R. H. Lutz, *The Fall of the German Empire, 1914–1918* (Stanford University, 1932), Vol. I, chapter iv.

[4] When the British battleship "Audacious" was sunk off the coast of Ireland, October 27, 1914, the British failed to make its loss public. Shortly

mans neglected to inform their people of the actual size of the American forces coming to the aid of France, the French failed to report the full facts of the military situation before the coming of the Americans. In other words, none of the warring nations allowed facts that would weaken the people's will to fight to be published. As Will Irwin, who was in charge of the Foreign Bureau of the American C.P.I., put it: "We never told the whole truth—not by any manner of means. We told that part which served our national purpose."[5] And Spencer Hughes expressed it well in a speech in the House of Commons. Arguing in favor of Lord Northcliffe for the Minister of Propaganda, he asked what that minister should do. Answering his own question he said: "It is to collect—I will not say to concoct—information and to get the people to believe the information."[6]

The first task of the Allied propagandists was, therefore, to impart to the German people those facts which their military leaders kept from them. A "Trench Newspaper" was published by the British and distributed to the German troops. This was a single-page "newspaper" which told of the victories of the Allies; it also illustrated the advances of the British from month to month by means of maps. The French issued the *Truppen Nachrichtenblatt,* which, though it was only a small leaflet, contained such pointed statements as these: "Foch Leading New Attack," "Entente Armies Press Forward on Another Wide Front," "Turkish Army in Palestine De-

after the battle of the Falkland Islands, Mr. Churchill made up his mind to go to the House of Commons and make a statement as to the loss of the "Audacious." "But just as he was about to go out of the admiralty door he was tackled by Lord Fisher, who cajoled him and threatened and browbeat him to such an extent that he [Churchill] allowed himself to be turned away from his intended course, and he remained silent on this point" (Rear-Admiral Sir Douglas Brownrigg, Bt., *Indiscretions of the Naval Censor* [New York, 1920], p. 46).

[5] Will Irwin, "An Age of Lies," *Sunset,* XLIII (1919), 54.

[6] Hansard, *Parliamentary Debates,* 5th ser., CIV, 82.

Deutscher General flüchtet.

Die Türken halten Liman von Sanders für ihr Unheil verantwortlich.

Zwei Armeen vernichtet.

Bulgaren werden auch auf ausgedehnter Balkanfront verfolgt.

Düstere Stimmung des Grafen Hertling.

Der Sieg der englischen Truppen in Palästina über die vom deutschen General Liman von Sanders befehligten türkischen Truppen hat sich entwickelt und hat viel größere Dimensionen angenommen als die ersten Berichte andeuteten.

Zwei türkische Armeen, die 7. und die 8., haben aufgehört zu existieren.

Ihr ganzes Train, alle ihre Geschütze, ihr ganzes Kriegsmaterial ist erbeutet worden. 30000 Mann ergaben sich.

Die wenigen, die dem Tode oder der Gefangenschaft entgingen, flüchteten in kleinen, zusammenhangslosen Gruppen über den Jordanfluß und treiben sich nun im Lande herum.

Jetzt verfolgen die Engländer die 4. türkische Armee, welche auch in Gefahr steht vernichtet zu werden. Auf jeden Fall ist der türkische Widerstand in Palästina entgültig gebrochen.

General Liman von Sanders, der deutsche Befehlshaber, der so vollständig überrascht und vom feindlichen Hauptquartier an Führung so übertroffen wurde, flüchtet vor den Engländern.

Die Türken behaupten sie seien verraten und von den deutschen Offizieren, die ihren Streitkräften vorgesetzt waren, ins Unglück geführt worden.

Palästina ist ihnen nun auf ewig verloren. Die Heiligen Stätten sind von der Muselmannherrschaft befreit. Die Entente hat sich verpflichtet Palästina dem jüdischen Volke zurückzugeben.

Der Sieg der französischen und der serbischen Truppen über die Bulgaren im Balkangebirge hat sich in schlagender Weise entwickelt.

Die Bulgaren ziehen sich jetzt auf einer Front von

160 Kilometern zurück.

Sie haben dem Vordringen der Ententetruppen keinen starken Widerstand entgegengesetzt. Die deutschen Niederlagen an der Westfront haben sie sehr niedergedrückt und ihren Kampfeifer geschwächt. Wir wissen, daß es nutzlos ist den Kampf fortzusetzen.

Dies weiß auch Graf Hertling, der Reichskanzler. Er hat dem Hauptausschuß des Reichstags gesagt, daß tiefe Unzufriedenheit weite Kreise der Bevölkerung ergriffen hat. Was empfiehlt er? Daß das deutsche Volk das alte, sichere Vertrauen auf Hindenburg und Ludendorff bewahren soll, in der Hoffnung, daß sie die Lage ein wenig bessern möchten. Aber er weiß, wir wissen und alle Welt weiß, daß sie sie nicht bessern können;

nur das deutsche Volk selbst

kann eine Besserung herbeiführen dadurch, daß es der Autokratie und dem Militarismus, dem Alldeutschtum und den veralteten Lächerlichkeiten, die andere Völker schon längst abgeschafft haben, ein Ende macht.

A Bit of Enlightenment

The *Truppen Nachrichtenblatt,* issued by the British, kept the Germans informed on the progress of the war on the various fronts. The pointed headlines told much.

stroyed," "No Further Opposition to English Expected," "20,000 Prisoners Taken."[7]

Charts and diagrams showing plainly the number of prisoners taken and the number of dead and wounded on each side were sent to the German trenches. So accurate were these estimates of the losses to Germany that Eugene Netter was prompted to write:

> The leaflets told the losses of the Germans in the first offensive. The number lost in one of our regiments as given in the leaflets tallied exactly with the actual loss. Hence thereafter the entire contents of the leaflets was believed and one was stunned at the greatness of our losses.[8]

When the French took the offensive in 1918, they also sowed the German trenches with maps upon which their gains were clearly marked.[9] They recalled the false hopes which the German leaders had held out to the people and the army. They circulated an alleged statement in a German newspaper which lamented that "a few weeks ago it appeared as if our armies were near their goal: The defeat of the enemy forces and peace. But what a change."[10]

Another method of enlightenment was to select special topics from time to time and, by means of a series of "London Letters," to get them into the neutral press and from there into Germany.[11] These invariably told of the food supply of the Allies and often contained stories of the shortage of food in the enemy countries.

Whenever the Allied propagandists could make the German officials appear guilty of falsification they did so. In October 1917 the Germans gave out an estimate of the tonnage of the Allies for transporting American troops across the

[7] *Truppen Nachrichtenblatt,* 1013; also *Leaflet A.P. 1000,* Hoover War Library collection.

[8] Eugene Netter, *Der Seelische Zusammenbruch der deutschen Kampffront* (Munich, 1925), p. 11. [9] *Fliegerabwurf-Schriften,* No. 15.

[10] Harold D. Lasswell, *Propaganda Technique in the World War* (New York, 1927), p. 165. [11] Stuart, *Secrets of Crewe House,* p. 99.

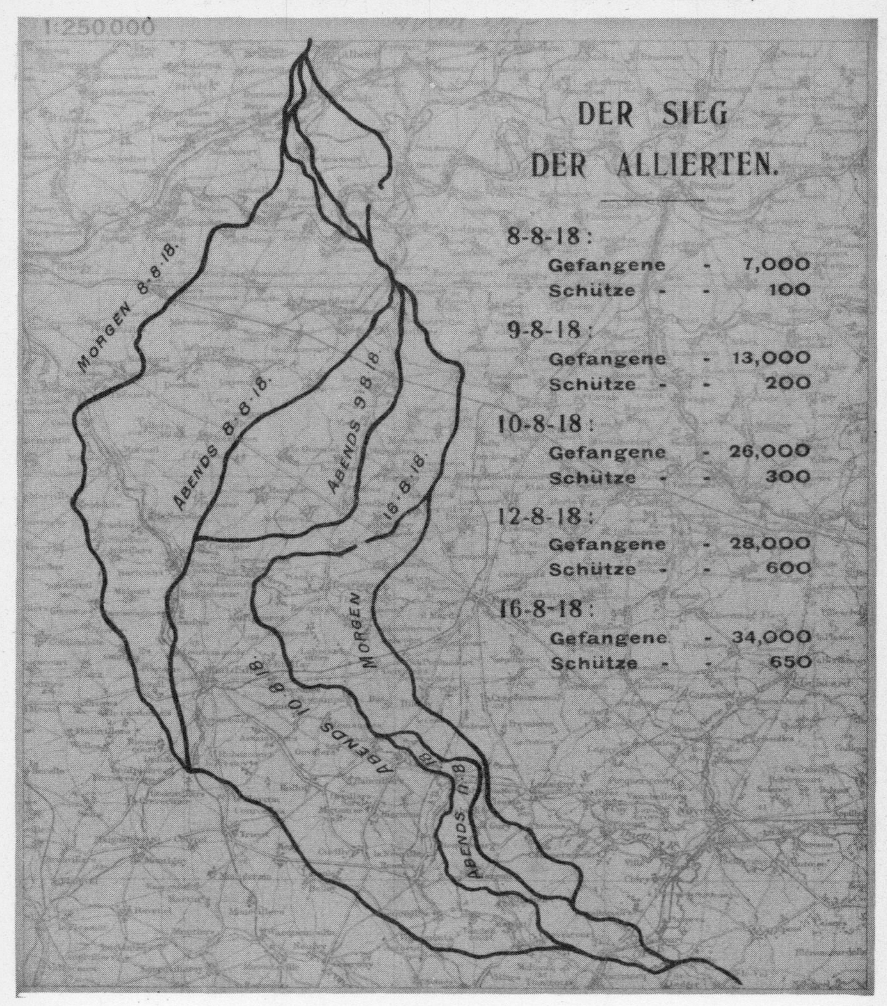

THE VICTORIES OF THE ALLIES

This map, showing with large red lines the gains of the Allies, was part of the intensive drive against the morale of the enemy in the last four months of the war.

ocean which showed that at best not more than 12 American divisions (250,000 troops) could be brought to France by the late summer of 1918. This estimate was published in the German papers in an effort to belittle America as a factor in the war.[12] Furthermore it was stated that these troops would still be unfit for battle—would have to be trained in France for several months yet before they could be pushed to the front. And again on May 17, 1918, the official news agency issued a statement for publication that the number of American fighting troops in France was to be estimated at about ten divisions—only four of these being at the front. "The total of all those back of the lines as well as in them, is at the most from 150,000 to 200,000 men." And the report continued, "Press notices should therefore state that America has not been able to meet its expectations in the way of sending troops and the earlier estimates of the German General Staff, as to what Ameria could do, has proved to be true."[13]

The propagandists corrected this misinformation by sending out, by leaflet,[14] the letter of Secretary Baker to President Wilson in which the Secretary of War gave the following monthly figures on the arrival of troops in France between May 1917 and June 1918:

Month	Troops	Month	Troops
1917			
May	1,718	September	32,423
June	12,261	October	38,259
July	12,988	November	23,016
August	18,323	December	48,840
1918			
January	46,776	April	117,212
February	48,027	May	244,345
March	83,811	June	276,372
Marines			14,644
Total to July 1, 1918			1,019,115

[12] Dr. Kurt Mühsam, *Wie wir belogen wurden* (Munich, 1918), p. 11.

[13] *Ibid.*, p. 1. As a matter of fact there were at that time nearly one million American troops in France.

[14] *Leaflet A.P. 61.*

A.P. 74.

BY BALLOON.
Durch Luftballon.

Die erste Million.

AMERICA IS COMING!

This Air-Post *Leaflet* was part of the campaign of despair, to show that the odds were against the Germans.

To emphasize the American help, another leaflet again listed the troop arrivals for the months of April, May, and June, 1918, which totaled 637,929. Commenting upon the efficiency of this transportation of troops the leaflet stated: "Lost at sea while coming over, 291."[15]

The Friends of German Democracy later informed the Germans that 1,500,000 American troops had arrived in France, while many more were ready to come over.

THE AMERICAN HELP

1,500,000 American soldiers are in France; more than twice that number is being trained in America. One single draft call in a single month gives almost as many recruits as a year in Germany. A fleet of 5 million tons, which can carry more than 13 million tons a year; a fleet which, together with the English fleet, would form between Europe and America, an unbroken line, and which brings an endless supply of steel, copper, explosives, grain, petroleum, and munitions . . . . These are the powers against which the cliques in Germany are struggling.

FRIENDS OF GERMAN DEMOCRACY IN AMERICA[16]

The propagandists impressed upon the Germans not only the facts of American military aid but also the greatness of America's economic strength. The aim, of course, was to convince the German people that the Allies had access to unlimited food supplies. *Leaflet A.P. 89* gave the International Agricultural Institute estimates of 1918 crop prospects in the United States and Canada as follows:

Wheat
U.S. 211,519,000 doublehundred weight (36% increase over 1917)
Canada 63,042,000 doublehundred weight (10% increase over 1917)

Oats
U.S. 186,238,000 doublehundred weight (9% less than 1917)
Canada 59,789,000 doublehundred weight (7% increase over 1917)

Barley
U.S. 44,762,000 doublehundred weight (10% increase over 1917)
Canada 16,472,000 doublehundred weight (53% increase over 1917)

[15] *Leaflet A.P. 84.*
[16] *Fliegerabwurf-Schriften,* No. 23.

Rye

U.S. 18,507,000 doublehundred weight (35% increase over 1917)

Corn

U.S. 716,680,000 doublehundred weight (same as in 1918)[17]

When the questions of war aims came up, the Allied propagandists saw another opportunity to push forward their campaign of enlightenment. No people will continue to fight, or to bear the hardships of a war if it does not know what it is fighting for. The German people had been told that the Fatherland was fighting a defensive war. But as the war progressed and the German troops penetrated farther into the enemy territories, some groups began to ask whether the "defensive war" was not turning into a war of conquest. Some of the press began to discuss the war aims; but that was soon forbidden. The German Chancellor's speech of August 19, 1915, led some newspapers to make inquiries regarding the Polish question. However, their attention was called to the order prohibiting any public discussion of the German war aims, "an order which covers the discussion of events that, in the future, may occur in the east."[18]

The excuse given by the officials for not wanting the Polish question discussed was that such discussion would be impossible without arousing party antagonisms.

> If opinions did not differ to such a degree, there would be no reason for such a demand. But if the discussion were permitted at this early date the quarrel of the parties would surely be carried by the papers into the conquered countries and would affect the Polish people.
>
> It is hardly necessary to point out how pleased our enemies would be to discover something that might be taken for a symptom indicating the disintegration of our inner solidarity, and that at a time when our armies are so victorious.[19]

[17] *Leaflet A.P. 89.*

[18] Hamburg-Polizeibehörde, *Zensur-anordnungen,* No. 6214, September 7, 1915, p. 177. Listed also as Document XIIf. of R. H. Lutz, *The Fall of the German Empire, 1914–1918,* I, 185.

[19] *Ibid.*

But the newspaper *Vorwärts* conducted a steady and insistent campaign for an open discussion of the German war aims. In January 1915 it printed arguments intended to show why the ban on such a discussion should be lifted:

> Even our diplomacy can profit by a sensibly restricted discussion in the press, as the public opinion of a people, of whom the highest demands are being exacted in all fields, expects to be enlightened in due time about important questions by official agencies.[20]

But those who favored such a "forward step" seemed to be making no headway, for the Chancellor, in response to an interpellation in the Reichstag on May 15, 1917, said:

> Gentlemen, the interpellations which have just now been brought forward demand from me a definite statement regarding the question of our war aims. To make such a statement at the present moment would not serve the interests of the country. I must therefore, decline to make one.[21]

This failure of the German government to announce its war aims was a great help to the Allied propagandists. What could be more effective than, on the one hand, to accuse Germany of imperialistic designs and on the other to tell the German people that the Allies had only idealistic interests in the war, and were fighting for the liberation of humanity from the yoke of militarism and greed. The French dropped packets of leaflets over Berlin which stated in part:

> Many clear-sighted Germans know today already that the war was instigated by the military degenerates of Berlin and Vienna.....
>
> The German people were lied to, to force them into a war which they did not want. They call it a war of defense, a war of liberation; but it is nothing but a war of conquest and stealing.[22]

[20] *Vorwärts,* January 30, 1915. Also quoted in Lutz, *op. cit.,* I, 354, Document 128.

[21] Germany, Reichstag, *Verhandlungen des Reichstags,* May 15, 1917, Band 109, pp. 3395–98. Also found in Lutz, *op. cit.,* p. 354, Document 128.

[22] Collection of French Military Documents, Hoover War Library; cited also in R. H. Lutz, *op. cit.,* I, 113. See also Hansi et Tonnelat, *À Travers les lignes ennemies,* p. 125.

The British called the attention of the German people to the supposed war aims of their government in a still more pointed manner when they said in a leaflet:

ONLY FOR A JOKE

Do you know that there is a man in Germany who regards this war as a joke. This man is your Crown Prince! He is a great admirer of Napoleon. Shortly before the outbreak of the war he showed an American woman his valuable collection of Napoleonic relics and remarked at the time that if war did not come soon it would certainly come after he became Kaiser. .... Today everyone except you knows that if the war had not come when it did, your Crown Prince would have started it just as soon as he became Kaiser, just for a joke!![23]

In this campaign of enlightening the German people as to the supposed war aims of their government the Allies made extensive use of the writings of Grelling, Muehlon, Balder, and Prince Lichnowsky. Extracts from Grelling's famous *J'accuse,* which blamed Germany for the war, were published in the *Zeitung für die deutschen Kriegsgefangenen,*[24] a "newspaper" issued by the French for the Germans in the French prison camps. Muehlon's *Die Verheerung Europas* was sent to Germany by various means, and extracts of it were distributed in leaflet form. In this book the former director of the Krupp Works gave a scathing indictment of the whole political, social, and moral structure of Germany. He arraigned its governmental system as repressive of individualism, freedom of speech, and independence of thought. He accused the German government of deliberately forcing war on Europe.[25]

[23] *Leaflet A.P. 6.*

[24] The edition of June 20, 1915, contains the first installment of *J'accuse.* This newspaper also told why America went to war, and attacked the Kaiser in various ways. The issue of June 10, 1915, contains a schedule of prices of foodstuffs for the months from July 1914 to March 1915, intended to impress the prisoners with the high cost of living in the Fatherland and the threat of a food shortage there.

[25] The book is translated into English by W. L. McPherson under the title of *The Vandal of Europe* (New York, 1918).

France and America! An army of 10 million is being prepared; soon it will come into the battle. Have you thought of that Michel?[30]

Perhaps the British felt that the German people were too much impressed with the slogan, "Für Gott und Vaterland"; so they sent out leaflets which showed that the Germans were fighting neither for God nor for the Fatherland:

"Wir kämpfen für den Kaiser,
Wir kämpfen nicht für Gott;
Wir kämpfen für die Reichen,
Die Armen gehn Kapott.[31]

Thus the German people were not lacking "information" as to why they were fighting. It was for annexation, for the Kaiser and his militarists, and for the rich who profited from the war. How sadly these reasons contrasted with the noble aims of the Allies! For were not the Allies fighting for humanity? Were not they fighting for peace and for justice? Coming to the aid of the propagandists, Lloyd George made a speech in which he outlined the supposed war aims of the Allies. This speech went to the Germans in another leaflet:

We are not waging an aggressive war against the German people. . . . . The destruction or the dismemberment of the German people was never one of our war aims, either at the beginning or today. Against our will and wholly unprepared we were forced into it in defense of the International Law of Europe, which was broken, and in justification of the sacred treaties upon which European society rested, and which were violated by Germany in a most cruel manner by the invasion of Belgium. We had to go to war or see Europe approach destruction and brutal strength triumph over international law and international justice. . . . .

We have not taken part in this war in order to disturb the constitution of the Empire, although we regard the militaristic, autocratic constitution in the 20th century as a terrible anachronism.[32]

President Wilson's speeches were used more extensively for propaganda purposes than those of any other statesman.

[30] *Leaflet A.P. 12.* [31] *Leaflet A.P. 73.*

[32] *Leaflet A.P. 1;* see also *Leaflet A.P. 3.*

The reason for this was that Wilson's idealistic aims fitted in well with the purposes of the propagandists. Throughout his speeches Wilson insisted that the United States was fighting for democracy and for humanity. He hammered continually upon the note that the war was being fought for the liberty of the German people no less than for the freedom of the people of the Western Powers. The disinterestedness of America as far as reward or conquest is concerned was also stressed. America's great desire, said the propagandists, was to help free the world from Prussianism, militarism, and Junkerism. Quoting from one of Wilson's speeches,[33] *Leaflet A.P. 3* says in part:

> What we want is that the world come to the point where security and prosperity is insured; security especially for every peace-loving nation which, like our own, desires freedom, the right to determine its own destinies, and to be assured of justice and fair dealing with other nations.[34]

As George Sylvester Viereck puts it, "the eloquence of Woodrow Wilson was the most powerful battering ram of the

[33] It is interesting to note here that some German writers considered Wilson's speech of January 8, 1918, in which he stated the Fourteen Points as motivated by propaganda purposes. Ernest Wrisberg points out that in January 1918, Edgar Sisson, the American commissioner of the C.P.I. in Petrograd, sent a dispatch to George Creel of the C.P.I. in Washington, stating that "if the president can give the anti-imperialist war aims and the democratic peace aims of America in a thousand words or less, in short, almost placard-like paragraphs and short sentences, then I can send them into Germany in the German translation in great quantities, and spread them here in the Russian version. It is necessary that the president show that he is thinking of their momentary situation and that he is talking to them. I can take care of the German translation and printing here." After a conference with Creel apropos of this dispatch, Mr. Wilson is supposed to have drawn up the Fourteen Points. Ernest Wrisberg, *Der Weg zur Revolution 1914–1918* (Leipzig, 1921), p. 108.

Edgar Sisson, *One Hundred Red Days* (New Haven, 1931), chapter xiv, discusses this matter in detail and intimates that his message to Creel was a deciding factor in the drawing up of the Fourteen Points.

[34] *Leaflet A.P. 3.*

Deutsche Soldaten!

Nun habt ihr die grosse Offensive, die — wie die früheren, wie der U-Bootkrieg und sämtliche Kriegsanleihen — den Feind wieder einmal «endgültig» auf die Knie zwingen sollte.

Nach dieser letzten Schlacht sollte ja unfehlbar der Frieden kommen. Diesen Frieden, den heissersehnten, um den eure hungernden und darbenden Frauen zu Hause täglich beten, hatte man euch versprochen und so gelang es wieder einmal, die deutschen Divisionen dem Feind entgegen zu treiben.

Und wieder liegen ein paar Hunderttausende mehr deutscher Männer in französischer Erde begraben. Ihr habt so ungefähr den Boden wiedergewonnen, den ihr im Früjahr 1917, nach gründlicher Verheerung, geräumt hattet. Er reicht gerade, um Eure toten Kameraden zu begraben..... Aber der Frieden ist weiter entfernt denn je. Denn ein wahrer Frieden, ein Frieden der Verständigung, der Versöhnung und des gegenseitigen Vertrauens ist unmöglich, solange nicht das deutsche Volk den Frieden schliesst, sondern die preussischen Junker und Generäle. Diese Leute kennen nur den Raubfrieden, der andere Völker vergewaltigt, ausbeutet und zu Sklaven eurer Agrarier und Schwerindustriellen erniedrigt.

Die Verhandlungen in Brest-Litowsk haben zur Genüge bewiesen, dass

KAMERADEN!

Den längst versprochenen Sieg, den vom ganzen deutschen Volke so heissersehnten Frieden sollte uns endlich diese Westoffensive «totsicher» bringen. Den Friedenssturm nannten sie das Morden und diesmal sollten die «Gelbe-Kreuz-Gase» die Franzosen, die Engländer und Amerikaner in Grund und Boden vernichten. Wieder hatten wir an die Lüge geglaubt, wie damals an den Verteidigungskrieg, oder an den Krieg gegen den Tsarismus, oder an den U-Bootkrieg, der uns den Sieg schon vor einem Jahre bringen sollte.

Und nun?

Schaut nach wieviel Tausende von Toten, wieviel blühendes deutsches Leben als Leichen von den blutgetränkten Fluten der Marne weggetrieben werden!

Hunderttausende Deutsche haben wieder ihr Leben lassen müssen, und von Sieg und Frieden sind wir weiter entfernt denn

Propaganda of Despair

These two examples are typical of the propaganda which aimed to discourage the German troops. They reminded the Germans of the thousands of comrades that they had lost in the last struggle. They informed them that the submarine campaign was a failure.

Only the front side of each is shown.

Allied and American propaganda against Germany."[35] And similarly Professor Harold D. Lasswell: "If the great generalissimo on the military front was Foch, the great generalissimo on the propaganda front was Wilson."[36]

PROPAGANDA OF DESPAIR

The second phase of the propaganda campaign aimed to bring despair to the Germans. The leaflets stressed the horrors of war and announced the intention of the Entente to fight to the bitter end. One leaflet was addressed "To you in the fields of death!" The German troops were told that wherever they marched there was death. "Look about you! All that you can see is the work of death!" The Allies then asked "Why are you here with the dead? Why are you marching over the dead?" And at the end of the leaflet the propagandists told the German soldier, "You will lie where your comrades are lying—in the field of death."[37]

In order that the Germans might not rejoice too much over their victories the propagandists told them that their rejoicing would not last long—soon the Germans would retreat, and in this retreat they would lose greatly.

> When your struggle began there were already 4 million fewer men, women and children in Germany than when the war began. A pretty high price to pay for a walk to and fro, isn't it?[38]

It was futile, according to the Allied propagandists, for the Germans to make further efforts to break the power of the Allies. The only result of these efforts would be death and the grave.

> Probably tomorrow you too will lie in a shellhole with your face up, looking toward heaven; then you will have peace, the peace of the field of slaughter! While at home your wives and children go hungry.[39]

[35] George Sylvester Viereck, *Spreading Germs of Hate* (New York, 1930), p. 207.

[36] Harold D. Lasswell, *Propaganda Technique in the World War*, p. 216.

[37] *Leaflet A.P. 37.* [38] *Leaflet A.P. 38.* [39] *Leaflet A.P. 39.*

A great deal of propaganda of despair had in it a touch of sentimentalism. It called attention to the suffering of the wives and children of the soldiers.

DOES IT PAY?

Tomorrow you will probably be killed! Why? Because your Kaiser wants it!

Does it pay?

At home your wives and children and mothers are starving. Will your death help them? Are you going to death for that reason? . . . . Why then are you offering up your life?—Are you certain it pays?[40]

The only thing that the German soldier could be certain of, according to the propagandists, was death: "For you the grave is numbered. Tomorrow, day after, or perhaps first next week, but certainly it is yours, if you continue to march westward. Only a few among you will return to Germany."[41]

Cartoons were also used to bring home to the German soldiers the situation at home. The French, for example, published a drawing in *Die Feldpost* in December 1915 which showed the kitchen of a German family. The table was bare, and two emaciated children were staring pitifully at the empty table. The father, nothing but skin and bones, remarks to his spouse, who still has a little life in her, "My insides are rumbling with hunger." Whereupon the wife replies, "Then don't go on the street or you will be arrested for disturbing the peace."[42]

With the coming of the Americans, the odds were against Germany and the propagandists made the most of that fact. Along with the attacks of gas, bombs, and shells during the great offensive, the Allies made increasing attacks with propaganda.

One hundred thousand more men lie buried in French soil, and thousands of others are being sent into the 80-kilometer-wide slaughterhouse. . . . .[43]

[40] *Leaflet A.P. 40.*
[41] *Leaflet A.P. 14.*
[42] *Fliegerabwurf-Schriften* (no number), entitled "Does it Pay?"
[43] *Ibid.,* No. 48.

As for the war itself, that "may last for years yet," the Germans were told. And to give the enemy troops a good tonic before they entered another battle, the Allies sent the following message to them:

GERMAN TROOPS

You are being dragged into another battle. The ghastly months of Verdun are being re-enacted. . . . . Your General Staff itself admits that the losses "in several places were greater than usual." This means that they were terrible.

Reports made by German officers, and which we found, bear this out. Whole companies were destroyed; whole regiments, except a very few men, were wiped out. Some divisions lost 70 per cent, many 50 per cent, of their number.[44]

In order to impress upon the Germans the determination of the Allies to fight to a finish, *Die Feldpost,* the French propaganda sheet, issued by the Hansi organization, said in its issue of October 18, 1915:

WHAT THE CENSOR KEEPS FROM YOU

Do you know that the Allied Powers have agreed to continue the war at least until the summer of 1916 and longer if necessary? Do you know that peace cannot be thought of until the last German has disappeared from French and Belgian territory?[45]

Another method of promulgating the propaganda of despair was to paint a picture of the rewards of the crippled soldiers after the war. Stories were circulated that veterans of the war of 1870 died of hunger in the parks of Berlin while begging from the rich who scorned their pleas for help. One leaflet shows a picture of a poor crippled soldier standing at the entrance of a large restaurant or hotel. Fat men and buxom women, dressed in the richest evening clothes, are coming out of the place with a look of contentment and happiness on their faces. Not one of them notices the war-exhausted, hungry cripple. The inference was that such a reward awaited

[44] *Leaflet A.P. 26.*

[45] Dr. George Huber, *Die französische Propaganda gegen Deutschland,* p. 252.

GRATITUDE!

The German soldier was told not only that he was fighting for the rich Junkers but also that these people were living in luxury while he was suffering and starving in the trenches.

And when the soldiers returned home wounded and in need, this shows how concerned the rich would be over their welfare!

the soldiers who were wounded while fighting for the Fatherland.

When the war entered its fourth year the Allied propagandists sent out leaflets which reminded the Germans of the suffering they had already undergone and assured them that more and worse was to come.

YOU POOR GERMAN PEOPLE!

Already you are in the 4th year of this war. One shudders to think of your suffering, which will increase this year. To the hunger, the pestilence, the cold, will be added the terrible campaigns on the front and the aeroplane attacks on your cities. . . . .

Three million dead, the flower of your nation, the future of your land, rest in foreign fields; one million of your best sons languish in prisons; millions of your children have become poor, helpless orphans. . . . .[46]

Such were the paper bullets by which the Allies attempted to put discouragement and despair into the hearts of the German troops and the people behind the lines. Such were the arguments which aimed to get them to thinking, to wondering if, after all, Germany was invincible, if after all the odds were not against them. The propaganda of despair was a powerful force, and it no doubt set many a German soldier to wondering if it really did "pay" to continue fighting.

PROPAGANDA OF HOPE

It was not enough to bring to the attention of the German troops the fact that they were fighting a losing battle, that they were the slaves of the military and Junker classes. They had to be given something better to strive for. The soldiers were told that they were being mistreated, and forced to fight for the wealthy aristocrats of Germany. But where would they be treated better? They were told that they were certain to meet death if they continued to fight for their militarists. But what else could they do? They were reminded that the

[46] *Fliegerabwurf-Schriften,* "You Poor German People," sent out by Der Ausschuss.

war was taking away their best, that it was destructive of their economic life and ruinous to the common people. But if they made peace, what assurance had they that the Allied peace conditions would not be equally as destructive to their economic life as the war? Here, then, was the task for the propaganda of hope.

One way by which the German soldier could hope to save his life, and perhaps return to his family unmaimed, was by surrendering to the Allies. Propaganda purporting to come from the German prisoners already in the Allied camps was used most extensively. These leaflets contained letters supposedly from prisoners in France or England which told of the good food, the comfortable quarters, and the fine treatment that they were receiving at the hands of their captors.

One of these letters from "a German prisoner" to his comrades still in the trenches said:

> Comrades!
>
> From the war prisons we are sending you a few words and hope that they will meet with a little success and bring the end of this war a little nearer.
>
> *First.* Do not believe those who tell you that you will be treated cruelly in prison. On the contrary we can assure you that we get more to eat in one day than you get from your murderous leaders in three.
>
> *Second.* Warm clothing and shoes and kind treatment from the English officers such as a German soldier can hardly imagine.
>
> *Third.* For whom are you taking your hide to market? For whom are your wives and children suffering? For the Hohenzollerns and Junkers. . . . . Don't you hear them laugh?[47]

The Allies wanted the Germans to desert as soon as possible. One leaflet calls:

> Come to us before it is too late. Report to us with the words, "We come to you by leaflet No. 1," and we will know who you are.
>
> Naturally, if you come only after your bullets are gone then your coming will not be as pleasant as otherwise. Don't hesitate; do as your common sense tells you; then you will soon be able to see your beloved wives and children again.[48]

[47] *Leaflet A.P. 66.*

[48] *Leaflet A.P. 68.*

Deutsche Kameraden!

Im Kampfe sind die Franzosen, Ihr wißt es ja,

gefährliche und unerbittliche Gegner.

Sobald aber der Kampf vorüber ist, zeigen sie sich als

gutherzige Menschen.

Sollte Euch Euer Weg nach unseren Linien führen, weil Ihr Euch vielleicht auf Patrouille verirrt habt oder etwa aus Ekel vor dem endlosen Blutvergießen,

so fürchtet Euch nicht.

Es wird Euch kein Leid angetan!

Es sind in dieser Beziehung den französischen Truppen strenge Befehle erteilt worden.

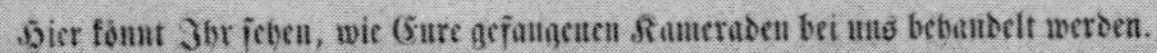

Hier könnt Ihr sehen, wie Eure gefangenen Kameraden bei uns behandelt werden.

A BIT OF FRENCH PROPAGANDA

Here is an appeal in word and picture to the German soldiers to desert. According to this, the French are terrible enemies to meet in battle, but when the battle is over they are very kind-hearted. The pictures show how well the German prisoners are treated by the French.

And the "Comrades in France" are supposed to have sent out letters asking the German soldiers to desert to the French. One of these letters states that more and more troops are coming over to the French every day.

> Comrades! They are the true friends of the Fatherland, for they are shortening the war, which can only bring suffering, sorrow and disappointment to the German people.
>
> COME OVER TO US!
>
> Your superiors are fighting for the rich, for the war-parasites, for the enemies of the people! . . . . Those who come over voluntarily are treated even better than the other prisoners. . . . .
>
> YOUR DEMOCRATIC COMRADES IN FRANCE[49]

Another leaflet from "a German prisoner" tells how, since he has been in the hands of the French, he has come to feel like a person "born anew.":

> Wake up, German Michel, be a man and make yourself free, that your posterity may not despise you. . . . . Come over to the beautiful France; here one not only has plenty of food to eat, but here you will also be treated like a human being and not like a beast.[50]

Still other letters lament the fact that their German comrades at the front continue to fight for the Hohenzollerns whose "thirst for blood is not yet quenched." They appeal to the men to think of their wives and children at home. "For you do not know why you are fighting," says one appeal, "while the French are fighting to recover their fatherland and for the rights of humanity. Come over! Break the bonds that hold you down, and see for yourselves how a free man is treated in a free land."[51]

But perhaps the most unique piece of propaganda of hope was the little card decorated in yellow, red, and black colors. It contained a short but pointed message.

[49] *Fliegerabwurf-Schriften,* No. 31.
[50] *Ibid.,* No. 29.
[51] *Ibid.,* No. 24.

REPUBLIC MEANS PEACE AND FREEDOM!

To the Comrades on the West Front!

The following order has been given out by the French Headquarters:

"He who permits himself to be captured (singly or in small groups) and cries out

RÉPUBLIQUE!

will no longer be treated as an enemy prisoner. If he desires, he can help free Germany."[52]

Fearing that some of the enemy troops would hesitate to obey this call because of the fear that they might be found out by the German officials and be disgraced, the propagandists, in their instructions on the reverse side of the card, told them not to fear, that their names would not be divulged to the officials. Furthermore, their action would help free Germany and "once Germany is free then the officials will have to be the ones to express fear."[53]

Letters supposedly written by German prisoners to their families were always good for propaganda purposes. These were known as *Grüsse an die Heimat, Briefe deutscher Kriegsgefangener.*[54] Emanating from Hansi's Service aérienne, they invariably painted a glowing picture of life in a French prison camp. How happy the writer of the following letter must have been.

To Herr Jacab Schmitt
Mainz
Rheinallee 53
Uzez, July 6, 1917

Dear Parents:

I thank God that I am at last out of the lazaret. You know how I disliked being in a German lazaret. . . . . I am in the most pleasant of officers' prison camps. Uzez is a beautiful little village of about 6,000

[52] *Fliegerabwurf-Schriften* (no number). See also Generalleutnant Altrock, *Deutschlands Niederbruch,* p. 32. Some time before this was sent out the French distributed instructions on how to pronounce the word *"République."*

[53] Altrock, *op. cit.*

[54] This was an 8-page sheet, lavishly illustrated with pictures of life in a French prison camp. It did not appear regularly, eleven numbers having appeared by May 1918.

inhabitants in the wonderful fruit district near Nimes. Our prison camp, a barrack before the war, is a good place for 200 of us comrades. There are large rooms in the barracks; a large library, concert hall, dining rooms, etc., are at our disposal. Daily the comrades give talks on geography, history, languages, sport, etc. Besides that we have a large ground at our disposal for games. . . . .[55]

And no doubt many a French soldier would have been envious of the German prisoners' rations as described in the following letter:

To Fräulein Martha Blumel
Villa Sprotte
Bertelsdorf (Schlesien)
Fort de Blaye

. . . . we got bread with oil sardines and a good flask of wine, that was, of course, the best of all. Then we bound grapes until 11 o'clock. When we went to dinner we were to receive our greatest surprise when we saw our dinner table. There stood two large bowls of soup, one plate full of meat and two jugs of grape juice, which tasted excellently to us.

Ernest Hampel, Pg. No. 1921
B II L.A.[56]

But perhaps the most ingenious scheme for getting the enemy troops to desert was that used by the Americans. Our propagandists dropped a "prisoner leaflet" over the German lines which contained an extract from the orders prescribing the treatment to be accorded by the A.E.F. to the prisoners of war. Appended to it was a list of rations issued to the American soldier and prescribed for enemy prisoners. More than a million copies of this were sent over to the enemy.[57] This was followed by postcards, in exact reproduction of the official German field postcard, which contained an invitation to desert.[58] The instructions on this card began:

Write the address of your family upon this card and if you are

[55] *Fliegerabwurf-Schriften* (no number).

[56] *Ibid.* (no number).

[57] E. A. Powell, *The Army Behind the Army*, p. 352; also *New York Times*, April 20, 1919, Section 7.

[58] Heber Blankenhorn, *Adventures in Propaganda* (Boston and New York, 1919), p. 78.

captured by the Americans, give it to the first officer who questions you. He will make it his business to forward it in order that your family will be reassured concerning your welfare.

The reverse side—the message side—had the following greeting to the homefolks all ready for the prisoner to sign and send off:

Do not worry about me. The war is over for me. I have good food. The American Army gives its prisoners the same food it gives its own soldiers: beef, white bread, potatoes, beans, prunes, coffee, butter, tobacco, etc.[59]

The greatest propaganda of hope, however, came from President Wilson. In his Fourteen Points and in his speeches the American President laid down the conditions of peace. He proposed a League of Nations which was to be a friendly association of nations for the maintenance of peace. There was to be freedom of the seas and open diplomacy. There was to be no discrimination between the victors and the vanquished when it came to a settlement at the end of the war.[60] A just and lasting peace was to be made with the German people. All they needed to do to obtain this just peace was to break away from the Hohenzollerns and establish a democratic government. Once the German people had set up a republic, a new day would dawn for Germany; a new freedom would come to them and they would again be received into the society of nations as citizens of an honorable and respected state.

Their hope then? Peace, freedom, respect, bread! These the Allies would help them to get if they but broke with their

[59] Many Germans immediately asked for these rations when they surrendered. Blankenhorn says that sometimes "their tired captors answered: 'That thing says that you get the same as me. I've had nothing for 24 hours. March!!'" Heber Blankenhorn, "War of Morale," *Harper's Magazine*, CXXXIX (1919), p. 512; also Powell, *op. cit.*, and *New York Times*, April 20, 1919, Section 7.

[60] Blankenhorn, "War of Morale," *Harper's Magazine*, CXXXIX (1919), p. 520.

autocratic and militaristic government. How many German soldiers deserted to the Allies because of this propaganda of hope no one knows. We know only that it played an important part in weakening the morale of the German troops and the people behind the lines.

PARTICULARIST PROPAGANDA

Conscious of the truth in the Biblical phrase that "a house divided against itself cannot stand," the Allied propagandists spared no effort to break the unity of the Empire. Despite its apparent unity, particularism was strong in certain parts of the German Empire. Alsace-Lorraine was French by tradition and had never become reconciled to German rule.[61] South Germany was Catholic, while the north was Protestant. Bavaria had always been more or less jealous of the power of Prussia, and this jealousy could easily be intensified by the propagandists. As Ungewitter put it, the Entente "spared nothing to tear us apart."[62]

The French concentrated upon Alsace-Lorraine from the very beginning of the war. The unwise action of Germany in making the relationship between Alsace-Lorraine and the Empire similar to that of a conquered nation to the vanquished made the feeling in these provinces still more bitter toward her. By the bill of incorporation the sole control of the two provinces had been vested in the Emperor and the Federal Council until the first of January 1874.[63] Although a few changes had been made in this original arrangement, Alsace-Lorraine had never been made to feel that it was a part of the Empire or on an equal footing with the rest of the states. This fact, together with the natural antipathy of the people in these provinces toward Prussia, made them very susceptible to the propaganda of the French.

[61] Alphonse Daudet's beautiful story, *La dernière classe,* gives a charming picture of the feeling of these people toward the Germans in 1870.

[62] Richard Ungewitter, *Wiedergeburt durch Blut und Eisen* (Stuttgart, 1919), p. 490.

[63] *Encyclopaedia Britannica* (14th edition), Vol. I, p. 702.

As early as August 1914 French aviators dropped leaflets in Alsace-Lorraine telling the people that France would fight until these provinces were freed from the Prussian yoke. Later the French propagandists recalled to the minds of these people the joys that were theirs while they were under the rule of the French, and told them that this joy could be real again if only they broke away from Prussia.

> For whom are you fighting? For whom did thousands of Alsace-Lorrainers offer up their lives? . . . .
>
> This nation took you under its control against your will in 1870. Thousands of Germans who brought their all in their handkerchiefs, came across the Rhine and settled in our beautiful Alsace-Lorraine. . . . .
>
> When the war started, thousands of Alsace-Lorrainers were dragged without reason to the prisons of Germany where they died in their misery.

The leaflet goes on to show how Germany has always treated the people in these provinces as second-class citizens of Germany. It accuses that country of censoring the mail of the soldiers and of discriminating against the troops of Alsace-Lorraine in the granting of leaves of absences:

> Therefore, dear fellow countrymen, come to us in France, where your ancestors, grandfathers, and fathers felt themselves fortunate; the land where you will not be slaves of the Prussian militarists and Junkers, but where you will be treated as equals.
>
> YOUR ALSACE-LORRAINE COMRADES IN FRANCE[64]

Another leaflet calls upon the Alsatian troops to surrender to the French. It assures them that they will be received with open arms, and that they will not be treated as prisoners but as friends.

> Come over, bring your Alsace-Lorraine comrades with you. Think of this! The more that come over now the sooner will our land become French. . . . . Come over, think of your family and your beautiful land, which we all want to see again.
>
> YOUR ALSACE-LORRAINE COMRADES IN FRANCE[65]

[64] *Fliegerabwurf-Schriften* (no number).

[65] *Ibid.,* No. 50.

Playing upon the pride of these people the French stated that the Germans considered the Alsace-Lorraine troops merely second-rate soldiers. Then picturing the enemy as a great demon that "forces your women and children to work like slaves in the fields; that permits the gendarmes to search your homes for wheat and potatoes," they assured the people that the Allies would see to it that a change would be brought about:

> France and her Allies will never make peace; they will lay down their arms at no price until the injustice of 1870 is made good again; until our land is again safe in the bosom of France. Thousands of Alsace-Lorraine troops have already come over here. They are not treated as prisoners but as full-fledged Frenchmen. They earn a good living and have good food.[66]

The Americans also sent out propaganda intended for the Alsace-Lorraine troops. Captain E. A. Powell tells how the American propaganda section of the Military Intelligence Division of the A.E.F. distributed some 20,000 copies of a leaflet designed to appeal to "those natives of Alsace-Lorraine who were serving in the German Army." These were the work of Captain Osaman of the G2, 4th Corps. Captain Osaman was familiar with German Army organization and knew the names of many German officers and men of the 224th Division, which was composed mostly of natives of Alsace-Lorraine.[67]

The attack upon Bavaria was more difficult than that upon Alsace-Lorraine. That principality had not been under the rule of the French; thus the method of attack had to be different. By the treaty between it and the North German Confederation on November 23, 1870, Bavaria, though becoming an integral part of the new German Empire, had reserved to itself a large measure of independence. From time to time, however, it had accepted a number of laws of the North German Confederation, thus drawing closer the bonds of the

[66] *Fliegerabwurf-Schriften,* No. 21.

[67] E. A. Powell, *The Army Behind the Army,* p. 352.

Empire.[68] When the war broke out, Bavaria, like the other states of Germany, gave up temporarily many more of its rights in favor of the Empire. Many leaders in South Germany opposed this centralization of power in Berlin. They feared that the Berlin government would make this war-time arrangement permanent by a change in the Imperial Constitution.[69] Thus it was evident that Bavarian particularism, which was founded upon traditional and religious antagonism to the Prussians, was by no means dead.[70]

The Allies understood this situation well. The French were the first to take advantage of the religious antagonism between the Bavarians and the Prussians. The Comité Catholique issued propaganda to the Catholics, stating that the war was a religious war and that the North Germans were trying to crush Catholicism. The one great piece of propaganda of this type was the book *La Guerre Allemande et le Catholicisme,* published by the Comité Catholique in May 1915. In this book the German government was pictured as the greatest enemy of Catholicism and the war as a war against the Church.

> This people, forged and hammered by Luther, still pursues with its hate the Roman cult and clergy. In thousands of German souls awakens the aggressive mentality which broke out under the pen of Wilhelm II when he wrote to the Landgrave of Hesse who had recently been converted to Catholicism: "I hate this religion that you have embraced."[71]

The German soldiers were accused of all kinds of sacrilegious acts. It was said that they entered churches and

[68] *Encyclopaedia Britannica* (14th edition), Vol. III, p. 550.

[69] *U.D.Z.,* VI, 238–40, quoting a letter of Crown Prince Rupprecht to the Bavarian Minister-President, Count von Hertling. Also cited by R. H. Lutz, *The Causes of the Collapse of the German Empire,* pp. 177–78.

[70] This antagonism dated back to the law of September 6, 1871, which expelled the Jesuits from the Empire.

[71] Alfred Baudrillart (ed.), *The German War and Catholicism* (published under the distinguished patronage of the Catholic Committee of French Propaganda, Paris, 1915), p. 98. The book came out in a number of different languages.

Geschrieben den ....

Hebe diese Karte auf, schreibe die Adresse Deiner Familie darauf, und wenn Du von den Amerikanern gefangen genommen wirst, gebe sie dem ersten Offizier, der Deine Personalien aufnimmt. Er wird es sich zur Pflicht machen, sie abzuschicken und so Deine Angehörigen über Deine Lage zu beruhigen.

Schreibe nichts auf diese Seite.

Streiche durch, was unzutreffend ist.

Ich bin gefangen { Leicht verwundet. / Schwer verwundet. / Unversehrt.

Seid ohne Sorge um mich. Für mich ist der Krieg aus. Ich habe gutes Essen. Die amerikanische Armee gibt ihren Gefangenen dieselbe Nahrung, wie ihren Soldaten: Rindfleisch, Weißbrot, Kartoffeln, Bohnen, Pflaumen, Bohnenkaffee, Milch, Butter, Tabak, u. s. w.

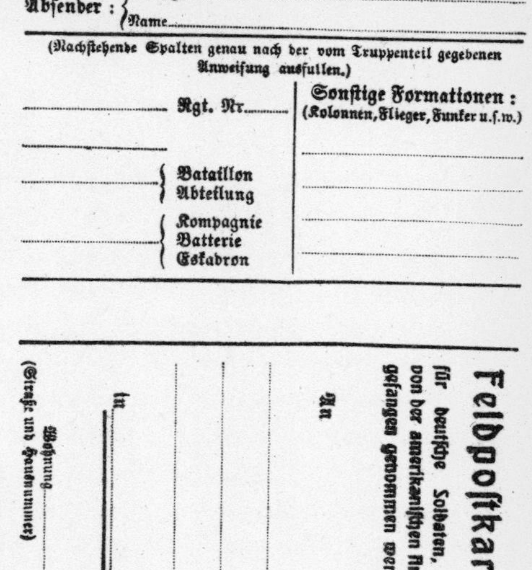

Absender: { Dienstgrad ....
Name ....

(Nachstehende Spalten genau nach der vom Truppenteil gegebenen Anweisung ausfüllen.)

.... Rgt. Nr. ....

{ Bataillon / Abteilung

{ Kompagnie / Batterie / Eskadron

Sonstige Formationen: (Kolonnen, Flieger, Funker u. s. w.)

Feldpostkarte

für deutsche Soldaten, die von der amerikanischen Armee gefangen genommen werden.

An

in

Wohnung (Straße und Hausnummer)

Aufgabestempel

(3)

Front and reverse of field postcard distributed by the Americans (photo from Heber Blankenhorn, *Adventures in Propaganda*).

Friends of German Democracy

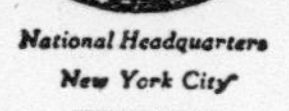

National Headquarters New York City

DIE AMERIKANISCHE HILFE.

1,500,000 (eine Million fünf mal hunderttausend) amerikanische Soldaten stehen in Frankreich; mehr als die doppelte Anzahl wird in Amerika ausgebildet: eine einzige Aushebung gibt in einem einzigen Monat fast ebensoviel Rekruten als ein Jahrgang in Deutschland; eine Flotte von fünf Millionen Tonnen, welche in weniger als einem Jahr dreizehn Millionen Tonnen betragen wird, eine Flotte, welche zusammen mit der englischen Flotte

Examples of American Propaganda

This little card distributed by the Friends of German Democracy told the Germans how many Americans had arrived in France to swell the ranks of Germany's enemies.

danced to the tune of the church organs, and that when they were tired of dancing they fiendishly set the churches on fire. Nuns, it states, were cruelly treated, priests were murdered, and women were violated by the German "savages." One German is quoted as having stated that it took him 57 shots of 210 millimeters to bring down the tower of a church.[72] In contrast to the "barbarism" of the Germans, the book tells of the nobleness and of the purity of the French troops, who prayed morning, noon, and night—the French were fighting on the side of God and for humanity.[73]

The political relationship between Prussia and Bavaria also was attacked by the Allies. Early in 1917 the French sent inflammatory leaflets into Bavaria, examples of which are: *Bayern und der Frieden* by Heinrich Sieger, *Bayern nimt Euch selbst den Frieden,* and *Seit Ihr Bayern ein Freies Volk?* In this work the French had the assistance of certain Germans who desired the liberation of their provinces from Prussianism. Jacob Feldner of Regensburg, Hans Suttner of Dietramszell, and Karl Ludwig Krause were outstanding in this work. Suttner was a German deserter who appropriated to himself the title of "Doctor" and who boasted of being an "antiboche."[74] His greatest contribution to the leaflet campaign was *Deutschland sein eigner Richter,* which appeared in 1917. Karl Ludwig Krause wrote the famous *Wofür stirbt das deutsche Volk?* He was very bitter toward Prussia and advocated that Bavaria break away from Prussia. In September 1917 he wrote an open letter to Count Hertling regarding separation.[75]

Most of the leaflets directed against Bavaria aimed to show, by reviewing the political relationship between North

[72] Baudrillart, *op. cit.,* p. 115. [73] *Ibid.,* p. 118.

[74] Wilhelm Ernst, *Die antideutsche Propaganda durch das Schweizer Gebiet im Weltkrieg, speziell die Propaganda in Bayern* (Munich, 1933), p. 6; hereafter referred to as Ernst, *Die antideutsche Propaganda.*

[75] Ernst, *op. cit.,* p. 6. Dr. Thimme (*op. cit.,* p. 92) expresses the belief that Krause is the "Heinrich Sieger" who wrote *Bayern und der Friede,* etc.

and South Germany, the many political errors that the Empire had made in the province. Thus: the Bavarians were supposed to be a "free" people, but the German Junkers and militarists were forcing them to fight for the interests of the Prussians. The leaflet, *Seit Ihr Bayern ein freies Volk?* states in part:

> Are you Bavarians a free people? No you are not! Why? Because you are subjected by the instigator of the war, Prussian Militarism. Why are you in the war? Why are you fighting? . . . . Must you defend your borders? . . . . Why then are you fighting? . . . . Because you are a free people only in a limited sense. In reality you are only, as history shows, an instrument for carrying out the Prussian desires. You are forced to fight against innocent women, children, and old people; to destroy everything that comes your way, to serve the Prussian militarists and Junkers. . . . . Ask yourselves why? . . . .
>
> All that you can say now is that you are slaves! When your eyes are open you will cry out, "We want to be free citizens of Bavaria and serve our king. We want to be free from Prussian influence." The sooner you come to this view the sooner will peace come.[76]

Another leaflet, *Bayern! Landsleute!!* sets forth the view that neither France nor England was to blame for the war, but only the Prussians, especially the king of Prussia. Far-sighted men, continued the leaflet, had all along warned against a union with Prussia which "has brought about the destruction of Bavarian independence so that now the King of Prussia has the right, in the name of Bavaria to declare war and make peace." After reminding the Bavarians that the war was being conducted in the interests only of the Junkers and militarists, it ended with the call:

> Leave work! . . . . Strikes and demonstrations, until this ruinous course is stopped, are your liberation. . . . . Stand up and resist! Everything for our beloved Bavaria!
>
> A BAVARIAN INTERESTED IN HIS NATIVE LAND[77]

[76] *Leaflet A.P. 20.*

[77] *Fliegerabwurf-Schriften,* No. 4. Hansi et Tonnelat (*op. cit.,* p. 120) state that many leaflets of a particularistic nature were written in Germany and sent to Holland or Switzerland, where they were printed and sent to Germany for distribution.

An appeal, *An die Süddeutschen,* which the Hansi organization sent out early in 1916, asked what interest the Bavarians had in the Hohenzollern dynasty. The people of Baden were reminded that their struggle for freedom in 1848 had been quelled by the "Prussian Junker-officers." At the close the leaflet asked if the South German people were going to continue to give material aid to the "bloody work of the Prussians." Free Germany from the Prussian yoke and the Prussian people from the yoke of Junkerism, it advised. Put an end to the World War, it continued, so that "a free Germany can be built on the wreckage of the Prussian castle."[78]

Different in its method, yet the same in its aim, was a leaflet entitled *Preussenherzen hoch!* This was sent to editors of Bavarian papers and marked "Confidential." In order to intensify the feeling between Prussia and Bavaria, the leaflet purported to be a Prussian appeal to the Prussians. "Help save Germany," ran its call. "All important offices are in the hands of South Germans. By particularistic hatred they are trying to break the power of Prussia." It then complained that Bavaria "made her continued support of the war contingent upon the making of Count Hertling the Chancellor." It told of the lack of discipline among the Bavarian high officials, and related that a number of Bavarian office holders had to be relieved of their positions because of their uncertain support of the war.[79] The purpose behind the leaflet was to create the impression in Bavaria that a spirit of enmity toward South Germany existed in Prussia, and thus to make the South Germans more susceptible to anti-Prussian propaganda.[80]

From the very beginning of the war there was consider-

[78] Dr. George Huber, *Die französische Propaganda im Weltkrieg gegen Deutschland 1914 bis 1918,* p. 259; also Hansi et Tonnelat, *op. cit.,* p. 121.

[79] Huber, *op. cit.,* p. 260. Some Bavarian newspapers did not suspect the propagandist purpose of this material and published it. On September 21, 1918, General Hoffmann forbade its publication.

[80] The *Müncher-Augsburger Abendzeitung,* September 27, 1918, informed its readers that this leaflet was a piece of propaganda emanating from enemy agents in Germany.

ELSASS-LOTHRINGER!

Für wen kämpft und leidet Ihr? Für wen haben Tausende und abermals Tausende Elsass-Lothringer ihr junges Leben opfern müssen? — Für Deutschland.

Dieses hat Euch im Jahre 1870 gegen den Willen Eurer Eltern unter seine Herrschaft gebracht. Tausende von Deutschen, die ihr ganzes Vermögen in einem Taschentuche mitbrachten, kamen über den Rhein und setzten sich in unserm schönen Elsass-Lothringen fest. Bald hatten sie die ersten und bestbezahlten Plätze inne und sorgten auch dafür, dass ihre Kinder ebensogut untergebracht wurden. Wenn sich Elsass-Lothringer und Eingewanderte für eine freigewordene Stelle meldeten, so waren die letzteren die Bevorzugten. Beim Steuerzahlen, bei Wahlen oder in letzter Zeit bei Zeichnung der Kriegsanleihen, da waret Ihr die «lieben wiedergewonnenen Brüder», sonst aber werdet Ihr seit 48 Jahren behandelt wie Bürger zweiter Klasse.

Als der Krieg begann, schleppte man Tausende von Elsass-Lothringern ohne Beweise ihrer Schuld in die Gefängnisse nach Deutschland, wo viele vor Elend starben. Selbst in Elsass-Lothringen waren die Gefängnisse überfüllt, denn bei dem geringsten Anlasse wurdet Ihr von bezahlten Spitzeln angezeigt und streng bestraft.

Und wie ging es Euch als Soldaten? Als Ihr bei der Mobilmachung mit Euren Regimentern wieder nach Elsass-Lothringen kamet, da sagten Euch Eure Offiziere, sobald der Rhein überschritten war: «So, jetzt befinden wir uns in Feindesland». Die ruchlosen Zerstörungen von Burzweiler, St. Moritz, Dalheim usw. geben Euch reichliche Beweise dieser deutschen Anschauung. Später wurdet Ihr wie Gefangene, manchmal ohne Gewehre, von der Westfront nach der Ostfront verbracht. Im Regiment oder in der Kompanie wurdet Ihr mit Wackes, Schangels, Landesverräter, Saubande oder mit anderen Schimpfnamen betitelt. Die Offiziere scheuten sich nicht, dieses vor versammelter Mannschaft oder selbst im Graben zu tun. Ein General sagte im Juni 1917 zu den vor einem Bataillon versammelten Elsass-Lothringern: «Euch bleiben nur zwei Wege übrig, entweder einen Strick zu kaufen um Euch aufzuhängen oder eine Kugel durch den Kopf.»

Und wie stand es mit dem Urlaub? Alle Eure deutschen Kameraden durften zu ihren Familien fahren, nur Euer Heimatland, Elsass-Lothringen, war für Euch gesperrt. Nur nach Baden durftet Ihr und dort konntet Ihr Eure Familien sehen. In letzter Zeit endlich, nach langen Reklamationen, gab man Euch Urlaub nach Hause und dann nur wenn es irgend einem «Herrn Gedarmen, der keine Not hatte», gefiel Euch ein gutes Zeugnis auszustellen.

A Call to the People of Alsace-Lorraine

The French made numerous appeals to the people of the "lost provinces." In this leaflet the Alsatians are reminded of the cruel treatment of the Germans were meting out to the people of these provinces. And yet thousands of their youths were offering up their lives for their German oppressors!

able friction between the two sections of the Empire, and the Allied propagandists made the most of this situation. The food question was one of the chief sources of this friction. The control of the food supply was left in the hands of the governments of the various federal states working through associations formed after a common model. The result of this was suspicion and accusation. The great landowners of East Prussia were said to be living in plenty while people in the cities were in need. In some German states there was enough food, and in others there was very little. Each state blamed the others for scarcity. In the Bavarian *Landtag,* on May 9, 1916, Deputy Schlittenbauer attacked the North German Agrarians, who, not being able to provide Berlin with butter or fat, blamed Bavaria for not coming to the rescue. The Deputy attributed Prussia's plight to her own selfish policy before the war when she preferred to import her supplies from Denmark instead of buying butter from Bavaria and encouraging dairy farming.[81] In Stuttgart, the *Oberburgermeister* and Council sent a protest to Berlin complaining that, while in South Germany the food regulations of the Bundesrat had been conscientiously obeyed, the North had refused to carry them out.[82]

Crown Prince Rupprecht brought the complaint of Bavaria to the attention of the Bavarian Minister-President Count von Hertling, on July 19, 1918, when he said that the Berlin government was catering to the big industrialists: "In Berlin, almost nothing is talked about but business and pleasure. By ruthlessly exploiting the distress caused by the war, businessmen in Berlin have been able to get the whole economic life of Germany under their control." He ended his complaint with the significant words:

The Bavarian Government is reproached with putting up with everything done in Berlin, and the opinion is constantly gaining ground

[81] *Verhandlungen der Kammer der abgeordneten des Bayerischen Landtags,* XII, Band 242, Sitzung von 8 Mai, 1916, pp. 832–33.

[82] *Supplement, Daily Review of the Foreign Press,* No. 69, June 16, 1916, pp. 4 ff.

that as, after all, everything is managed from Berlin, our government is nothing but superfluous and expensive ballast. . . . . For reasons which I cannot go into here, the Kaiser has forfeited all respect and the feeling goes so far that serious thinkers doubt whether the Hohenzollern dynasty will outlive the war.[83]

Further evidence of this feeling between Bavaria and Prussia is the fact that at the Press Conference in Berlin on May 21, 1918, the complaint was made that Bavaria permitted agitation against Prussia because of the belief that she was being cheated of her just bread rations.[84]

Another source of jealousy between the two leading German states was the war reports. The Bavarians felt that these were partial to the Prussians, who got more credit than they deserved. Princess Blücher makes the following observation in her memoirs:

The Bavarians have a special complaint that the war reports are always partial to the Prussians. They say that as long as losses of life and materials are sustained by the Crown Prince's Army, no mention is made of them, but as soon as Prince Rupprecht's Army is being beaten, every detail of the defeat is being made public, and an open confession is made of the enemy having penetrated the German lines.[85]

Allied agents in Bavaria nursed along this feeling of discontent by circulating stories to the effect that great animosity existed between Bavarian and Prussian troops. One of these stories related that at Verdun the Bavarian troops refused to attack and that at Colmar there was actual fighting between Bavarian and Prussian contingents.[86] The South Germans

[83] *U.D.Z.*, VI, 238–40; also quoted as Document 41 in Lutz, *Causes of the German Collapse*, p. 178.

[84] *U.D.Z.*, V, 221.

[85] Princess Evelyn Mary Blücher von Wahlstalt, *An English Wife in Berlin* (London, 1921), p. 243.

[86] The origin of this story is a letter to one Herr Guerbach in Berne. The confidential agent who wrote it was offered 5,000 marks if he would name the regiment and the officers of the troops engaged in this "fight," but he refused. It was found later that Guerbach was the "cover name" of the French Military Attaché in Berne, Col. Pageot. Ernst, *Die antideutsche*

A.P. 20. **BY BALLOON.**

Durch Luftballon.

Seid Ihr Bayern ein freies Volk?

Nein, Ihr seid es nicht. Warum? Weil Ihr dem Urheber des Krieges, dem preußischen Militarismus unterworfen seid.

Warum seid Ihr im Kriege? Zu welchem Zwecke führt Ihr den Krieg? Habt Ihr die Absicht Euere Grenzen auszudehnen, oder tragt Ihr Euch mit der Absicht einen anderen Volksstamm zu vernichten? Gewiß nicht, Ihr fühlt Euch wohl hinter Eueren Pfählen in Euerem Lande und unter Euerem Herrscher. Aber warum kämpft Ihr denn? Warum wollt Ihr andere Völkerstämme ausrotten, ohne Nutzen daraus zu ziehen? — Weil Ihr ein freies Volk seid nur in beschränktem Maße; in Wirklichkeit seid Ihr, wie die Geschichte augenblicklich lehrt, nur ein Werkzeug zur Ausführung der preußischen Gelüste. Ihr seid gezwungen Euch an unschuldigen Frauen, Kindern und alten Leuten zu vergreifen, in fremde Ortschaften einzufallen, zu morden, zu brennen und Alles, was Euch in den Weg tritt zu vertilgen und zu vernichten, um den preußischen Militarismus, vertreten durch das Junkertum, zu unterstützen. Viele von Euch haben einen Abscheu davor, aber Ihr müßt, sonst trifft Euch auf der Stelle die eigene Kugel; Ihr habt keinen Ausweg.

Habt Ihr je darüber nachgedacht, ob „Kultur" in der Vernichtung von Volksstämmen besteht? Habt Ihr je darüber nachgedacht ob „Fortschritt" in der Erfindung von Mordwerkzeugen zur Ausrottung von Volksstämmen besteht? In den Augen des preußischen Junkertums unbedingt und die unter dem sogenannten Schutze desselben stehenden Völker sind das Werkzeug zur Ausführung der Gelüste. Es besteht ein himmelweiter Unterschied zwischen Verteidigung der Landesgrenzen und Eroberungsgelüsten.

Der preußische Herrscher giebt sich als das Werkzeug Gottes aus! Wehe Euch und allen anderen Volksstämmen, wenn das so wäre! Aber der Gott lebt noch, der Euch Allen in Euerer Kindheit vorgestellt wurde und die Zeit wird kommen wo dieser Dünkel und Hochmut des Preußentums zerschmettert auf der Erde liegen wird.

Denket einmal nach und seht zurück was Euch seit Kriegsausbruch versprochen, und was gehalten wurde!

Ihr könnt ruhig sagen: „Viel bekamen wir versprochen, aber erreicht haben wir nichts weiter, als daß wir unsere Mägen immer mehr zuschnüren müssen."

Was hat Euch die Eroberung Belgiens, Serbiens, Montenegros gebracht? Doch keinen Frieden, im Gegenteil weitere Zerstörungswut seitens des Junkertums unter dem Deckmantel des preußischen Militarismus.

Dann mußte Rumänien daran glauben! Warum? Weil es gewagt hat die Hand gegen das hochheilige Preußentum zu erheben. Ist dann der versprochene Friede gekommen? Nein! — Seid Ihr Euerer Nahrungssorgen überhoben worden? Wieder einmal „Nein"!

Der Einfall nach Italien erfolgte darauf, um Euch zu verblenden und wieder etwas als Erfolg auftischen, respective vorgaukeln zu können. Ihr werdet vielleicht sagen, die Länder da unten gehen mehr Österreich an; Ihr, die Ihr aber sozusagen von früher her mit Österreich noch verkettet seid, wißt doch ganz genau, daß Österreich ganz so wie Bayern vollkommen unter dem Einflusse Berlins, also Preußens steht.

Jedenfalls kam der Friede auch dann nicht, als Italien dem weiteren Einfall „Halt" gebot.

Durch Bestechung mit ärarischen Geldern, herausgezogen aus den Taschen der ohnehin schon stark mitgenommenen Bevölkerung in Form von Kriegsanleihen, ist es gelungen Spitzbuben zu finden die in einem ihnen gar nicht gehörenden Lande als Volksvertreter aufgetreten sind und einen ehrlosen, sogenannten Frieden am Papier abgeschlossen und unterzeichnet haben. Ist der Krieg zu Ende gekommen? — Nein! — Ist Rußland, ausgenommen die sich Regierung nennende Sippe, einverstanden und zufriedengestellt? — Nein! — Ist der Frieden in Rußland dadurch hergestellt? — Nein! — Ist der Frieden geschlossen mit Rußland seitens des Preußentums eingehalten? — Nein! Immer weiter dringt der freche preußische Moloch vor, denn Papier ist geduldig, und was ihm nicht paßt, wird einfach niedergetreten und zermalmt. Ihr könnt es ja im eigenen Lande sehen. Habt Ihr einen freien Willen? — Nein! Wer von Euch der preußischen Militärgewalt die Wahrheit sagt, wird ins Loch geworfen oder kurzerhand an die Mauer gestellt. Werden dazu Kinder erzogen?

Nehmen wir an, der Frieden mit Rußland wäre seitens Preußens eingehalten worden wie es abgemacht war. Glaubt Ihr, daß es nicht nachher im Volke Rußlands weitergefressen hätte wie ein Krebs und Euere Kinder wieder in einen Krieg verwickelt werden würden? Habt Ihr die versprochenen Nahrungsmittel von Süd-Rußland nach dem Friedensschluß bekommen? —

(12389)

An Appeal to the Bavarians

In an effort to drive a wedge into the Empire the French tried to arouse the particularist spirit in Bavaria. This leaflet informs the Bavarians that they are not free but are slaves to Prussia.

were also told that the Prussians regarded their soldiers as second-rate men and that the Bavarian troops were pushed to the front where they had to bear the brunt of the fighting.

BAVARIANS!

It was clearly shown that the German General Staff expected another attack from the enemy at the end of September.

You know yourselves how many Bavarian Divisions were hurriedly established to intercept this attack.

So the Bavarians were again, as has so often been the case, sacrificed. The Prussian used the Bavarians again. He always sees to it that the bitterest struggles and the heaviest losses are assigned to the Bavarians.[87]

To bolster the argument that the Bavarians were always sent into the hottest fighting, while the Prussians were held back and saved, the propagandists circulated leaflets giving the comparative losses to the various German states.[88]

Yes, yes, what you say is common knowledge. The losses to date of the various German States are as follows:

Bavaria	46%
Württemberg	26%
Baden	24%
Prussia	11%

And the following issue of the *Kriegsblätter für das deutsche Volk* was sent out by the Allies to show that the non-Prussian German troops were bitter against the Prussian soldiers.

The accursed Prussians, the favorite children of Wilhelm. With each charge against a stronghold the South German regiments are

Propaganda, p. 17, quoting *Bayer. Kriegsarchiv,* Akten des Kriegsministeriums: "Verbreitung revolutionärer propagandaschriften—Abwehr." Vol. J, 1917 mit 1918.

[87] "Französischen Methoden," *Süddeutsche Monatshefte,* April 1924, p. 7.

[88] Huber, *op. cit.,* p. 255. Statistics of the the actual loss of men by the different states in Germany during the entire period of the war tell a story other than that in the leaflet cited above. The figures are taken from Friedrich Felger, *Was wir vom Weltkrieg nicht wissen,* p. 625: Of the 2 million dead, Prussia lost 1,500,000, Bavaria 250,000, Saxony 150,000, and Württemberg and the rest of Germany 75,000.

sent ahead until just before the surrender of the enemy; then the Prussian regiments step in and earn the honor of heroes by completing our victory and are then "my brave Brandenburgers, my dear children," etc.[89]

The French worked for a definite split between North and South Germany. In Heinrich Sieger's pamphlet *Bayern und der Frieden,* a parallel is drawn between France under Napoleon I and Germany in the World War. Both had to break under the weight of the enemy coalitions. France was able, a few weeks after her surrender, to deal upon an equal footing with her enemies. "How was that possible? The word *dynastiewechsel* explains all." It then asked if Wilhelm II was prepared to make the same sacrifice for Germany that Napoleon made for France. In other words, the pamphlet suggested that Germany should get rid of the Hohenzollerns and come before the Allies with a new king, a Bavarian king.

Bavaria is the natural intermediate state between Germany and France. On the horizon—perhaps not such a distant horizon—beckons the German-French understanding, yes, the German-French Alliance. This is possible under the democratic Germany under the kingship of a liberal, popular man of Wittelsbach, tied to France by old traditions.[90]

In the second chapter of this pamphlet the possibility of an enlarged Germany was held out to the Bavarians. This enlarged democratic state was to be under the rule of a Wittelsbach. After the fall of the Dual Monarchy of Austria-Hungary, the non-German portions were to become independent states and the German portion—present-day Austria—was to come under German control. These promises could, of course, be fulfilled only after the overthrow of the Kaiser and all the existing German dynasties.[91]

The Allies used a variety of schemes to get particularist propaganda into Germany. One scheme was to distribute leaflets among the exchange prisoners who came to Germany by

[89] Huber, *op. cit.,* p. 255.

[90] Heinrich Sieger, *Bayern und der Frieden,* p. 13, in "Pamphlets," *German Revolution,* Vol. III, Bavaria.

[91] *Ibid.,* chapter ii, *passim.*

way of Switzerland.[92] Another trick was to smuggle leaflets into Germany by means of brass shells, which were sealed on both ends with cork and stamped with the words, "Printed matter, pass on." These were thrown into the Rhine and carried by the current into Germany.[93] Another means was to put the propaganda into book form and give false titles to the books. For example, Grelling's *Das Verbrechen* (*J'accuse*) had the title *Die Europäische Lage,* by Dr. Fr. Arndt; and Grumbach's *Das Annexionistische Deutschland* was sent into Germany as *Grossdeutschland* by W. Siegwart.[94]

Another method was to use a falsified seal and falsified envelopes of the Austro-Hungarian Legation in Berne and with the help of these send propaganda to certain persons or groups in South Germany. The imprint on these was "K. u. K. *Österr. Konsulate, Cs. es. K. Osz.—Tr. Magy. Konsulatus Basel.*" This method was first followed in March 1917, when a number of Heinrich Sieger's pamphlets were smuggled into Bavaria. At that time they were addressed to Bavarian burgomasters. It was again used in the summer of 1918 when Siegfried Balder's pamphlets were circulated in Germany. Balder's material was addressed to the locomotive-fireman, and polytechnic unions, the workers and handicraft associations in all South Germany, and to two members of the Royal family.[95] Among the other leaflets sent out in this manner was *Die lustige Witwe,* by Eric Mühsam. This contained a picture of the Kaiser going to the scaffold and implied that if the Hohenzollern dynasty were destroyed the Bavarians would be a free people.[96]

[92] Ernst, *op. cit.,* p. 20.

[93] *Ibid.,* p. 22, citing *Bayer. Kriegsarchiv,* Akten des stellv. Generalkommandos I b. AK, "Einfuhr von Druckschriften—Allg.," Bund 345.

[94] *Ibid.*

[95] Ernst, *op. cit.,* p. 25, quoting *Bayer. Kriegsarchiv,* Akten des stellv. Generalkommandos I b. AK.

[96] The original of this leaflet is said to have been produced in Germany, smuggled into Switzerland by Jakob Feldner, and printed by Meyer & Larcheveque in Geneva in the latter part of 1917. *Ibid.*

That smuggling leaflets into Bavaria was an active enterprise is demonstrated by the fact that the German customs officials were kept busy. At the head customs house in Munich a 42-kilogram trunkful of material by Leonard Frank was taken on December 8, 1917. At the port of Lindau, the following cargo was apprehended at the fast freight inspection in September 1918:

150 copies of the pamphlet, *Kaiser und Krieg oder Republik und Frieden.*

200 copies of the pamphlet, *Wilhelm II annoch deutscher Kaiser wir klagen dich an.*

2,000 leaflets, *Zeichnet die Kriegsanleihe!* by Ludwig Thoma von Eheden.

2,000 leaflets, *Das Genossen Karl Liebknecht Brief an das Kommandanturgericht.*

2,000 leaflets, *Die lustige Witwe,* gedicht von Erich Mühsam.[97]

According to a report of the Bavarian Legation in Berne in the fall of 1917, the German and Swiss guards took many propaganda leaflets, letters, and revolutionary writings, and arrested a number of propaganda agents. They took more than 200 copies of the leaflet *Deutsches Volk wach auf.* In June 1917 they intercepted a transport of the pamphlet *Wie deutsche Geschichtsschreiber einst urteilen werden*—written by a German deserter in Switzerland—and at the end of July they made 100,000 copies of Wilson's speeches "harmless." They also arrested two under-agents, Fritz Demeter and Karl Schneider, at Basel, because they had thrown a floating leather sack containing 50,000 copies of the pamphlet *Bayern und der Friede,* into the Rhine.[98] And again in September 1917, some 90,000 copies of the leaflet *Du armes deutsches Volk* were taken from Anderson, an agent of the French government.[99]

[97] Ernst, *op. cit.,* p. 30, citing *Bayer. Kriegsarchiv,* Atken des stellv. Generalkommandos I v. AK: "Einfuhr von Druckschriften—Überwachung München"—Bund 346; "Einfuhr von Druckschriften—Überwachung Lindau"—Bund 346.

[98] This was a common method used to get material into Germany. The leather sacks had cork on each end.

[99] Ernst, *op. cit.,* p. 29.

From the foregoing discussion we get a fair idea of the first four types of propaganda with which the Allies attacked Germany. Each type had a specific purpose, and the writers of the propaganda were clever enough to make this purpose stand out clearly. Having "enlightened" the German people, having brought despair into their hearts, having given them something to hope for—to look forward to—and having finally striven to break the unity of the Empire, the Allied propagandists were ready to bring on the revolution in Germany.

CHAPTER V

REVOLUTIONARY PROPAGANDA

> On the day the Kaiser of Berlin falls, you will be liked in Paris, London, New York, and Rome, as well as we like the Russian soldiers today.
>
> —Leaflet distributed by the Allies

The cause of every revolution exists among those against whom the revolution is directed. Realizing this fact, the Allied propagandists directed their efforts against "Kaiserism," "militarism," and "Junkerism," and promoted a "cause" for revolution in the minds of the troops and the masses in Germany. And taking their cue from the words of Goethe, who said, "The revolution from below is always due to the habits of those above," the producers of "word bullets" directed their ammunition at the Kaiser and the military leaders.[1]

The French propaganda sought from the very beginning to inoculate the German people systematically with the thought

[1] It is interesting to see how the revolutionizing of Germany became a war aim of the French very early in the war. *L'Humanité* was the first of the Left press to attack the Kaiser and make a distinction between the German people and the ruling class. The war aims of the French Socialists became the destruction of the system which was to blame for the war. Said *L'Humanité,* in its issue of August 16, 1914: "and though he [William II] calls himself Frederick, or Napoleon, or Bismarck, his defeat is certain. This defeat will tear away the whole hated Prussian military system, as well as his throne, which is the seat of the most shameful reaction of modern times. On the ruins of the Hohenzollern family will arise, as soon as possible, the German Republic with which the French Republic can conclude an honorable and lasting peace." Soon the phrases, that the war was a struggle "against militarism," against German "imperialism," and for a "lasting peace" found their way also into the papers of the Right. *Le Matin,* on September 18, 1914, stated that it was important for the French to determine to fight, not alone for victory, but that "victory should carry through the destruction of German Imperialism."

of revolution. They strove to soften the fear which the word "revolution" naturally evokes, and in one of Siegfried Balder's pamphlets it was pointed out that a person who went against the Kaiser was not an enemy of the Fatherland:

> He who opposes his government does not fight against the Fatherland. Even if the Fatherland is the Kaiser, it is the duty of every German to oppose him and his government.[2]

The revolution, the Germans were told, was to lead only to the Republic and a rebuilding of Germany. They were told that the Allies were fighting only Prussian militarism, "that military caste in Berlin which has unchained the mass murder."[3] The impossibility of a peace as long as the Kaiser ruled in Germany was continually called to the attention of the German people. In September 1917 *Das Freie Deutsche Wort* stated that peace negotiations could take place only between such countries as are ruled by the people. "In Germany such a fact does not exist." The leaflet continues by quoting from the reply of the American government to the peace offer of the Pope, in which it is stated that there could be no dealings with an irresponsible government; that the word of the German rulers could not be accepted "unless supported by conclusive evidence of the will and purpose of the German people themselves." Without such guaranties, "treaties of settlement, agreements for disarmament, covenants to set up arbitration in place of force, territorial adjustments and reconstitution of small states, if made with the German government, no nation could depend on."[4] In other words, no peace could be made as long as the Hohenzollerns were in power.

[2] *Kaiser und Krieg oder Republik und Frieden,* p. 13.

[3] *Flugblätter für das deutsche Volk,* No. 16, April 1916.

[4] Dr. George Huber, *Die französische Propaganda im Weltkrieg gegen Deutschland 1914 bis 1918,* p. 269; hereafter cited as Huber, *Französische Propaganda.* See also the reply of the United States government on August 27, 1917, to His Holiness Benedict XV in Joseph Tumulty, *Woodrow Wilson as I Knew Him* (Garden City, New York, 1926), pp. 281 ff., or any collection of Wilson's state papers.

On August 2, 1917, a soldier of the 7th Army received a leaflet which said:

> On the day the Kaiser of Berlin falls, you will be liked in Paris, London, New York, and Rome as well as we like the Russian soldier and worker today. . . . . German soldiers, think of this. Have counsel with your comrades. Oppose the continuation of the war as forcefully as you oppose your enemies.
>
> Please pass this on to your comrades.[5]

The attack upon the Kaiser and the ruling family was made with pictures as well as words. One leaflet displayed two pictures. The one at the top showed the Kaiser and his official staff seated at a table in a beautiful garden. Upon the table there was an abundance of food and beverages. A look of contentment showed on the faces of the members of the "party." The picture is captioned: "How the war looks at Headquarters." Below this is another picture, this one showing the explosion of a shell and two soldiers being blown to pieces. This is labeled: "How the war looks in the trenches."[6]

In another leaflet a drawing shows the Kaiser and his six sons, in full dress uniform, with feathered caps, leather boots, and medal-bedecked topcoats, smartly traversing a pathway flanked by thousands of black figures of death. This ghastly horde is stretching out skeleton arms toward the proud family. The caption of the picture reads: "One family which has not lost a single member."[7]

Leaflet A.P. 47 shows the Kaiser riding his horse into a dark wilderness filled with the bodies of dead soldiers. Skeleton forms are pointing accusing fingers at their former ruler. One deathlike figure is seen in front of the Kaiser's horse, with a long rope and noose, ready for action. The caption beneath this reads: "The King of Prussia goes to meet his death."[8]

And *Leaflet A.P. 48* contains a picture of a heavy throne labeled "Militarism" resting on a hill of dead bodies. A huge form is seated on the throne. One hand of this image of mili-

[5] *U.D.Z.*, VI, 20.
[6] *Fliegerabwurf-Schriften* (no number).
[7] *Leaflet A.P. 18.*
[8] *Leaflet A.P. 47.*

BY BALLOON.
Durch Luftballon.

Eine Familie welche kein Mitglied verloren hat.

AN ATTACK UPON THE KAISER

This leaflet shows the Kaiser and his six sons, all unscathed by the war, marching proudly by as thousands of clamoring arms reach out to them in anguish.

tarism is holding a bloodstained document and the other hand is clasping a sword. A general, pointing to the hill of dead, is saying to the Kaiser, who is smiling, "A few more dead, Your Majesty, and the foundation will be safe."[9] And the next issue of the leaflets shows the Kaiser and Hindenburg, seated in the midst of ammunition and heavy implements of war, being carried on the shoulders of wounded, emaciated human beings. Hindenburg says to his chief, "Your Majesty, the people are depressed and are murmuring constantly," to which the Kaiser replies, "Why do they murmur? We feel no burden."[10]

In their attack upon the Kaiser, the English made further use of their prisoners of war. In the leaflet entitled "What a German soldier, recently taken prisoner by the English, told an English officer," the prisoner gives vent to his feelings as follows:

> This war is the greatest crime the world has ever seen. . . . . Here on this front the Germans are falling like flies. Many are killed by German bullets. The Germans are driven into the slaughter like beasts. And why? Only because the Kaiser and his so-called statesmen fear what would happen should the people know all. . . . .
>
> The Russians rose up and broke their chains, but not our people. But our tyrants are sly; they not only have the body but the will of the people in chains. No German will has been free in Germany since 1870! . . . . Thank God, I am out of it.

At the end of this the English propagandists added their call: "German soldiers, follow the example of Russia! Drive your tyrants to the devil."[11]

As much as possible the propagandists tried to bring about antagonisms between the officers and men, and to destroy discipline. In one leaflet we find the following:

> Your Kaiser, German soldiers, your Kaiser desires to play the part of the ruler of the world and the representative of God on earth. . . . . Are you going to continue to fight so that the German steel barons, the worst of all enemies of labor, can enslave the French workers of

[9] *Leaflet A.P. 48.*

[10] *Leaflet A.P. 49.*

[11] *Leaflet A.P. 16.*

Longwy and Briey? . . . . It is up to you to put a stop to this world butchery.[12]

In this campaign against the officers the military leaders were accused of prolonging the war for selfish reasons. They were accused of living the life of heroes, amid splendor and luxury, while the poor soldiers in the trenches were tired and hungry:

> . . . . And that isn't the worst yet, soldiers! A Lieutenant General in Berlin takes bribes to firms, soldiers! in order to supply goods to the war officials . . . . It is a known fact but it is hushed up! . . . .
>
> And in the big hotels in Berlin champagne flows every night at 80 marks to the bottle! . . . .
>
> Do not die, soldiers! Live if you can! Save yourself if it is possible. Live and look the great revolution in the face! Weepingly she arises from the sorrow which your war lords have spread over you.
>
> She comes to bring you back to the "Heimat."[13]

The strike was suggested as the quickest means of bringing on the revolution. In the leaflet *Volk nim dir selbst den Frieden!* the suffering of the people and the soldiers is contrasted with the contentment of the militarists and the Junkers. After speaking of humanity and peace, of a universal peace and brotherhood, it cries "Down with the Government! Down with the oppressors!" And at the end it gives a formula by which peace can be hastened:

> The only means is: Refuse to continue the war! Refuse to shoot at the orders of your superiors! Refuse to work in the munitions factories! Strike! In the field! On land!
>
> Strike! Strike!
>
> Assemble by the thousands and cry out Peace and Freedom![14]

---

[12] *Fliegerabwurf-Schriften,* No. 37.

[13] *Leaflet A.P. 42.*

[14] *Fliegerabwurf-Schriften,* No. 9. See also E. Drahn and Susanne Leonhard, *Unterirdisches Literatur im revolutionären Deutschland während des Weltkrieges* (Berlin, 1920), p. 190. This is perhaps the best study of the revolutionary agitation in Germany, especially the Bolshevik agitation, that has appeared to date. It will be referred to hereafter as Drahn and Leonhard, *Unterirdisches Literatur.*

Hindenburg: „Majestät, das Volk ist gedrückt und murrt unaufhörlich."

Majestät: „Weshalb murren sie? Wir spüren keine Last."

"Why Do They Murmur?"

This is another example of the attack upon the German high officials. The supposed heartlessness and greed of the Kaiser were depicted in word and picture.

And in the latter part of 1917 the French dropped over the German lines the following leaflet, the front side of which read:

FORESIGHT PASS THIS ON

3 days of universal strike and victory is yours.

The reverse side strove to create a class war by stating:

FORESIGHT

Can this war still end with a victory? Certainly! And with a great victory of the workers over the manufacturers, war-wagers, the Junkers and Princes; the victory of the proletariat over their exploiters. How? Three days of universal strike and the victory is yours.

Against your will the war cannot be carried on. Three days of universal strike and the war and your suffering will be ended.[15]

A versified piece of propaganda called upon the German troops to lay down their arms and stop fighting. If the Kaiser should insist that they continue the struggle, they were to tell him to go into the trenches himself, for they were through with the war. Reading like an old English ballad this leaflet said:

Wenn ich der deutsche Michel wär
So wüsst ich was ich tät;
Ich legte meine Waffe hin
Und spräch' zu Majestät:

"Nun ist's genug! Ich mach nicht mehr
Im Schützengraben sein;
Wenn du noch länger kriegen willst
So steige selbst hinein!

"Drei Jahre und ein halbes schon
Kämpft ich fürs Vaterland,
Stritt für den Kaiser und fürs Reich
Und lag im Unverstand;

"Ich litt an Hunger, Durst und Frost,
Ich stand im Kampfgebraus;

[15] Drahn and Leonhard, *Unterirdisches Literatur,* p. 181.

Das Toten ist ein schrecklich Ding—
Ich sehne mich nach Haus!

"Hast du noch nicht genug vom Krieg,
So rücke selbst ins Feld,
Und kämpf im heissen Schlachtgewühl,
Als braver deutscher Held."[16]

When the Kaiser gave Hindenburg a high military decoration the propagandists asked the German troops:

What has he given you? Suffering, poverty, hunger for women and children, misery, pestilence and tomorrow the grave! They say you are fighting for the Fatherland—but what is your fatherland? Is it Hindenburg, who with Ludendorff is many kilometers behind the front lines, making more plans to give the English more cannon-fodder?[17]

Attacking all of the ruling families in Germany, a little pink card stated that all princes should be sent to the lower regions. These rulers weaken, it said, the power of the people.

They are leading you to slaughter to make your children more submissive. Millions should yet be offered up, but this revolution should prevent it. . . . . Save yourselves in the French camps. Who wants to can. God will help him. Stop obeying and learn to think! Make yourselves free![18]

"Mother Revolution," stated another leaflet, "will save you."

And what comes now? Who comes from this region of death? Mother Revolution! And weeping she brings you back to the *Heimat*.

Do not die, soldiers! Live if you can! . . . . Live and look the great revolution in the face. Weepingly she arises from the sorrow which the war lords have spread over you. She comes to bring you back to your homes.[19]

The French often suggested to the German soldiers that they unite with the radicals in Germany who were working for international peace. After the arrest of Liebknecht, for in-

[16] Liste I, Hoover War Library collection.
[17] *Leaflet A.P. 12.*
[18] *Fliegerabwurf-Schriften* (no number).
[19] *Leaflet A.P. 42.*

stance, the French *Kriegsblätter für das deutsche Volk,* No. 21, dated July 1916, warned:

> Workers, Liebknecht's cause is your cause. Through Liebknecht they want to strike at you, to kill you, to silence you, so that the human slaughter shall continue. Through Liebknecht it is hoped that the opposition of the German proletariat to the war criminals will be broken. Will you stand for that? . . . . Down with the war, down with the Government.[20]

By publishing, in neutral newspapers, stories of conflict between German soldiers and officers, and supposed incidents of mutiny among the troops, the Allies tried to make it appear that there was a strong hatred among the troops for their officers. An article in the *Tribune de Genève* for July 24, 1918, which reached the hands of the German soldiers, stated:

> From information from a good source we are certain that discontent is spreading in the German army. Many acts of disobedience are known and the High Command has not succeeded in stopping them. A regiment which was to go to rest quarters had been sent to the Western Front; the men mutinied and threw their rifles out of the windows, stopped the train and fled across the field.[21]

There is no doubt that the military failures of the spring and summer of 1918 had a demoralizing effect upon the German troops. There is evidence that, in many sections of the army, discipline was broken. Many officers stood face to face with opposition from some of their troops. One observer at the front said: "As yet their doubled-up fist remained in their

[20] Huber, *Französische Propaganda,* p. 262. From a report of a confidant in Switzerland, we learn that regular conferences were held by Haguenin, the chief of the French propaganda section, in which the revolutionary propaganda, especially the smuggling of leaflets into Germany, was discussed. In these conferences the French ambassador Dustata took a lively interest and Haguenin gave him regular reports on the conversations. In these conferences, also, most of the known foreign propagandists took part, e.g., Flesch for the Italians, Delmar for the Americans, and Dr. Schlieben, Hugo Ball, and Dr. Bloch for the German Democrats. Ernst, *op. cit.,* p. 11, citing *Bayer. Kriegsarchiv,* "Akten des stellv. Generalkommandos," I b. AK, Bund 345.

[21] *Press Review,* Second Section, United States General Staff, No. 212, August 4, 1918.

Soldaten der deutschen Armee!

Scheut nicht die russische Gefangenschaft! Laßt euch mit ruhigem Gewissen gefangen machen. Ihr beschleunigt dadurch die Beendigung dieses für euch hoffnungslosen Krieges und bringt euer Leben und Gesundheit in Sicherheit.

Wir, zurzeit in russischer Gefangenschaft sich befindenden deutschen Soldaten in gesamt schon über 150 Tausend, die tapfer und ehrlich viele Monate hindurch gekämpft und alle Schwierigkeiten dieses furchtbaren Krieges ertragen haben, wenden uns an Euch, Kameraden, mit einem guten Rate: „werfet die Flinten von euch, wie es die meisten von uns getan haben, und laßt Euch freiwillig von den Russen gefangen machen! Ihr bringt wenigstens euer Leben und Gesundheit in Sicherheit!". Der Krieg wird noch sehr lange dauern und gewinnen können wir Deutsche ihn doch nicht. Wenn dich die Kugel auch noch verschont hat, so kannst du doch sicher damit rechnen, daß du von ihr morgen oder übermorgen getroffen wirst. In Deutschland sind durch diesen Krieg schon zwei Millionen Männer Krüppel geworden. Vergrößert doch nicht durch euch die Zahl dieser Unglücklichen, die ein Hungerstot erwartet, denn der Staat kann unmöglich so viel Krüppel ernähren, zumal die Zahl derselben schon jetzt das Friedensetat des Deutschen Heeres ums dreifache übersteigt.

Glaubt nicht dem Geschwätz euerer Offiziere über die großen Siege. Trotzdem von Deutschland alles aufgeboten worden ist, haben wir bis jetzt nur Teilerfolge zu verzeichnen, die für den Ausgang des Krieges von garkeiner Bedeutung sind. Im Osten haben wir nicht einmal Warschau nehmen können, im Westen stehen wir noch immer an der französischen Grenze. Da wollen wir doch lieber über unsere Siege schweigen.

Von uns hat es noch niemanden gereut, daß er in Gefangenschaft geraten ist. Wir werden gut behandelt und bekommen ausgezeichnetes Essen. Viele von uns wollen überhaupt nicht mehr nach Deutschland zurück und werden auch nach dem Kriege in Rußland bleiben. Was erwartet uns in Deutschland? Die Kolonien sind uns abgenommen, unsre Fabriecken haben bankrott gemacht und unsre Handelsflotte ist in den Besitzt anderer Staaten übergegangen. Schon jetzt findet der größere Teil der Befölkerung keine Arbeit und nach dem Kriege wird es noch viel schlimmer werden. Bei uns spricht man, daß die, welche sich freiwillig ergeben, in Rußland kostenlos Land bekommen werden.

Kameraden! nur durch Gefangenschaft könnt Ihr euer Leben in Sicherheit bringen. Ihr werdet es nicht bereuen, wenn Ihr unserem Rate folge leistet.

An Invitation from Russia

This is another call for the German troops to desert. It assures them that they have nothing to fear in the Russian prison camps, and it offers free land to those Germans who come over to the Russians voluntarily.

pockets, but how long yet?"[22] And Richard Ungewitter admitted that "It finally came to the point where the leaders no longer had the troops under their control."[23]

When the attitude of the German people toward the Kaiser in the last year of the war was analyzed by Princess Blücher; she wrote in her memoirs:

> The feeling toward the Kaiser is steadily diminishing, and the same people who greeted him with "Ave, Caesar," a short time ago, are now distributing leaflets in the back streets of Berlin proclaiming "down with the Kaiser; down with the government."[24]

And the viewpoint of the troops is given in an entry in her diary of February 1917. She had talked to a German soldier just returned from the front, and he said:

> We all do our best for our country, and if we meet as prisoners or otherwise we are perfectly friendly, but there must be something wrong somewhere, to make us so hated by all other nations, as well as by our allies. Who is to blame for it? That is what my comrades and I are trying to find out.[25]

Yes, who was to blame? If there was any doubt in the minds of the German soldiers on this point in February 1917, that doubt must certainly have been dispelled by late summer 1918, thanks to the propaganda of the Allies.

The sentiment of the revolutionary propaganda is well summarized in a leaflet, *"Comrades, Awake!"* After criticizing the German government and blaming the Kaiser for the sufferings and tribulations of the nation, it closes with

> For a more beautiful, higher, and nobler end our strength should go. The holy aim of our strength should be: A free and fortunate German Republic! . . . . Comrades, awake! Realize your strength.[26]

[22] Ludwig Lewinsohn, *Die Revolution an der Westfront* (Charlottenburg, 1919), Foreword.

[23] Richard Ungewitter, *Deutschlands Wiedergeburt durch Blut und Eisen* (Stuttgart, 1919), p. 491.

[24] Princess Evelyn Blücher, *An English Wife in Berlin,* p. 190.

[25] *Ibid.,* p. 177.

[26] Richard Müller, *Vom Kaiserreich zur Republik* (Vienna, 1924), 2 vols., I, 117.

The dissemination of revolutionary leaflets among the German troops led to a dispute between Germany and the Allies as to the legality of such activity. Even before the World War experts in international law had discussed the question whether the law of nations recognized the right of a warring nation to induce the subjects of opponents to treason by means of revolutionary leaflets. Vattel held that there is nothing in strict international law to prevent a belligerent from sowing disaffection and treason among the armies of his opponent and the population. But he thought that such a course could not be compatible with good conscience.[27] Although there are modern writers who condemn this practice, yet the actions of the states during the World War certainly showed that they did not accept such condemnation.

The German government, despite the fact that it had been the first to distribute leaflets to enemy troops by means of the airplane, considered such acts a serious breach of international law. The leading case on the subject of leaflet-dropping that came up during the war is that in which two British officers, Captain E. Scholtz and Lieutenant H. C. Wookey, were concerned in the latter part of 1917. These two officers, carrying propaganda leaflets, were shot down and captured by the Germans near Cambrai on October 17, 1917. They were taken to the 2d Army Headquarters at Le Cateau and there interrogated by Captain von Loehnegsen of the Intelligence Staff, who informed them that the German government had notified the Allies in April 1917 that the dropping of pamphlets was considered illegitimate and that the airmen guilty of the practice were liable to be brought before a field-general court-martial and to be shot. On November 22, 1917, the officers were shown the charge sheet, which referred to two separate alleged offenses: The distribution, in September 1917, of pamphlets detrimental to the German troops; and the attempted distribution, on October 17, 1917, of pamphlets de-

[27] H. Lauterpracht, "Propaganda by Governments," transactions of *Grotius Society,* XIII, 152–53.

scribing the favorable conditions in the English prison camps and intended to induce the German soldiers to desert. On December 1 the two British airmen were placed on trial before a court composed partly of civil and partly of military judges sitting with a jury. They were found "guilty of treason" and were sentenced to ten years of hard labor.[28]

The British government learned of the case and took immediate steps to obtain the release of the officers. The German government was informed through the Dutch representative at Berlin that unless the airmen were released His Majesty's government would take reprisals. The stand of the British government was that the distribution of leaflets from the air was not a breach of international law. Consequently, the condemnation of Captain Scholtz and Lieutenant Wookey to a long term of penal servitude for this "offense" was held to be abusive. Furthermore, it was pointed out that German and Austrian airmen had committed similar offenses and no punitive measures had been undertaken against them upon capture.[29] The German government was given one month—the period fixed by the Hague Mission for giving notice of intended reprisals—to release the airmen and cancel the sentences before adequate retaliatory measures would be taken. The Prisoners of War Department announced, on March 11, that the two men had been released and returned to their camp.[30] Hence reprisal action was not necessary.

The question of the legality of fomenting political disturbances in an enemy state or inciting enemy troops to desert or surrender was cleared up by the Commission of Jurists who drew up a draft code of rules for air warfare at The Hague

[28] J. M. Spaight, *Air Power and War Rights* (London and New York, 1924), pp. 305 ff. Mr. Spaight got his information concerning the details of the case directly from Lieutenant Wookey, who wrote him a personal letter regarding the matter.

[29] *The Times* (London), February 2 and 6, 1918; also Spaight, *op. cit.*, pp. 306–7.

[30] *The Times* (London), March 12, 1918.

in February 1923. This commission included an article in the following terms:

Art. 21.—The use of aircraft for the purpose of disseminating propaganda shall not be treated as an illegitimate means of warfare. Members of the crews of such aircraft must not be deprived of their rights as prisoners of war on the charge that they have committed such an act.[31]

BOLSHEVIK PROPAGANDA

No attempt is made here to analyze all of the propaganda which was issued by the Bolsheviks. A book could easily be written on that subject.[32] The Bolsheviks were interested in a world revolution. They hoped that the war would be the beginning of that world revolution which would result in the overthrow of the capitalistic system. Hence their propaganda was directed against all capitalist nations. In September 1914, a month after the outbreak of the war, Lenin wrote his famous theses on the war. *Number One* declared:

The European and World War has the sharp definite character of a bourgeois imperialist and dynastic war. The struggle for markets and looting of countries, the tendency to fool, disunite, and kill off the proletarians of all countries by instigating the hired slaves of one nation against the hired slaves of another for the benefit of the bourgeoisie—such is the real meaning and purpose of the war.

And in the thesis *Number Seven* he asserted:

The slogans of social democracy at the present time should be: First an all-sided propaganda (spread also in the army and the area of military activity) of a socialist revolution and of the necessity of turning the weapons, not against brothers, hired slaves of other countries, but against the reaction of the bourgeois governments and parties of all countries. To carry on such propaganda in all languages it is

[31] Spaight, *op. cit.*, p. 309. The article makes no distinction between military and political propaganda.

[32] The most complete study of Russian propaganda that has appeared thus far is E. Drahn and Susanne Leonhard, *Unterirdisches Literatur im revolutionären Deutschland* (Berlin, 1920).

absolutely necessary to organize illegal cells and groups in the armies of all nations. . . . .[33]

On October 6, 1917, the Central Committee of the Russian Social Democratic Labor (Bolshevik) party issued a call, through its paper, *Bote der Russischen Revolution,* "to all workers, sailors and soldiers of all lands":

> Five months have passed since the revolutionary proletariat and the army brought to an end the government of the whip and put Nicholas Romanov behind lock and key. The worker has stripped off the fetters of the police regime. The soldier has become a free citizen. . . . . Workers of all lands! We reach you the hand of brotherhood over mountains of dead bodies. . . . . We call you to make firm the international unity. . . . .
>
> We bid you heed our call. Do not show this manifesto to your officers. Spread it among your artillery comrades.[34]

Although the ultimate aim of the Bolshevik propaganda was a world revolution, a considerable amount of it was directed against the German government. It is to this phase of the Bolshevik propaganda that we will limit ourselves in this study.

The designs against Germany were well summarized in the newspaper, *Rabochii Soldat,* on October 17, 1917, almost a month before the Bolsheviks got into power in Russia, when it stated:

> The German Kaiser, covered with the blood of millions of dear people, wants to push his army against Petrograd. Let us call to the German workmen, soldiers, and peasants, who want peace no less than we do, to stand up against this damned war!
>
> This can be done only by a revolutionary government which would really speak for the workmen, soldiers, and peasants of Germany, and appeal over the heads of the diplomats directly to the German troops—fill the German trenches with proclamations in the German language. . . . . Our airmen would spread these proclamations all over Germany.[35]

[33] R. H. Lutz, "World War Propaganda," in Quincy Wright (ed.), *Public Opinion and World Politics* (University of Chicago Press, 1933), p. 168. Also Lenin, *The Imperialist War* (International Publishers, 1930), pp. 61 and 63–64.

[34] Drahn and Leonhard, *op. cit.,* p. 132.

[35] John Reed, *Ten Days That Shook the World* (New York, 1919), p. 31.

On December 5, 1917, Lenin and Trotsky sent a proclamation to the German soldiers as follows:

RUSSIAN PROCLAMATION TO THE GERMAN SOLDIERS

The Provisional Government has fallen. The power is now in the hands of the Russian people, and the new government considers the immediate conclusion of peace as its foremost duty. . . . .

We charge you soldiers to stand by us in the fight for peace and socialism, for socialism alone can give to the proletariat a lasting peace. . . . .

Brothers, if you support us, the cause of freedom is assured success. . . . .

Our soldiers have laid down their arms. It is now for you to follow this standard of peace.

May peace triumph! May the Socialistic and International Revolution live!

For the Council of the People's Commissars.

(*Signed*) LENIN, TROTSKY[36]

A similar message was addressed to the German sailors on February 15, 1918. This, which was sent out by wireless, said:

TO THE SAILORS OF THE BALTIC FLEET AND ALL OPPRESSED PEOPLES

Do you hear our voice, and do you hear the cries and groans of our brothers, the soldiers who are drowning in their own blood, and the sailors who are meeting their death day by day in the misty sea and the cold depths of the seas and oceans? Do you hear the heartbreaking lamentations and the despairing sobs of mothers, brothers, and children throughout Europe which is drenched in blood? Do you not see the approaching shadow of the black specter of famine and his bony hand?

If you hear and see all this, why do you keep silent? Give answer to our cry and to the appeals of your brothers. Follow the example of the Russian people. . . . . Rise up like a hurricane, tear off the fetters of bondage, overthrow the thrones of tyrants, and free yourselves from the god you have created with your own hands—Capitalism. . . . .

[36] This message was picked up on April 11, 1918, near Ancerviller by Americans. It is printed in full in *Secret Summary of Intelligence,* A.E.F. General Staff, No. 97, p. 395. It is also found in the *Russian Daily News,* December 24, 1917.

Therefore raise boldly the standard of revolt. Leave the sepulcher of the trenches; make an end to the despots.[37]

In their propaganda activities before the Brest-Litovsk Treaty the Bolsheviks paid special attention to the German troops on the Eastern front. Beginning as early as October 1917, a continued and ever increasing stream of propaganda found its way to these soldiers. A number of periodicals designed to arouse a revolutionary spirit among the German prisoners in Russia and the German troops on the Eastern Front were established. The largest and most influential of these was *Der Völkerfriede,* which was published in Petrograd and was distributed along the northern sector of the German line in the East.[38] Another newspaper, *Die Fackel,* made its appearance on December 6, 1917. It emanated from the People's Commissar for Foreign Affairs in Petrograd, by whom it was published for free distribution among the German troops. According to the *New Russian Daily News* this paper was "to publish the proclamations of the Council and secret diplomatic documents. It will set forth and defend the Internationalist ideas."[39] The issue of December 9 contained a proclamation by Trotsky which called upon the laboring masses to form a united front against capitalism.[40]

Appeals were also made to the German people at home. In No. 24 of *Das freie deutsche Wort* appeared the "Call of the Central Commitee of the Bolsheviks to the Socialist Proletariat of Germany," by Lenin and Trotsky. In this the German soldiers, workmen, and workingwomen were called upon to emulate the Russian proletariat and unite with the Russian Revolution.

[37] *Fliegerabwurf-Schriften,* No. 36; also *British Daily Review of the Foreign Press,* VI, 904.

[38] Drahn and Leonhard, *Unterirdisches Literatur,* p. 139.

[39] *New Russian Daily News,* December 8 (21), 1917.

[40] *Norddeutsche Allgemeine Zeitung,* January 5, 1918, announced the establishment of *Die Fackel.* See also Germany, Reichstag, *Verhandlungen des Reichstags,* February 26, 1918, Band 134, 4171–75.

Go to the streets! Let the factories go! There must not be a fourth winter of fighting. Not another shot must be fired. . . . .

An immediate Armistice! Do not fire another shell. On to the peace negotiations! Come out and struggle for the peace made by the free will of the people.[41]

When, at the peace conference at Brest-Litovsk, the German government disclosed her plans for a *Gewaltfrieden,* she put another powerful propaganda subject into the hands of the Russians. As soon as the annexationist demands of Germany became known, the Russians sent their protests to all of the world.[42] In a series of brilliant speeches Trotsky declared to the world that Russia's desire for a peace without annexations and reparations was being thwarted by the lust for conquest displayed by the German militarists.[43]

Following the same theme, Maxim Litvinoff, while in England, made a stirring appeal to British labor to help end the war. In this appeal, delivered on January 10, 1918, he said

[41] Huber, *Französische Propaganda,* p. 268.

[42] The French used these protests to educate the German troops to the policy of their government. Thus in No. 26 of *Das freie deutsch Wort* there appear three official telegrams of the Russian peace commissioners (the first without date and the others dated January 23, 1918). In the third it is stated: "The Austrian and German delegates have refused to give a definite statement regarding the evacuation of the occupied territory. The matter at stake is a monstrous annexation." Then it concludes with the regret that the German working class has not taken the opportunity to work for the good of the class and the "good of mankind" (Huber, *op. cit.,* p. 267).

[43] Arthur Rosenberg, *The Birth of the German Republic,* translated from the German by Ian F. D. Morrow (London, 1931), p. 205.

The German delegate, Kühlmann, was no match for Trotsky in this verbal duel. The man on the street was on Trotsky's side in arguing that whoever desired peace without annexations and reparations must at once be prepared to withdraw his troops from districts they occupied beyond his own frontiers. If he were not prepared to do so, then it seemed clear that he must be entertaining plans of conquest. When matters became too entangled in the coils of Trotsky's dialectics, General Hoffmann intervened (January 12) by bluntly informing the Russians that Germany was the victor and that the Russians had better take this fact into account in making her proposals. This declaration showed clearly to the mass of people what were the war aims of their militarists. Rosenberg, *op. cit.,* p. 205.

that the Russian revolutionary propaganda among the German soldiers on the Western Front and among the prisoners of war "is undermining the strength of German autocracy and militarism more effectively than military victories could, and has already provoked a strong peace movement in Germany and Austria."[44]

When the 12th regiment of the Russian Army evacuated Riga, it left behind the following summons for the German troops:

German Soldiers! The *Vollzugsausschuss* [Executive Committee] of the 12th Army calls your attention to the fact that you are fighting for absolutism and against the Revolution, freedom, and justice! Your victory signifies the death of democracy and freedom. We leave Riga, but we know that the revolution will prove itself stronger and more powerful than the power of cannons. We are certain that the German soldiers will finally march with the Russian Revolutionary Army to the victory of Freedom. . . . . Throw your entire strength against imperialism and, in union with us, hurl the enemy to the ground.[45]

Another appeal issued by the Petrograd Soviet on February 8, 1918, and addressed to the "Council of Workmen's Delegates in Berlin and Vienna," calls upon the troops to stop fighting and the workers to strike and make huge demonstrations. The working class of Germany must not permit the "hangmen and spoilers to impose a peace of violations and annexations on the Socialist Republic of the Soviet." The call continued:

Brothers, we cordially believe that you will do all that is possible to ensure that the peace *pourparlers,* begun by the Russian Workmen's and Peasants' Government with the government of Kühlmann, shall end in *pourparlers* between the Russian Workingmen's and Peasants' Government and the German Government of Liebknecht. . . . .

Long live the Councils of Workmen's and Soldiers' Delegates of Berlin and Vienna! Long live Communism![46]

[44] The *Labor Leader,* January 10, 1918.

[45] Richard Müller, *Vom Kaiserreich zur Republik,* I, 113.

[46] *The Times* (London), February 8, 1918.

A Russian government wireless message to German soldiers, on February 15, 1918, lamented that the German workingmen had not yet overthrown their government. "Chase the Kühlmanns, the Hindenburgs, and the Tirpitz's to the devil," ran the appeal, "and send us Karl Liebknecht and Fritz Adler."[47]

The protracted negotiations at Brest had their effect upon the German soldiers. This is attested by von Hindenburg, the Chief of the General Staff, in his report to the Kaiser in January 1918, where he stated that the manner in which the peace conference was being conducted left a poor impression upon the German troops. The German diplomats, according to the veteran warrior, had been more diplomatic than forceful, which gave the German soldiers the impression of compliance.

> This same impression is current in many quarters in the army and is certainly calculated to call forth unfavorable criticism of the attitude adopted by General Ludendorff and me . . . . I cannot prevent this happening, for the long trench warfare and the confused conditions in the country have also increased the pleasure taken in criticism at the front. I am unable to suppress the apprehension that the manner and results of the negotiations in Brest have unfavorable influence on the frame of mind in the army.[48]

The effect of the Bolshevik propaganda was to become even more evident when the Germans withdrew their troops from the Eastern Front and sent them to the Western Front. These men had seen the Russian Army deprived of its leaders and had been impressed with the methods of the Bolsheviks.

> Not only did these 1½ million troops swell the West Front in numbers but also a great many of these troops had been inoculated with Bolshevism so that the foundation for the Revolution was laid.[49]

The spirit of disintegration among the German troops may already be read in the lines of a letter written by a gunner on the Eastern Front as early as September 5, 1917. He writes

[47] *British Daily Review of the Foreign Press,* VI, 905, February 19, 1918.

[48] R. H. Lutz, *Causes of the German Collapse,* p. 27.

[49] Richard Ungewitter, *Deutschlands Wiedergeburt durch Blut und Eisen,* p. 586.

in part: "That Socialism has already gained the upper hand in everything is characterized in our battery by the fact that a so-called Soldiers' Council has its hand in everything. All the doings of an officer which are not free from objection are most sharply criticized by the non-commissioned officers and men. But in doing this, everyone is cunningly serving his own interest."[50] And on September 19, 1917, a member of a labor battalion wrote:

> The longer the war lasts the more obvious it becomes that the officers of all arms of the service consider it as a most favorable opportunity to enrich themselves. The few exceptions prove the rule. Everything is taken from the men, the officers are given everything and besides this these gentlemen steal in Russian fashion. An institution on the model of the Russian Soldiers' Councils would be a great blessing for us and a good education for them.[51]

Bolshevik propaganda was further strengthened by the return of German prisoners from Russia. Many of these refused to fight again and "poisoned their comrades on the front with Bolshevism."[52] Many of these troops were more active in agitating against their own government than they were in fighting the enemy.[53] One of the leaflets distributed by the German soldiers transported from the Eastern to the Western Front closed with the words:

> Take heed where your government and your Kaiser are leading you. Unite yourselves with the main conditions which are declared by the Allies and force your government to do likewise. Then we can end this war without trouble and conclude an honorable peace for all.[54]

The revolutionists in the German Army and the revolutionary circles within Germany were richly supplied with printed matter from Russia. At the Dresdener Hof in Moscow a German Propaganda Centrale had been set up which sent out leaf-

[50] *U.D.Z.*, V, 151, statement of Dr. Philipp. [51] *Ibid.*

[52] Generalleutnant Altrock, *Deutschlands Niederbruch*, p. 36.

[53] Richard Müller, *op. cit.*, I, 114.

[54] *Süddeutsche Monatshefte*, April 1924, "Die Vermittlungsstellen im Neutralen Ausland," p. 13.

lets and pamphlets in great numbers.[55] Propaganda agencies were established in Berlin, Leipzig, and other important cities.[56] The German government permitted the Petrograd Telegraph Bureau to establish a filiale in Berlin,[57] and this was a great boon to the revolutionists. Russian agitators in Germany were numerous and some 200 couriers came to Germany from Russia between April and November 1918, bringing propaganda material with them.[58]

The material which came into Germany from Russia was much more inflammatory than that which came from the Allies. During the January strikes in Germany the Russians stated in one of their leaflets sent to the German workers:

> The German workingmen are rising. For the first time in the history of Germany all the factories throughout the country are silent by the command of the proletariat. . . . . The Russian Revolution has staked its cards on the German and Austrian proletariats. Do not allow yourselves to be used as the hangmen of the Russian proletariat.
>
> German Soldiers! The hour has struck in which a decision must be made. Decide for the Russian Workingmen's Revolution or for German Generals and capitalists; for peace or for war without end.[59]

Another appeal from the Russians called upon the German soldiers to throw off their yoke of slavery and force the capitalists out of existence.

> GERMAN SOLDIERS, WORKERS!
>
> For four years your wives have wept their eyes out while you gave yourselves as cannon-fodder in order to give world dominion to German capital. Now the time has come to end German Imperialism, to drive out the vermin that has drunk your blood and hold high the standard of the revolution to drive out the bloodstained capitalistic system.[60]

[55] Drahn and Leonhard, *Unterirdisches Literatur,* p. 146.

[56] Walter Nicolai, *The German Secret Service,* p. 49.

[57] Knesebeck, *Die Wahrheit über den Propaganda Feldzug und Deutschlands Zusammenbruch,* p. 117.

[58] *U.D.Z.,* V, 32.

[59] *British Daily Review of the Foreign Press,* VI, 905, February 18, 1918.

[60] *Ibid.,* p. 176.

When the German officials tried to appeal to their people to defend the Fatherland, the Bolshevik propagandists said to the workers: "You have no Fatherland to defend."[61] The Fatherland, they said, was in the hands of the oppressors of the workers; let the workers end the war and take the Fatherland; then they will not need to defend it, for no one will attack a peace-loving Socialist government.

In this campaign against the German government the Russians were aided by the revolutionists in Germany. The Spartacists and the Independent Socialists worked hand in hand with the Russian agents in Germany. Since the re-establishment of diplomatic relations with Germany, the Russian Ambassador, Joffe, had maintained a close connection with the Independent Socialists.[62] On May 1, 1918, Deputies Haase, Cohn, and Mehring took part in a May-Day celebration in the marble room of the Russian Embassy where Haase proposed a toast to the *International*. The Russian Embassy in Berlin became the center for the agitation against the German government.[63] Couriers traveled freely between Berlin and Moscow, and agitators were brought from Russia to Berlin to work for a revolution.[64] The Russian telegraph agency, "Rosta," was set up at Friedrichstrasse 118, in Berlin, ostensibly for business

[61] *Tägliche Rundschau*, March 4, 1919, *abends*.

[62] *U.D.Z.*, V, 31. This circle of Russian sympathizers grew larger and took in other deputies, notably Deputy Bernstein. Oscar Cohn became financial intermediary for money from Russia and M. Rosenberg maintained connections with the Independent Socialist press, while Madame Markowska kept in contact with the radical youth. Ledebour was also connected with the Russian Embassy (*ibid.*).

[63] Haase, Cohn, and Barth were accused of having received some 100,000 marks from Joffe for revolutionary purposes. No attempt is here made to prove or disprove the many charges made against the Independent Socialists and the Spartacists in Germany regarding alleged money received from the Bolsheviks to agitate for a revolution in Germany. A separate study could well be made of the relationship between the German Left parties and the Russian Bolshevists during 1918.

[64] Walter Nicolai, "Die Gesamtlege," *Süddeutsche Monatshefte*, April 1924, p. 34.

purposes, but really for propaganda activity. Russian consulates were set up in Stettin and Hamburg for the same purposes.[65]

Joffe and his friends in Germany had a great deal of money at their disposal. Much of this money came from sympathizers in Germany who contributed to the revolutionary cause, and some of it came directly from Russia. Dr. Cohn, a member of the Reichstag, received large sums from Joffe, which was used to "good advantage." A declaration of the Undersecretary of State to the former Imperial Ministry quotes Dr. Cohn as having stated:

> Is any formal statement or justification required that I was only too glad to receive the money which our Russian friends put at my disposal through Comrade Joffe for the purpose of the revolution? . . . . I applied the money to the purpose for which it was destined, that is, propagating the idea of a revolution.[66]

The German government soon became suspicious of Joffe's activities. In the beginning of November the German Secret Service, having long suspected the dozens of couriers who traveled regularly between Moscow and Berlin, bringing heavy trunks to the Russian Embassy, obtained direct evidence which proved that Joffe was taking advantage of his extraterritoriality rights for purposes of propaganda. It was arranged that one

[65] Nicolai, "Die Gesamtlege," *Süddeutsche Monatshefte,* April 1924, p. 34; see also Ewald Beckmann, *Der Dolchstossprozess in München von 19 Oktober bis 20 November 1925* (Munich, 1925), p. 212, testimony of Roeder. General Hoffmann foresaw the danger of allowing a Bolshevik Embassy to be established in Berlin or consulates to be opened which would serve as centers for Bolshevik propaganda against Germany: "Not for a moment had the Bolsheviks left it in doubt that their object was a World Revolution and that they considered the revolutionizing of Germany as the first step towards it. They used every opportunity for propaganda. Radik, a member of the peace delegation even went so far as having propaganda writings thrown out of railway coaches to be distributed among our soldiers." General von Hoffmann, *The War of Lost Opportunities* (London, 1924), p. 231.

[66] *Deutsche National Versammlung,* stenographisches Bericht, Sitzung 15, February 25, 1919.

of the twelve incoming trunks should "accidentally" fall down the steps of the Friedrichstrasse station in Berlin. This accident caused the trunk to break open, and the contents to fall to the ground. As had been suspected, the trunks proved to be loaded with leaflets directed against the German government.[67] The German Consul General at Moscow was instructed to inform the Russian government that Germany had been obliged repeatedly to protest against Russia's contravention of Article II of the Brest-Litovsk Treaty.[68] Further, Russia was reminded that though the Soviet government had often promised to apprehend the murderer of Count Mirbach,[69] the instigators and the murderer were still at large. The Russian government was requested to withdraw all of the official representatives from Germany until such time as it would guarantee that, in the future, no revolutionary agitation and propaganda would be carried on.[70]

Joffe and his Russian co-workers were now out of Germany, but the Independent Socialists and the Spartacists were still there. And the clouds of revolution were becoming heavier and heavier and drawing ever closer. The propaganda of the Allies alone did not bring the revolution, nor did the propaganda of the Bolsheviks and the revolutionary parties within Germany bring it on. It was the propaganda of all three that stirred the Germans to take up arms against their rulers, their militarists and Junkers. The capitulation of Germany was inevitable after a psychological change had been brought about among the rank and file of the Germans both at home and at the front. And this psychological change was accomplished by the revolutionary propaganda of the Allies and the archpropagandists of Russia.

[67] Walter Nicolai, *The German Secret Service,* p. 233; also *The Times* (London), November 7, 1918.

[68] This article stated that a foreign representative should not interfere in the internal affairs of a country.

[69] The German Ambassador to Russia who was murdered in Moscow.

[70] *Norddeutsche Allgemeine Zeitung,* November 6, 1918, *Morgen Ausgabe.*

CHAPTER VI

INTERNAL CONDITIONS OF GERMANY AN AID TO PROPAGANDA

> Since the Entente parties were certain that there would be internal dissensions in our country they spared nothing to tear us apart.
>
> —UNGEWITTER, *Wiedergeburt durch Blut und Eisen* (p. 490)

The vision of victory had buoyed up the rank and file of the German people for almost four years. The Kaiser, Hindenburg, and the various German Chancellors had all promised victory to them. Yet by the summer of 1918 the average German had begun to see that the vision of victory was after all only a mirage, that retreated as he pressed on after it. This realization, together with the shortage of food, the scarcity of clothing, and a general war-weariness, produced a restlessness in the public mind of Germany.

THE DOLCHSTOSS QUESTION

In an article in the *Star* of November 30, 1918, entitled "The Watch on the Rhine," the British General, Sir Frederick Maurice, asked how it was possible that an enemy which was so united, so determined to win, should collapse. He answered the question by stating that it could all be attributed to the moral collapse of Germany. This opinion of the British General was the kernel of the *Dolchstoss* theory.[1] German generals

[1] There is an abundance of literature on the *Dolchstoss* question. A few of the books that deal with the matter are: Emil Barth, *Aus der Werkstatt der deutschen Revolution;* Drahn and Leonhard, *Unterirdisches Literatur im revolutionären Deutschland während des Weltkrieges;* General von Wrisberg, *Der Weg zur Revolution 1914 bis 1918;* Drahn and Friedegg, *Deutscher Revolutions Almanach für 1919;* and, of course, *U.D.Z.*, especially Volume VI. The *Süddeutsche Monatshefte* is one of a number of periodicals that gives considerable space to the question.

and German leaders immediately accepted this view and enlarged upon it. It was their explanation for the defeat of Germany: The militarists had been "stabbed in the back." The Army was still intact, but the collapse of Germany came because the home front had broken down.[2] There had developed, behind the lines, a strong anti-war sentiment, and this sentiment spread from the home front to the troops and thus tore down the will to fight among the soldiers at the front.

Those who hold to the "stab in the back" theory say that the tactics of the *Dolchstoss* were threefold. First, it centered upon the intellectual revolutionizing of the front through the spread of leaflets, pamphlets, and manifestos. Second, it centered upon the psychical or spiritual revolution of the front through organization of deserters. Third, it concentrated upon the organized revolutionization of the home front "through the centralization of all the forces of the revolution."[3]

When comparing the loyalty of the people at home with the soldiers at the front one has to remember that the civilian population was confronted with more complex problems. The people became despondent. Little irritations arose in the course

[2] Winston Churchill, in *The World Crisis 1916–1918* (New York, 1927, I, 40 ff.), makes some comparisons which throw light on the strength of the German Army at the end of the war. "During the whole war," he says, "the Germans never lost in any phase of the fighting more than the French whom they fought, and frequently inflicted double casualties upon them. In no one of the periods into which the fighting has been divided by French authorities did the French come off the best in killed, prisoners and wounded. Whether they were on the defensive or were the attackers, the result was the same. Whether in the original rush of invasion, or in the German offensive at Verdun, or in the great French assaults on the German line—it always took the blood of 1½ to 2 Frenchmen to inflict a corresponding injury upon a German.

"The second fact which presents itself from the table is that in all the British offensives the British casualties were never less than 3 to 2, and often nearly double the corresponding German losses."

[3] *U.D.Z.*, VI, 12 (von Kuhl's Report); see also Wolfgang Breithaupt, "Die Auswirkung des Dolchstosses, Erinnerungen von Teilnehmern," *Süddeutsche Monatshefte,* May 1924, p. 80. Von Kuhl's report is also given in Lutz, *The Causes of the German Collapse,* pp. 132–66.

of daily wartime activities. The numerous decrees of the government administrators and the police were not always comprehended by the people, who grew weary of regulations. The poorer classes were jealous of the situation of the newly rich classes, who often showed a lack of consideration for their less-fortunate fellow countrymen. The heavy work, coupled with the decreasing food allotments, caused discontent among the masses of the people. All of these facts tended to make the people receptive to any type of propaganda.

Among the fighting forces the spirit could easily remain stronger than at home. The party struggles and the fight over the "war problem" did not reach them. The mass of the soldiers were too busy to be bothered with such things. They marched, they went into the trenches, bled, and died in obedience to the call of their Fatherland. Eventually, however, they became war-weary. In burning longing they looked toward home. They wanted peace, an honorable peace.

This feeling was already noticeable in the autumn of 1915, when there was a change in the attitude of the reserve forces. The reserves disliked to go to the front. They felt that they had done their share in the war—in short, the service in the army no longer appealed to them:

> So, already at this time one found evidence of extensive propaganda—among the reserve forces. This propaganda said that Germany was responsible for the war; otherwise the number of Germany's opponents would not increase daily. We would be certain of losing the war from which only munitions manufacturers and the high officials would profit.[4]

Speaking of the cause of the Kiel revolt, Lieutenant Captain Erich Galster von Seydlitz said:

> The mutiny was not the result of discontent despite the fact that there were sufficient causes for it . . . . It would be too unjust to our men to say that this discontent led them to turn against their flag at such an inopportune moment. This mutiny was rather the result of the

[4] *Kölnische Volkszeitung* (Abends), February 3, 1919.

systematic efforts of the betrayers among our own people and the systematic work of the enemy propaganda.[5]

The long duration of the war, the unprecedented demands of the military situation upon the people, and the oppressive economic burdens led to an ever increasing sentiment for peace among the masses of the German people. There is no doubt that this sentiment found it way from home to the front. There is no doubt that the conditions at home were exaggerated by the Allied propagandists and the propagandists of the revolutionary groups within Germany. The complaints about the suffering at home told on the soldiers. The manufacturers had raised the prices to such an extent that the one thought of the people was "How shall we get enough to eat?" Ever stronger became the wish and the call for peace.

However, if the situation at home had its effect upon the army, it must be admitted that the army also had its own complaints:

> The Army was weary and embittered. Great injustices and unfulfilled promises demoralized the troops. The absolute separation of the officers' corps, the scandalous stories of provision stores, opened the eyes of all the men. The means of strengthening their morale, defensive war for the homeland, was decried as a lie. The *Vaterlandische Unterricht,* which was conducted by young officers, was laughed at. Hate was in the troops. Hate, not for the enemy who were suffering the same, but hate for those who prolonged the war.[6]

Hints of the threatening revolution in Germany come from both the Right and the Left. One of the earliest proofs of this is the well-known letter of May 5, 1915, from the Pan-German, Freiherr von Gebsattel, to the Imperial Chancellor von Bethmann-Hollweg. Von Gebsattel said that the war aims of the government did not justify the heavy burdens which the people

[5] *Deutsche Zeitung,* December 28, 1918.

[6] Ludwig Lewinsohn, *Die Revolution an der Westfront* (Charlottenburg, 1919), Foreword. Although Herr Lewinsohn hoped, in this book, to wipe out the "historical falsity" that the breakdown of the Army was the result of the "revolution at home," he admits that "those who came from home told of unspeakable conditions there."

were forced to bear, and that if the German people were not promised more suitable compensation for their efforts they would undoubtedly rebel against the monarchy.[7]

The first really revolutionary remark in the Reichstag was made, not, as might have been expected, by a representative of the Labor Union (Arbeitsgemeinschaft), but by the Majority Socialist Hoch. On July 5, 1917, he uttered the following sentence in the Main Committee of the Reichstag: "There is always talk of whether the revolution will come or not; we can only say that the German people are already in the midst of the revolution." He then went on to discuss the discontent in Germany and said:

> The feeling in Germany is such that things cannot go on as they are at present, for otherwise it will come to conflicts of the worst kind. The Government ought to take to heart Goethe's words: "The revolution from below is always due to the sins of omission of those above."[8]

In considering the moral collapse of Germany it must be remembered that the war had lasted much longer than had been expected. The old Reich had not provided during the war what the German people had a right to expect of its institutions. It had neither established a close connection between the "spirit of the people and a strong external leadership, nor had it harnessed the industrial powers of the nation for the most terrible war Germany has ever waged."[9]

These two factors explain the internal conditions of Germany which played into the hands of the Allied propagandists. The old Reich had not counted upon a blockade that would cause a shortage of food, and it had not prepared the moral force of the people for a long war. We shall now consider these two factors more in detail.

[7] *U.D.Z.*, V, 151–71, statement of Dr. Philipp; also R. H. Lutz, *The Causes of the German Collapse*, pp. 113 ff.

[8] *U.D.Z.*, V, 151–71, statement of Dr. Philipp; also in Lutz, *The Causes of the German Collapse*, p. 113.

[9] Rochus Albrecht K. von Rheinbaben, *Stresemann, The Man and the Statesman* (New York and London, 1929), p. 143, quoting an article Stresemann wrote for the *Deutsche Stimmen* in August 1918.

THE FOOD SITUATION

As has been noted in a previous chapter, the food supply in Germany was left in the hands of the governments of the different federal states working through associations formed after a common model.[10] This system was very unsatisfactory. Because there was no central agency for the control of the food supply some states had enough food and other states had very little. Suspicion and jealousy resulted. When, for instance, the meat supply reached the point of exhaustion in Prussia, the Saxons were blamed. The *Leipziger neueste Nachrichten,* coming to the defense of the Saxons in May 1916, said:

> At present Saxony has no meat. This is partly due to bad distribution. Saxony is dependent on imports and only gets its share of meat from the Prussian provinces when these have satisfied their own needs; and when they have done that practically nothing is left for Saxony. This must be altered. Prussia must reduce its consumption.[11]

The growing difficulty in the supply of food caused great anxiety among the people. They were, however, forbidden to speak openly about the actual amount of food available in order that the facts regarding the food situation would not reach the Allies. But much information on this matter leaked out through the newspapers, which gave space to rumors "partly spread by enemy agents, which hinted at profiteering and imperfect organization at home."[12]

The Allies made the most of the food situation in Germany. They tried to make the German soldiers believe that the people at home were starving. Leaflets entitled "Slow Starvation" were sent across the lines in great numbers. These traced the food situation from 1915 to 1917. By giving the menu of the German worker in 1915 and comparing it with that of 1917,

[10] *Supra,* chapter iv.

[11] *Confidential Supplement to the Daily Review of the Foreign Press,* No. 69, June 16, 1916, pp. 4 ff.

[12] Rochus A. K. Rheinbaben, *Stresemann, the Man and the Statesman,* translated from the German by Cyrus Brook and Hans Herzl (New York and London, 1929), p. 110.

the propagandists tried to show that Germany was headed toward starvation. Said one of these leaflets:

The workers' menu of 1915 was:

1. Early morning lunch (5:45 A.M.)
   4 slices of bread with butter or fresh lard, cheese or sausage, coffee.
2. Breakfast at 8:00 A.M.
   Bread and cheese sandwich and coffee.
3. Noon meal
   Meat or fish, potatoes (any amount).
4. Supper
   Soup, meat or fish, potatoes, peas, rice or hominy.

In April 1917 it was different.

1. Breakfast—2 pieces of dry bread and potatoes.
2. Dinner—cooked beets one day, the next day cooked sea weeds or beets and a few potatoes.[13]

After making this comparison of menus the leaflet called upon the Germans to revolt against their government.

After the revolt of the German people, the Allies, who have no hate for them, will supply them with food and clothing even as they are supplying the war prisoners now. But these provisions will be withheld until the military authority in Germany collapses.

News of the various hunger riots in Germany in 1916 reached foreign countries despite the efforts of the censors. The *Briefe aus Deutschland* leaflets spread among the German troops the news of these riots and kept before the eyes of the German soldiers the picture of a Germany short of food. *Die Feldpost* also made it a point to keep the German soldiers informed regarding the food situation behind the lines. Such phrases as "Carry through, suffer long, hunger long, kill long," were used often in this propaganda sheet of the Allies. Another leaflet contained an "Apostle's Creed" which ended with: "I believe in the Holy War, a great universal usury, the community of hamsters, the increase of taxes, the shortening of meat rations, and an everlasting shortage of bread. Amen."[14] *Leaf-*

[13] *Leaflet A.P. 9.*

[14] Dr. George Huber, *Französische Propaganda,* p. 233.

let A.P. 87 contained a number of quotations from various German newspapers which showed what the situation was in Germany. One of these from the *Arbeiter Zeitung* says:

From München it is reported that a ministerial decree orders that the dead be clothed with paper clothing to give the living the linen of the dead, because of the scarcity of clothing.[15]

Letters to German prisoners in the hands of the Allies were intercepted and those that complained of the conditions at home were printed in the *Briefe aus Deutschland* series and sent to the soldiers at the front. One of these letters gives the prices of certain articles of food.

June 26, 1917

DEAR PAUL:

A year ago bread could be had without limit at nine marks. Now there is no more. Now to give you some of the prices: 2 eighths (*achtel*) butter 70 pfennigs; a pound of marmalade (not eatable) 1.40; a pound of potatoes 8 pfennigs.[16]

Another letter complains:

In a word, here in Germany it has come to the point of starvation. The people just creep about, and now this terrible heat on top of it all. Sickness is everywhere. A terrible dysentery has broken out here in Berlin and surroundings.[17]

A letter dated April 9, 1916, and sent from Dresden, found on a prisoner of war by the British said in part:

We are sending you less and less. Now they have made tickets for meat. It is impossible to buy even a sausage. I tell you everything is going from bad to worse. They have seized everything, or one can only sell for coupons. What is going to become of us? It is high time that we had peace.[18]

[15] *Leaflet A.P. 87.*

[16] The *Briefe aus Deutschland* came from the Hansi organization, the *Service aérienne*. They appeared irregularly beginning in April 1916. Thirteen numbers appeared by November 1917. Hansi et Tonnelat, *op. cit.*, p. 40; also Huber, *op. cit.*, p. 230.

[17] *Briefe aus Deutschland,* No. 13, quoted by Huber, *op. cit.*, p. 232.

[18] *Confidential Supplement to the Daily Review of the Foreign Press,* No. 54, May 30, 1916, p. 2.

Another, also sent from Dresden and dated April 10, 1916, stated:

> Let us hope that peace will not be delayed much longer. Otherwise we shall be quite dead of hunger. Are we not already half dead? Even for meat tickets are now necessary. One has the right nowadays to 600 grams of sausage, fat, and meat per week. There is something to get fat on![19]

Other letters complained of the lack of coffee, salad oil, and beer. The butcher shops, they said, "look as if they had been swept bare from top to bottom."[20] Bread also was very scarce. As early as April 1916 each family was allowed two loaves of bread a week without a ticket: "And now a loaf costs 2.60 marks. It is a shame."[21]

Princess Blücher, who lived in Germany throughout the period of the war, gives a picture of the conditions within Germany when she says in her diary in May 1918, regarding the situation:

> Food is growing scarcer from day to day and we have been reduced to killing and eating our kangaroos. They have been kept here as a curiosity and rarity for years past. Yesterday my husband received a letter from a provision dealer in Breslau saying he would give any price my husband asked if he would sell him a kangaroo.[22]

Because of the high cost of food and the difficulty of obtaining the necessities of life, there developed a feeling of enmity between the poorer class and the well-to-do. The poor felt that the rich were not subjected to the same restrictions as they were, and that the upper class of people were making a profit out of the war. The working class became hungry and resentful. "The feeling of hatred daily grew stronger for the factory owners, the rich shopkeepers, and business men who dealt in

[19] *Confidential Supplement to the Daily Review of the Foreign Press*, No. 54, May 30, 1916, p. 2.

[20] *Ibid.*, p. 3.

[21] *Ibid.*

[22] Princess Mary E. Blücher, *An English Wife in Berlin*, p. 22.

army supplies of all kinds, and for officers of the army and navy."[23] A letter to a German prisoner of war intercepted by the British pictures the food situation in the following words:

LANDSBERG, April 30, 1916

We are having an infernal time here with regard to food. I feel like smashing the shopwindows. Nothing can be had for love nor money. There is food enough for us all, but the wretches will not part with it. They feed themselves fat, fill their purses, and leave us to eat dirt. And what is going to happen by and by? Nothing good; there is nothing that we can hope for. The luckiest are the men who are killed and dead. The others, the wounded and the mutilated, are patched up only to be sent back to the front to be martyred again. . . . . There is precious little food fit for human beings; meat, bacon, sausage, and all fats are short. We are vegetarians, we are salad-soldiers and as limp as rags. They can't take us out on long marches any more, else they would have to come and collect us in hay carts.[24]

Deputy Haase gave his observations on the food question in a speech in the Reichstag on April 6, 1916, in which he pointed to the internal discontent in Germany as a result of the food situation. On the previous day the Chancellor had spoken of the great moral reserve which had enabled the German people to maintain the enormously improved standard of living which had come into being during the last decade. Haase pointed out, however, that large groups of the labor and middle classes did not participate in the rising standard of living. Continuing his speech he pointed out that

even the better-situated circles have been forced away below the previous level. And in what would the masses restrict themselves more? Prices of food products are as a rule beyond their means. . . . . The well-to-do and the rich—that we admit openly—are subjected to some restrictions and annoyances at this time. However, anyone having money is still in a position to buy sufficient food materials and sweets. The poor and those with lesser means suffer want again and again. . . . .

[23] Arthur Rosenberg, *The Birth of the German Republic,* translated from the German by Ian F. D. Morrow (London, 1931), p. 91.

[24] *Confidential Supplement to the Daily Review of the Foreign Press,* No. 55, May 31, 1916, p. 2.

The differences between various classes become more apparent than ever.[25]

Making capital of the growing bitterness of the people as a result of the food shortage, the radical Socialists within Germany sent out leaflets blaming the capitalists and the government for the plight of the people. One of the leaflets states:

HUNGER!

What was bound to come has come! Hunger!! In Leipzig, in Berlin, in Essen, and many other places there are riots started by hungry masses of the people.

Herr Bethmann-Hollweg says England is the cause of the hunger in Germany, and the other officials repeat this. The German government should have known it would come to this. War against Russia, France, and England had to lead to the blockade of Germany. . . . .

Why has the government done nothing? Because the government, the capitalists, the Junkers do not feel the pangs of hunger of the masses. . . . .

The workers can either continue in silent obedience and go to a sorrowful end, or they can rise up, do away with the government and the ruling classes, and force peace. . . . .

Arise, you men, you women!

Down with the War!

Hail to the International Solidarity of the Proletariat![26]

When food became more scarce in the army, the feeling of envy and resentment became noticeable among the men in the ranks. They cast angry and envious glances toward the officers' mess. This was especially true in the reserve battalions, among the garrisons at home, and among the crews of the battleships which were virtually inactive throughout the war and on whom a barrack routine was enforced.[27] Of this situation, one German authority states:

The student seeking the causes of the revolution in the German Army returns continually to the food question and the embitterment

[25] Germany, Reichstag, *Verhandlungen des Reichstags,* April 6, 1916, Band 40, pp. 881–89; also cited in R. H. Lutz, *The Fall of the German Empire,* I, 226.

[26] *Fliegerabwurf-Schriften,* No. 5.

[27] Arthur Rosenberg, *The Birth of the German Republic,* p. 91.

of the soldiers and sailors who believed they were less well-fed than their officers.[28]

Just what was the actual food situation in Germany during the war period? In 1915 Paul Eltzbacher and a group of experts made a study of the food supply of the Fatherland and the methods of conserving it. They came to the conclusion that England could never starve Germany by the blockade, nor by otherwise isolating her, if Germany adopted the various measures which the experts recommended.[29] Another German, Dr. W. Robert de Fiori, stated, in a conversation with Dr. George Herron of the United States, that Germany could last ten years.[30] The fact was, however, that the German food supply became more and more critical, and that it reached a dangerously low point before the end of the war. Dr. Philipp, in discussing this question before the *Untersuchungsausschusses,* presented the facts in calorie form when he stated:

> At the end of the war the German people were allowed only 1,100 calories each day, whereas before the war they had 3,300 calories per day. The bread ration was 160 grams per day, whereas before the war it was 320 grams per day; meat, 135 grams per week, before the war was 1,050 grams; lard, 7 grams per day in 1918, while it was 28 grams per day before the war.[31]

[28] Arthur Rosenberg, p. 91.

[29] Paul Eltzbacher, ed., *Germany's Food: Can It Last?* English version edited by S. Russell Wells (London, 1915). The Committee concluded (p. 232) that the English "starvation scheme, in spite of closed frontiers and raids on shipping will be shattered by the willing co-operation of millions."

[30] "Herron Papers, Germany, First Conversation between de Fiori and Herron, June 14, 1918," Vol. I, Document XXV B (manuscript, Hoover War Library), p. 58. In a later conversation between de Fiori and Herron, the former admitted that the "economic condition of Germany was not nearly so good as he first asserted. People are literally starving in Bavaria. The Ukranian harvest bids fair to be a failure this summer, and the expected food supplies of the Ukraine were a delusion. Germany is not in an economic condition to continue the war, except the people accept great and continuous misery."

[31] *U.D.Z.,* V, 137.

A Memorandum of the Public Health Office, dated December 16, 1918, gives further light on the food question.

> Among the foodstuffs, the shortage of animal foodstuffs (butter and other animal fats, eggs, meat, milk, and dairy produce) was felt particularly acutely. In densely populated industrial districts and in large cities the regular feeding of small children was often rendered difficult by the shortage of milk. Vegetable fats and oils were also available in such small quantities, owing to the insufficiency of imports, that even the most pressing needs could not be met.[32]

When we consider the fact that the Inter-Allied Food Commission allowed 75 grams per head per day as the minimum amount of fat necessary, and that this amount had to last an individual in Germany for from 12 to 14 days, we get an idea of the food situation in Germany in 1918.

What effect did this have upon the people of Germany? Writing in her diary in May 1918, Princess Blücher said of the situation:

> I notice a great change in the people here from what they were last year. They are all "tired of suffering," as they express it. "We want our sons and husbands back, and we want food," is all they say.[33]

The German government was helpless before the rising storm. When it started a strict food-control system, which covered practically every article for home consumption, the peasants complained bitterly. The proletariat in the cities became restless. Even the men at the front became bitter as a result of the ever increasing number of complaints that came from home—complaints that told of the advantage that the usurers were taking of the food situation to increase their wealth while the mass of the people were on the point of starvation.[34]

[32] *U.D.Z.,* VI, 434, Annex C to the Memorandum of the Public Health Office; also cited by R. H. Lutz, *The Causes of the German Collapse,* pp. 180–87.

[33] Princess Blücher, *An English Wife in Berlin,* p. 224.

[34] *Kölnische Volkszeitung,* February 3, 1919.

Failure, therefore, on the part of the German government to distribute its food supply scientifically and to prepare her industries for the greatest war in history resulted in hunger and starvation. Germany had not counted on the blockade; she had not planned for a long war; and when the war dragged out and the blockade became effective, the result was bound to be disastrous. Thus the student seeking the cause of the German Revolution cannot overlook the food question and the hardships resulting from a long-drawn-out conflict against great odds.

THE POLITICAL SITUATION

On August 4, 1911, the International Labor Conference convening in London adopted the following resolution:

> The German, Spanish, English, Dutch, and French delegates of the Workers' Organizations declare that they are ready to oppose any declaration of war, whatever the grounds may be. Every national representative will, accordingly, undertake to oppose any criminal act of the ruling classes.[35]

Just three years later, the German Reichstag voted the necessary war credits. The German Socialists, forgetting the resolution of three years before, now supported the government in the war. The various political parties in Germany not only agreed to a truce between themselves but also agreed to abstain from all opposition to the government during the period of the war.[36] The Social Democrats voted in favor of the war credits demanded by the government on August 4, 1914. In a speech before the Reichstag, Deputy Haase justified the stand of the party by stating that, although the Social Democrats had always opposed imperialism and competitive armaments, support

[35] Drahn and Leonhard, *Unterirdisches Literatur,* p. 7.

[36] The Social Democratic group in the Reichstag was composed of 110 members. At a party meeting it decided, by a vote of 96 to 14, to support the government in the war credits. The 14 dissentient voters, however, submitted to party discipline and voted for the war credits in the Reichstag. Rosenberg, *op. cit.,* p. 73.

of the war was necessary in order to render secure the civilization and independence of Germany.

> Much, if not all, is at stake for our people and its freedom in the future, in case victory should be on the side of Russian despotism sullied with the blood of the best of its own people. It is necessary to ward off this danger, to render secure the civilization and the independence of our own country. And we shall do what we have always maintained: In the hour of danger we do not leave the Fatherland in the lurch. In so doing we feel ourselves in agreement with the International, which at all times has recognized the right of every people to national independence and self-defense, just as we, in agreement with it, condemn every war of conquest.[37]

A party truce was thus declared. So pleased were the military leaders with this party peace and the united support for the war that they lifted the restrictions upon the literature of the Social Democratic party, a restriction which had been in effect since 1894. General von Falkenhayn wrote to Comrade Stadthagen, who represented the newspaper *Vorwärts:*

> Referring to your letter of the 17th inst. the War Office informs you that Section 3 of the ordinance of the War Office, dated 24.1.1894, prohibiting the subscription to, and the distribution of revolutionary or Social-Democratic literature, as well as the dissemination of such literature in military barracks or other buildings used for military purposes, has been repealed as far as Social-Democratic literature is concerned, if published after 31.8.1914.
>
> The Minister of War takes the occasion to state that this repeal has been made in the expectation that nothing will be published which might endanger the spirit of loyalty in the army. If this should not be the case every Chief Command is empowered to put the ordinance in force again.[38]

However, the *Burgfrieden,* as the party truce was called, could not withstand a long war and, when the German General

[37] Germany, Reichstag, *Verhandlungen des Reichstags,* August 4, 1914, pp. 8–9; also R. H. Lutz, *The Fall of the German Empire,* I, 15–16.

[38] *Vorwärts,* September 2, 1914; also cited in Lutz, *The Fall of the German Empire,* I, 20.

Staff was unable to give to the nation the speedy victory that had been hoped for, the political and class warfare broke out again. All hope of a speedy victory for Germany was destroyed with the miscarriage of the Schlieffen Plan. After the first battle of the Marne it became evident that the war would last much longer than had been anticipated. The longer the war continued the more clearly did political and class differences manifest themselves within Germany.

Although the workers readily offered themselves for the defense of the Fatherland, they could not understand how it was that their old enemies, the Prussian militarists and the great industrialists, were all of a sudden to be regarded as friends. They knew that the military and police regime in Prussia was the same as it had been before the *Burgfrieden*. They soon discovered that the workers had actually lost influence as a result of their action on August 4, 1914, and that the promise, which had often been made since the early part of the war, of reform in the Prussian electoral system was not to be fulfilled. The result was a "depression which held the working men and women in its grasp," and a "deep-seated discontent" which animated the masses of the German people throughout the first winter of the war.[39]

This discontent grew stronger with each passing month of the war. Questions began to be raised as to the war aims of Germany. The Social-Democratic workmen had formulated their war aims, but the government refused to tell what Germany was fighting for. A certain portion of the populace gained the impression that the war was started by the industrialists and the militarists for their own selfish interests. The Peace of Brest-Litovsk gave proof of the annexationist designs of the militarists in Germany.

From the end of August 1916 until shortly before the Armistice in 1918, Germany was ruled by a small military and

[39] Rosenberg, *op. cit.*, p. 90; also Lutz, *The Causes of the German Collapse*, p. 98.

Junker class whose chief was Ludendorff.[40] The Kaiser was regarded by this ruling party as a fool and was completely disregarded so far as the councils of government were concerned. Nor did the Chancellor count greatly, for many of the most important decisions were made and actions were taken without reference to him. In fact, Ludendorff even claimed the right to name the Imperial Chancellor. Bethmann-Hollweg was dismissed because Hindenburg and Ludendorff refused to work harmoniously with him. The two generals agreed upon Michaelis as the successor, and the Kaiser accepted him, "although he was forced to confess that he did not know Michaelis."[41]

But from the very beginning of Ludendorff's dictatorship there was evidence of a breach between the German people and their rulers. There was a growing liberal movement that perceived that the war was ruining Germany. However, this liberal movement was not organized and it lacked leaders. Only after the split in the Social Democratic party did opposition leadership develop.

The Social Democrats divided because of differences regarding the party attitude toward the war. The party leaders were convinced that it lay in the interest of the German workmen to defend the country to the utmost. They felt that the party should live up to the *Burgfrieden* and content itself with emphasizing that Germany should not attempt conquests in the war. This official policy of the party encountered increasing opposition. This opposition ultimately crystallized into two groups: the Spartacus Association, and the Independent Social Democratic party of Germany.

The Spartacus group grew out of the extreme Left Wing of the Social Democratic party and was under the leadership of Karl Liebknecht, Rosa Luxemburg, Franz Mehring, and

[40] "Herron Papers," Germany, First Conversation between de Fiori and Herron, June 14, 1918, Vol. I, Document XXV A, p. 6; also Rosenberg, *op. cit.*, pp. 125 ff.

[41] Arthur Rosenberg, *op. cit.*, p. 126; see also Germany, *Verhandlungen des Reichstags,* 116 Sitzung, July 19, 1917, p. 3586.

Klara Zetkin. Liebknecht broke the *Burgfrieden* pledge when he refused to vote for the war credits in the Reichstag on December 2, 1914. Liebknecht justified his action in a speech before the Main Committee of the Reichstag. This speech was put in leaflet form and circulated throughout Germany. Among other things Liebknecht said:

> This war, which the people did not want, did not blaze up for the welfare of the German or any other people. It is an imperialistic war, a war for the capitalistic monopoly of world markets and the political control of worthwhile settlements for industry and capital.[42]

From December 1914 to the end of the war the Spartacus group hammered at the capitalists, the government, and the militarists. Pacifist and revolutionary sentiment was stirred up by pamphlets, leaflets, and a certain portion of the press. Rosa Luxemburg, in her *Junius Pamphlet,* which was printed in Switzerland in 1915, and distributed secretly in Germany, attacked the Social Democrats for their "treacherous action" in supporting the war policy of the German government. The war, according to the *Junius Pamphlet,* was a capitalistic war. The desire for imperialistic expansion, the hope of "subjecting all the riches of the earth and all means of production to capital, to turn all the laboring masses of the peoples of all zones into wage slaves," were the forces that brought on the war. But this "brutal triumphal procession of capitalism through the world has one bright spot: It has created the premise of its own final overthrow."[43]

[42] Ernst Meyer, ed., *Spartakus im Kriege; die illegalen Flugblätter des Spartakusbundes im Kriege* (Berlin, 1927), Document No. 3. After the break with the Social Democratic party Liebknecht regarded it as his duty to protest publicly against the *Burgfrieden.* He was drafted into the army, but despite this he took part in the street demonstration in Berlin on May 1, 1916. For this he was court-martialed and sentenced to four years. He thus became a martyr for the Socialist peace movement. See Dr. Max Adler, *Karl Liebknecht und Rosa Luxemburg* (Vienna, 1919), p. 9.

[43] *The Crisis in German Social-Democracy* (*The Junius Pamphlet,* New York, 1915), p. 124. At a conference in January 1915, the Spartacus group adopted the principles as set down by Rosa Luxemburg in her pamphlet as the program of the Spartacus Association.

In the winter of 1915 Liebknecht began to circulate letters which he wrote under the name of "Spartakus." These *Spartakusbriefe* were open letters to the German people in which Liebknecht denounced the war and advocated the overthrow of the German capitalist government.[44] These letters were hectographed at first, but from September 1916 on they appeared in printed form. For the most part they were distributed from headquarters in Berlin in editions of from 5,000 to 6,000 copies. In some provincial towns they were reprinted or were recopied on typewriters for distribution. The distribution of the Spartacus letters was also simplified by the fact that Baumeister's *Internationale Korrespondenz,* which was under the special patronage of the General Commission of Trade Unions, reprinted the letters for purposes of information and sent them to thousands of trade-union officials. From this source they also reached the official press of the Social Democratic party.[45]

The purpose of the propaganda of the Spartacus League was summarized by Liebknecht when he said:

> Universal peace cannot come without the overthrow of the ruling powers of Germany. . . . . The German workers are now called upon to carry the message to the East and to the West.[46]

Like the Russian Bolsheviks, the Spartacists believed that they should take advantage of the war to get their system established. As Liebknecht stated in a speech in January 1915:

[44] Dr. Ernst Meyer, ed., *Dokumente des Kommunismus,* No. 2, *Spartakusbriefe,* Band II, Vorwort. This collection contains the *Spartakusbriefe* from September 1916 to October 1918. The hectographed copies are not included. Dr. Meyer, in discussing the amount of money spent on Spartacus propaganda, states that it is not true that the Spartacus group spent 20,000 marks weekly on propaganda. The expenditure of the head office up to November 1918 was from 3,000 to 5,000 marks monthly at the most. "These figures do not include the expenditure of the provincial organizations, but their total expenditure was naturally far less than 20,000 marks. . . . . Funds were placed at our disposal by the Russian party which was friendly to us, but they were only small amounts. . . . ." See also *U.D.Z.,* V, 115–16.

[45] Dr. Ernst Meyer, *Dokumente des Kommunismus,* No. 2; also *U.D.Z.,* V, 116.

[46] *U.D.Z.,* II, 112.

> Class struggle is the watchword of the day. Class struggle not after the war, class struggle during the war. If the party does not take up the struggle today, during the war, people will not believe in its fighting spirit. Now is the time to prove it true.[47]

To further their propaganda activities the Spartacists obtained the support of certain German newspapers. The *Arbeiter Politik,* a weekly published in Bremen, often contained articles by leading Spartacists.[48] The *Leipziger Volkszeitung* was also favorable to Spartacan propaganda, while the *Internationale,* the *Internationale sozialisten Deutschlands,* and the *Bremer Linksradikale,* were others of a definitely revolutionary character.[49]

These newspapers and others of the same character were freely circulated among the troops at the front. This fact caused General Galwitz to state, before the Session of the Secretaries of State on October 28, 1918:

> The fact that we have permitted newspapers of all political opinion to be freely distributed throughout the army has also been proven to have a bad effect.[50]

The Spartacus organizations spread over Germany like a net. Provincial organizations were founded, and these in turn started local groups. All were in close connection with the central organization in Berlin. In the beginning of 1918 these revolutionary groups began an attack upon the morale of the German troops with such leaflets as *Der deutsche Soldat als Hänker der Freiheit* and *Kameraden erwacht.* The former attacked the government for the Brest-Litovsk Treaty, which "took by force, from the Russian Revolution, a territory twice the size of Germany." The German soldiers, it said, "are being used as the gendarmes for capitalist reaction in all of Europe," and

[47] *Voices of Revolt,* "Speeches of Liebknecht" (New York, 1927), IV, 75.

[48] Walter Nicolai, *Nachrichtendienst Presse und Volksstimmung.*

[49] Drahn and Leonhard, *Unterirdisches Literatur,* p. 10.

[50] *Preliminary History of the Armistice* (Official Documents, Germany), No. 86, p. 123.

thereby they are blocking the progress toward the freedom of the German proletariat and the coming of Socialism:

Arise German Worker! Rescue in these last hours, the freedom of Europe.

Down with Imperialistic murder! Down with the war!

Awaken again the international solidarity of the workers![51]

The leaflet, *Kameraden erwacht,* also attacked the policy of the German militarists in the Brest-Litovsk negotiations. It lamented the fact that the German people were being "lied to" by the much-censored press. It ended with the appeal:

For a more beautiful, higher, nobler aim, our fight should continue. The holy aim of our struggle should be: A FREE AND FORTUNATE GERMAN REPUBLIC! . . . .

Comrades awake and realize your strength![52]

When the German government court-martialed Liebknecht and imprisoned him for his activities in the 1916 May-Day riots in Berlin, it gave the Spartacists new material for their propaganda. Liebknecht was a martyr to the cause of the Revolution. The Spartacus letter of November 5, 1916, addressed to Karl Liebknecht, said:

No, you have not fallen! You are gone from us, but . . . . you remain at your post as a fighter and leader for our holy cause and each day that you spend in the prison is a thorn for the German working class, and each clanging of your chains is a trumpet-call to us all: To the fight! To the fight for yours and our liberation![53]

The same note was struck in the leaflet No. 14, when it called:

Do you hear the voice of Liebknecht? Does it not come to your ears through the prison walls? Are you not ashamed to know that he is right? And yet you leave him alone . . . . you have betrayed him. . . . . Only when he is free will you be free.[54]

[51] Dr. Ernst Meyer, *Spartakus im Kriege,* Document No. 47, p. 199.

[52] *Ibid.,* Document No. 48, p. 201.

[53] Meyer, *Dokumente des Kommunismus,* No. 2, p. 22.

[54] *Fliegerabwurf-Schriften,* No. 14. More than 60,000 workers in Berlin went on strike as a protest against the trial of Liebknecht in July 1916. Meyer, *Dokumente des Kommunismus,* Band I, No. 1, "Aus dem Reich."

The restrictions upon the food rations also furnished material for an attack upon the government by the Spartacists. In March 1918 they protested against the "starvation of human beings" in a leaflet which said in part:

> After April 16 the bread rations for the hungry emaciated people are to be reduced by more than one-fourth. While our sons and brothers are being murdered and crippled in the trenches and battlefields, the working people have to live in misery until their strength is gone and they fall to the ground exhausted.

Then the leaflet tells how the Russian workers took matters into their own hands and set up a people's government.

> And we?
>
> Should we carry patiently the old misery, the hunger, the human murders—the cause of all our torment and pain?
>
> No! A thousand times No! Leave your work and the factories! Let the work rest!
>
> Man der Arbeit aufgewacht!
> Und erkenne deine Macht.
> Alle Räder stehen still
> Wenn dein starker Arm es will.
>
> Down with the war! Down with the government.
> Peace! Freedom! Bread![55]

Another group which differed in many respects from the Spartacists but which worked for the cessation of hostilities and for a republic in Germany was the Independent Socialist party. This group differed from the radical Liebknecht group in that they were opposed to any revolutionary action. They believed that, since no enemy stood on the frontiers of Germany, the question at issue was no longer one of national defense but rather that of a Pan-German war of conquest. In December 1915 twenty Social Democratic members of the Reichstag, inspired by the belief that in order to prevent the annexationist policy of the government from being carried out it was necessary to refuse the war credits, separated themselves from the rest

[55] "Die Tätigkeit deutscher Organizationen," *Süddeutsche Monatshefte,* April 1924, p. 15.

of their party and voted against a proposed credit. This split of the Social Democratic party in the Reichstag was carried into the party organization throughout the country, until the opposition was expelled in 1917 and formed itself into the Independent Social Democratic party.[56]

Although the U.S.P.D., as this party was known, was not as revolutionary as the Spartacists were, it carried on a lively propaganda with the object of ending the war by a peace by agreement and without annexations. Its chief weapon was the strike, with which it hoped to force the government to initiate peace negotiations. Deputy Dittmann expressed the views of the U.S.P.D. in a speech on June 17, 1917, before the Main Committee of the Reichstag as follows:

> The workmen are helots but they want to be free men after the war. . . . . It must therefore be said openly that Germany wishes a peace which will not make it necessary to continue competitive armaments after the war, but a peace with disarmament and arbitration.[57]

On April 14, 1917, a number of strikes began in the munitions factories in Berlin. These had been prepared by the U.S.P.D. and came close on the heels of the announcement by the government of further reductions in the food rations which were to become effective on April 16. Though many people participated in these strikes because of the food situation, there was a political side to the disturbances. This is proved by the fact that work was not resumed in all quarters even after the wishes of the strikers in regard to the food provisions had been met. General Gröner declared at the hearing of the *Hauptausschusses* of April 26, 1917:

> Where did these political things come from? You are all acquainted with the Leipzig Program and the shameful telegram to the Chancellor. Their contents is a whole series of political demands, above all, the establishment of a Workers' Council patterned after

[56] Arthur Rosenberg, *The Birth of the German Republic,* p. 121; also R. H. Lutz, *The Fall of the German Empire,* II, 4.

[57] *U.D.Z.,* V, 160; cited also in Lutz, *The Causes of the German Collapse,* p. 121.

those of the Russians, and for this purpose the Chancellor was to receive a deputation. This political momentum was carried into the German arms and munitions factories. We have evidence that agitation material was smuggled in from the outside. Some of these smuggled articles fell into our hands.[58]

At first the party committee of the U.S.P.D., led by Haase and Dittmann, was skeptical about the prospects of a Socialist revolution in Germany. But the party gradually adopted a sharper tone, and established connection with the Dresden International Youth Organization, which had been organized to tear "the mask from the face of the humbug of war and peace at home," and which appealed to the young men not to obey the orders calling them to the colors and not to give themselves up like cattle to militarism.[59] Also, many radical Socialists and Spartacists joined the U.S.P.D. and these inoculated the party leaders with revolutionary ideas. Concerning this Dr. Philipp said:

> Owing to the numbers of Left Radicals who belonged to the Independent Socialist Party, its active propaganda was doubly dangerous to the conduct of the war and to the state; it was the preliminary condition which made the revolution the great mass movement on which men like Eisner, who belonged to the Independent Socialist Party but was a Left Radical at heart, could build up their work.[60]

Haase, one of the leaders of the U.S.P.D., went even farther when he said:

> Right from the beginning of the war, from the beginning of 1915 we worked systematically for the revolution in the navy. We subscribed 50 pfennigs from our own pay every ten days, got into touch with the members in the Reichstag, and drew up, printed, and distributed revolutionary leaflets in order to create the conditions necessary for the events of November.[61]

[58] "Der Berliner Metallarbeiterstreik im April 1917," *Süddeutsche Monatshefte,* April 1924, pp. 25 ff.

[59] *U.D.Z.,* von Kuhl's Report, VI, 1–39.

[60] *Ibid.,* statement of Dr. Philipp, V, 164.

[61] *U.D.Z.,* von Kuhl's Report, VI, 10.

Among the propaganda materials against the militarists which the U.S.P.D. distributed was a little card which contained an appeal for peace without annexations or indemnity and was signed for the central committee of the party.[62] On the reverse side of the card the following appeal was printed in large letters:

Stand up!
Go to the streets!
Leave the factories!
We don't want a fourth winter campaign! Do not fire another shot!
Long live peace![63]

Propaganda in the navy was especially effective, since the prolonged inactivity of the fleet brought on a state of mind among the men that made them readily susceptible to the activities of the agitators. On July 31, 1917, on board the battleship "König Albert," some four hundred sailors signed the following proclamation:

PEACE PROCLAMATION!

We whose names are appended to this declaration herewith claim our membership in the U.S.P.D. and our approval of its policy. At the same time we wish it to be known that we are in favor of a peace without annexations and reparations, and that we are therefore anxious for a conclusion of hostilities. . . . . The U.S.P.D. has up to now been the most determined champion of our interests in Germany and hence alone possesses our confidence as is proved by our entry into its ranks.[64]

By the summer of 1917 it was evident that the German government had lost the confidence of those people in Germany who desired peace. Through Erzberger a majority in the Reichstag informed the Imperial Government that it no longer enjoyed their confidence. Erzberger, with von Richthofen, had

[62] The committee was composed of Dittmann, Haase, Adolph Hofer, Gustav Laukant, Ledebour, Wengels, and Louise Zeits.

[63] *Fliegerabwurf-Schriften* (no number).

[64] Arthur Rosenberg, *op. cit.*, p. 185.

made a journey to the Eastern Army Headquarters, where General Hoffmann had revealed the true state of affairs to them. From his observations and his conversations with Hoffmann, Erzberger resolved to induce the Reichstag to bring the war to a conclusion as quickly as possible.[65] On July 6, 1917, therefore, he delivered his famous speech in the Reichstag in which he demonstrated that since the government had been completely mistaken in the question of submarine warfare it could no longer expect to enjoy the confidence of the Reichstag.[66] The Reichstag, said Erzberger, must give the government to understand that it desired a peace of compromise without any forcible subjection of peoples or annexations.

Following the lead of Erzberger, the Center, the Majority Social Democrats, and the Progressives united as a solid majority upon the famous Peace Resolution of July 19, 1917, favoring a peace without annexations.[67] The significance of the resolu-

[65] *Ibid.,* pp. 153 ff. The genesis of the Peace Resolution was tested with particular care by the Committee of Inquiry. All the material on this question can be found in *U.D.Z.,* VII and VIII. For details, see especially Vol. VII, Part I, pp. 282 ff., and Vol. VIII, pp. 69 ff.

[66] *Echo de Paris* of July 11, 1917, for instance, said of it: "The good speech of Herr Erzberger is a joyous announcement."

[67] The National-Liberals were opposed to the idea of the Peace Resolution, not because they considered that territorial expansion or war indemnities were an essential condition of peace, but because they believed that the German government ought, in practice, to make it clear to her opponents, without any public announcement, that readiness to make peace without annexations or indemnities was the basis of its foreign policy. The Conservatives were opposed on principle to the Peace Resolution because they regarded such action by the Reichstag as a danger for the conclusion of peace and because they wished to prevent the adoption of parliamentary government, which they considered to be unsuitable. The military situation did not appear to them to demand the complete renunciation of all territorial and economic claims.

After opposing it at first, the Supreme Command accepted the adoption of the resolution and co-operated in its final wording without approving it at heart. The Kaiser approved it in principle but refrained from adopting a decisive attitude with regard to it in public. Chancellor Michaelis supported the resolution with the famous reservation, "as I interpret it." Michaelis made it clear to the world at large that he interpreted the resolution was that it united for the time being the parties in the Reichstag against the policy of the government. One German authority goes so far as to state that the Peace Resolution "hindered a German victory in that it strengthened the enemy will to victory and weakened the will to victory in our own land."[68]

Opposition to a war of conquest became stronger and stronger in Germany. When the policy of the German government at Brest-Litovsk became known, the U.S.P.D. encouraged strikes as a demonstration against the measures that the militarists were taking against Russia. So serious was the strike threat that the high officials issued an order on January 29, 1918, as follows:

> We are still in a difficult struggle. Everyone who quits work at home sins against our brothers in the field who are sacrificing their all to fight off the enemy who is looking forward to the overthrow of Germany, the destruction of our industries, and thereby the pauperization of the German people and the German workers.[69]

The National Workers' and Professional Union issued an appeal at about the same time as follows:

> From various sources the attempt is being made to put into the minds of the German workers the idea of a general strike for political purposes. The German worker is being betrayed, in the critical moment

---

tion very differently from the interpretation placed upon it by Erzberger and Scheidemann. On July 25 the Chancellor elaborated upon his reservation when he wrote to the Crown Prince (*U.D.Z.,* Vol. VII, Part II, p. 390, or Part I, p. 294): "I have deprived it [the Peace Resolution] of its greatest danger by my 'interpretation.' One can, in fact, make any peace one likes, and still be in accord with the Resolution." (For the attitude of the various individuals and groups toward the Resolution see *U.D.Z.,* Vol. VII, Part I, pp. 3–13; also Lutz, *The Causes of the German Collapse,* pp. 190–91.)

[68] Oscar Müller, *Warum musten wir nach Versailles?* Kriegspresseamt publications, No. 1, p. 59.

[69] Dr. Friedrich Purlitz, ed., *Deutscher Geschichtskalendar, Der Europäische Krieg in aktenmäsziger Darstellung,* 34 Jahrgang, Band I, 1 hälfte, Januar-März 1918 (Leipzig and Vienna, 1918), p. 102; also *Norddeutsche Allgemeine Zeitung* (Abend Ausgabe), January 29, 1918.

of the war, when all our strength in the field and at home should be dedicated to the effort to deprive the struggling brothers in the field of war necessities and thus bring on a catastrophe. These propagandists are hard to discover. Loyal to our Fatherland, we call upon our fellow members, and all loyal workers to oppose with all means and energy such a move and to heed Hindenburg's warning: "To strike is treason."[70]

After the strike of January 1918 the conviction grew among the Independent Socialists—and especially among the more radical element who had associated themselves with this party—that if trouble started again they should not be content with a strike but should resort to arms. From that time onward preparations were made by such U.S.P.D. leaders as Barth, Däumig, Eckert, Wegmann, and Neuendorff for the Revolution. As Ledebour said in a speech on December 17, 1918, at the General Congress of Workmen's and Soldiers' Councils of Germany:

> They obtained weapons, they enlisted recruits, and we others who co-operated with them to a certain extent, influenced our workmen. . . . . Besides, we had not only made preparations in Berlin but had established relations with all the provinces.[71]

The Independent Socialist Vater gave further proof of his party's machinations when he boasted in a speech at Magdeburg in December 1918:

> The Revolution did not come as a surprise to us. We had been systematically preparing for it since January 25, 1918. The work was difficult and dangerous. . . . . The party saw that big strikes did not lead to revolution; so some other way had to be taken. . . . . We induced our men who were going to the front to desert. We organized these deserters, supplied them with forged papers, money, and unsigned pamphlets. We sent these men out in all directions, but principally to the front, in order that they should work on the feelings of the men at the front and bring about its dissolution. They persuaded the

[70] Purlitz, *Deutscher Geschichtskalendar,* p. 104.

[71] See *U.D.Z.,* Vol. V, Annex VIII, pp. 117–21, for the complete speech of Ledebour.

soldiers to desert and so the work of destruction was slowly but surely completed.[72]

Ernst Lorenz, in a pamphlet, *Fünf Jahre Dresdner U.S.P.*, provides additional proof that the revolution did not come as a surprise,[73] when he states:

> It was a dangerous venture to attack the monster militarism by the printing and distribution of leaflets during the war. . . . . Nevertheless we in Dresden did excellent work with regard to the production and distribution of anti-war printed matter.

He continues by stating that the Dresden group did not limit itself to distribution of material in and around Dresden but took to mass production of blanket distribution throughout Germany. "Hundreds of thousands of these warning, accusing, and inciting leaflets left the press by night, under cover of the protecting darkness, and then . . . . found their way to every town in Germany."[74]

Making one last attack upon the government in the Reichstag before its adjournment on July 12, 1918, the Independent Socialist Deputy Geyer said, among other things:

[72] *U.D.Z.*, VI, 10; Wrisberg, *Der Weg zur Revolution*, p. 103; and Erich Ludendorff, *My War Memories* (London, 1919), II, 645. The German government, desiring to get rid of the strike agitators, sent many of them to the front or to prison. The result was that everyone sent to the front or punished in any way became an agitator for the Revolution. *U.D.Z.*, V, 117–21.

[73] The Revolution came as a surprise to the Right Wing of the Social Democratic party. The leaders of that wing did not really want the overthrow of the government, but for various reasons they did not withdraw from it in the end. *U.D.Z.*, V, 151–71, statement of Dr. Philipp; also Lutz, *The Causes of the German Collapse*, p. 113.

[74] *U.D.Z.*, VI, 7. It is interesting to note here that Deputy Haase had said shortly after the outbreak of the war: "We will undermine the Army in order to bring on the World Revolution." And in the session of the Prussian House of Delegates on February 23, 1915, Delegate Ströbel, the editor of *Vorwärts* said: "I admit openly that a complete victory of the Reich will not be suited to the interests of the Social Democrats." *U.D.Z.*, von Kuhl's Report, VI, 1–39; also Lutz, *The Causes of the German Collapse*, p. 135.

The boundless distress of the people increases to an unbearable degree. Hunger and misery destroy all that the war does not claim in human lives. We say "Down with the War!"[75]

Revolutionary agitation and sentiment was not confined to the Spartacists and the Independent Social Democrats. In the middle of 1918 the Majority Socialists joined with the U.S.P.D. in voting against the budget. Scheidemann, in explaining the vote, said that the war should be ended as quickly as possible:

The greatest military victory by itself can never bring peace, but only an armistice. The exasperation of the masses has reached the highest pitch. There is now only one cry, namely to make an end of the war, but of course, an end with honor.[76]

In November 1917, on the occasion of the celebration of the anniversary of the Reformation, a group of Berlin and Hanoverian clergy issued a proclamation, which was endorsed by many hundreds of influential men, to other parts of Germany. This proclamation said in part:

We German Protestants, conscious of the Christian principles and aims, heartily stretch out a brotherly hand to all co-religionists, including those of enemy countries.

We recognize as the deepest cause of war the anti-Christian powers dominating the lives of the peoples, e.g., suspicion, idolatry, or force and covetousness; therefore a peace based on mutual understanding and reconciliation is in our opinion the peace that must be brought about.[77]

Thus the German government and militarists were confronted with opposition at home as well as at the front. The longing for peace grew stronger and stronger after the middle

[75] Germany, Reichstag, *Verhandlungen des Reichstags,* Band 313, 191 Sitzung, July 13, 1918, p. 6146.

[76] *Labor Leader,* July 11, 1918.

[77] *Ibid.,* June 20, 1918. Another source of attack upon the German government was the International Socialist Women's Organization. At a conference in Berne in March 1915 this group agreed upon a propaganda campaign against the war. Women from Germany, France, England, Russia, Italy, Holland, and Switzerland took part in this campaign.

of 1916. In a letter from a traveler in Germany, written from Switzerland, we find a sentiment typical of those expressed in the many letters intercepted by the Press Service for the British General Staff.

> Among the middle class they say with the Chancellor, "Look at the map. We have advanced too far into the enemy country for him ever to recover all the territory he has lost. We can therefore now talk peace." This is the language of those who argue—officials, professors, bank managers, and Socialistic intellectuals. But the crowds do not argue. They merely say: "When will the end come?"[78]

In a letter that a German soldier had written from Hauseberge we find similar sentiments expressed when he says:

> Everybody here wants peace, that this horrible shedding of blood may have an end. Only purveyors of army supplies think it is a good thing that the war is lasting so long, because they make a profit out of it.[79]

Another intercepted letter from a German residing at The Hague to a friend in New York demonstrates the feeling of the masses of the German people. Dated June 14, 1917, it said:

> About revolution yes, I have great hopes that it will break out in Germany this autumn. According to what I have heard at the frontier, not only the people wish for it but the soldiers, and the non-commissioned officers, lots of them speak about it among themselves in secret, saying that the only way to get peace is to depose the Kaiser. May this soon be! It would be a mercy and a blessing not only for the whole of humanity but especially for us Germans. . . . .[80]

The whole internal situation of Germany was well summarized in the report of the Bureau for Social Policy when it stated:

> The common people with large families have made great sacrifices at the front and at home. A strong feeling of war weariness in these classes is comprehensible and undeniable. The result of short rations,

[78] *Confidential Supplement to the Daily Review of the Foreign Press*, No. 58, July 8, 1916, p. 4.

[79] *Ibid.*, No. 102, August 1916, p. 9. Letter dated July 22.

[80] *Ibid.*, No. 148, July 14, 1917, p. 4.

combined with undiminished and increased work is a feeling of nervous irritation and mental susceptibility to all embittering impressions and influences.[81]

That is why the *Burgfrieden* broke up. That is why many people lost faith in their government during the latter years of the war. The people were hungry, weary, and irritable. Erich Volkmann, in his study, *Der Marxism und das deutsche Heer im Weltkrieg,* states:

> In August 1914 one rejoiced with it. At that time it was in truth the representative of the people's will and the universal spirit. Since then a grey layer of increasing disenchantment has come over the entire land.[82]

It was obvious that the longer the war lasted and the greater the burdens and miseries it brought in its train, the more powerful became the forces that threatened the truce that had been concluded between the rival parties, until the day should be reached when war and revolution would be synonymous terms.

Thus we see the conditions in Germany which aided the Allied propagandists in their campaign to tear down the morale of the German troops and the people behind the lines. Dr. Philipp summed it up well when he said before the *Untersuchungsauschusses:*

> The saddest thing in this dark chapter of the question of war guilt is the assertion, continually confirmed by fresh material, that the enemy's revolutionary work would have been in vain without the co-operation of certain German circles.[83]

[81] *U.D.Z.,* V, 102.

[82] Alfred Niemann, *Revolution von Oben, Umsturz von Unden* (Berlin, 1927), p. 54.

[83] *U.D.Z.,* Dr. Philipp's statement, V, 151–71; also Lutz, *The Causes of the German Collapse,* p. 127.

CHAPTER VII

MEASURING THE EFFECT OF PROPAGANDA

If the historian ever has an opportunity to delve into the files of the German Intelligence Bureau, however, I imagine that he will find ample evidence that the showers of leaflets played no inconsiderable part in the collapse of the German machine.

—E. ALEXANDER POWELL, *The Army Behind the Army* (p. 355)

On July 31, 1917, the Chief of the German General Staff of the Field Army issued a circular in which he lamented the feeling "of profound depression" at home. This symptom was to be attributed in part to the real distress, the difficult situation with regard to the foodstuffs and the coal, financial worries, the length of the war, and the loss of relatives. But for the greater part this situation was due, said the circular, to the agitation of certain enemies of state who "so unscrupulously endeavor to exploit this state of distress in order to further their political aims and cause discontent, irritation, etc. of all kinds."[1]

The spirit of the people in Germany is further described by Dr. George Herron after his fifth conversation with Dr. de Fiori:

The peasants and workers of Germany are already asking questions which predict the possibility of a revolution, continued Dr. de Fiori. All through Germany, he declared, the peasants and workers are saying to each other that if the whole world is against Germany there must be some reason for it. It must be that their masters have not told them the truth. It must be that they have been deceived about the war

[1] *U.D.Z.*, von Kuhl's Report, VI, 20. The circular was signed by Ludendorff. Also found in R. H. Lutz, *The Causes of the German Collapse,* p. 148.

from the beginning. And why should they go on being killed and starved for masters who tell them only lies? It is better that they should kill their masters.[2]

The observing Princess Blücher described the mood of the German people in February 1917, when she wrote in her diary:

. . . . the heroic attitude has entirely disappeared. Now one sees faces like masks, blue with cold and drawn by hunger, with the harassed expression common to all those who are continually speculating as to the possibility of another meal.[3]

The *Süddeutsche Monatshefte* went so far as to credit the Allied propagandists with having taken over the leadership of the German people in the last few months of the war. By the fall of 1918 "the majority of the German people placed greater trust in Woodrow Wilson than in their own leaders."[4]

However, in estimating the effect of Allied propaganda upon the German troops and the people behind the lines we must consider: first, the Reports of the Psychological Subsection of the United States Army; second, the efforts on the part of Germany at counter-propaganda; third, the desertions among the enemy troops; fourth, the letters from German soldiers to their relatives at home; and, fifth, the German army orders dealing with propaganda.

REPORTS OF THE PSYCHOLOGICAL SUBSECTION OF THE UNITED STATES ARMY

The Psychological Subsection of the United States Army kept a closer watch on the morale of the German troops and the German civilian population than any of the other propaganda agencies or intelligence sections of the Allied countries. This subsection set up a detailed system for watching the progress of the deterioration of the German morale. Agents of the Intelligence Division prepared daily reports which contained all news in any way relating to the morale of the Germans in their par-

[2] "Herron Papers," Document XXV, de Fiori Conversations, I, 126.
[3] Princess Evelyn Mary Blücher, *An English Wife in Berlin,* p. 162.
[4] *Süddeutsche Monatshefte,* April 1924, p. 1.

ticular sections. After studying these daily reports carefully, the officers in charge prepared weekly reports which gave a general interpretation of the drift of the enemy morale.[5] Using as a basis for its estimates material contained in these weekly reports, supplemented by information obtained from other sources open to the Military Intelligence, the Psychological Subsection worked out its famous "Chart of German Civilian Morale," which recorded the upward and downward trend of enemy morale. This chart also recorded the variation in Germany's military position, the degree of political unity in Germany, the food situation in North Germany, and the U-boat sinkings.[6]

To get information for their daily reports the agents of the subsection interviewed prisoners in the Allied prison camps. They held long conversations with prisoners in camps near Toul and Souilly, where men of all ranks and from all parts of the German Empire were kept, and from these interviews they got valuable information concerning the feeling among the German troops and the people beyond the Rhine.[7]

During these conversations the German officer was "often bored," while the private was gratified and "we found him sick of the war, doubtful of his leaders and passionately curious about America's war and peace."[8] Occasionally, however, they

[5] Major E. Alexander Powell, *The Army Behind the Army,* p. 356.

[6] The writer encountered considerable difficulty in locating this chart. Major Powell referred me to Mr. Newton D. Baker, in whose office the chart was kept during the last few months of the war. Mr. Baker, however, did not recall the chart but stated that there might have been such since the General Staff made continuous studies of the enemy morale. He referred me to the Army War College, where it might be located. A letter from Colonel W. S. Grant of the Army War College states that they have no record of such a chart. Mr. Powell, however, insisted that there was such a chart. After considerable more correspondence, the writer finally received a letter from the Intelligence Division, General Staff, War Department, stating that photostat copies of the chart were being sent. These have been turned over to the Hoover War Library.

[7] E. Alexander Powell, *op. cit.,* p. 350.

[8] Heber Blankenhorn, "War of Morale," *Harpers' Magazine,* CXXXIX (1919), 518.

found officers also who talked freely. An artillery Lieutenant L—, who was described as an "admirer of Ludendorff," said in one of these interviews concerning the effect of propaganda:

> I can only talk as a soldier at the front, but there its effects were disastrous and especially so in the last six months. Even the little *Flugblätter,* after you read them, you imagined you read the truth, that our government was lying to us. I remember one, after I read it, I felt like blowing my brains out. I never let one of our men read them—but it was difficult—they were everywhere.[9]

In the summary of the reports of the Intelligence Section of the United States Army we find statements regarding the conditions in the various sectors of the German Army. Regarding the 41st Division, 20th Corps District, we find that the Commanding General issued an order on June 6, 1918, indicating an increase in the number of instances in which subordinates emphatically refused to accompany their units into line and in which officers neglected to enforce obedience to orders.[10] Of the 45th Reserve Division, 2d Corps District, we read:

> According to the statement of prisoners, when the 212th Reserve Infantry Regiment came from the Verdun front to Flanders it refused to attack on September 30, 1917. . . . . About the 16th of October it received a very large draft of replacements among which were a considerable number of elements of decidedly Bolshevistic tendencies. Men deserted to the rear, to the enemy, and quite a few were punished for insubordination to officers, and some for refusing to fight.[11]

The 6th Bavarian Landwehr Division was considered by the American Intelligence Section a fourth-class division.

> Morale was low, discipline poor. Several prisoners stated that the men did not hesitate to say even in front of their officers that the war had been lost by Germany and that they were thoroughly sick of it.[12]

[9] *Ibid.,* p. 524.

[10] *Histories of Two Hundred Fifty-one Divisions of the German Army Which Participated in the War, 1914–1918,* compiled from records of Intelligence Section of the General Staff, American Expeditionary Forces, at General Headquarters, Chaumont, France, 1919 (Washington, Government Printing Office, 1920), p. 450; hereafter referred to as *Histories of 251 Divisions.*

[11] *Ibid.,* p. 266.

[12] *Ibid.,* p. 143.

In the 15th Bavarian Division the political discontent and the "dissatisfaction with Prussia continued to give the division a low morale."[13] The 30th Bavarian Division possessed very little value: "The men are, for the most part old, and the fathers of several children. Moreover, Bavarians came to believe that Prussia was 'using' them."[14]

From the German authorities we learn that, when the Alpine Corps was sent up to the front occupied by the 18th Army to the west of Nesle and the 2d Army to the north of Péronne, men belonging to the divisions which had held the line up to then streamed back in a more or less disorganized state. In spite of the energetic work of the advancing line of the Bavarian Regiment of Foot Guards, they did not succeed in inducing the men to stop and renew the fight. The fact that this was due to lack of fighting spirit and to wilful breach of discipline caused by agitation "is proved by the repeated use of the expression that the men of the Alpine Corps were prolongers of the war."[15] Later on the report states that on August 10 men opposite Hallu said: "The war won't come to an end like this; we shall have to put an end to it."

According to a report made by the 2d Jäger Regiment, the men of the regiment were grossly insulted by retreating infantry soldiers for holding out so long in the firing line. The general commanding the 2d Division of the Foot Guards stated: "Everyone who spends his time among the troops knows that the mood of some of the men is becoming depressed and that this is due to influence from home and to agents, leaflets, etc."[16]

In a *Summary of Information,* A.E.F. General Staff, we learn that after having been "bombarded with literature picturing the superior strength of the Allies, and the determination to victory, the morale of the German soldier was lowered. Evidences of nervousness in the face of what he thought an attack

[13] *Histories of 251 Divisions,* p. 261. [14] *Ibid.,* p. 394.

[15] *U.D.Z.,* von Kuhl's Report, VI, 21; also cited in Lutz, *The Causes of the German Collapse,* p. 148.

[16] *U.D.Z.,* VI, 22; Lutz, *op. cit.,* p. 150.

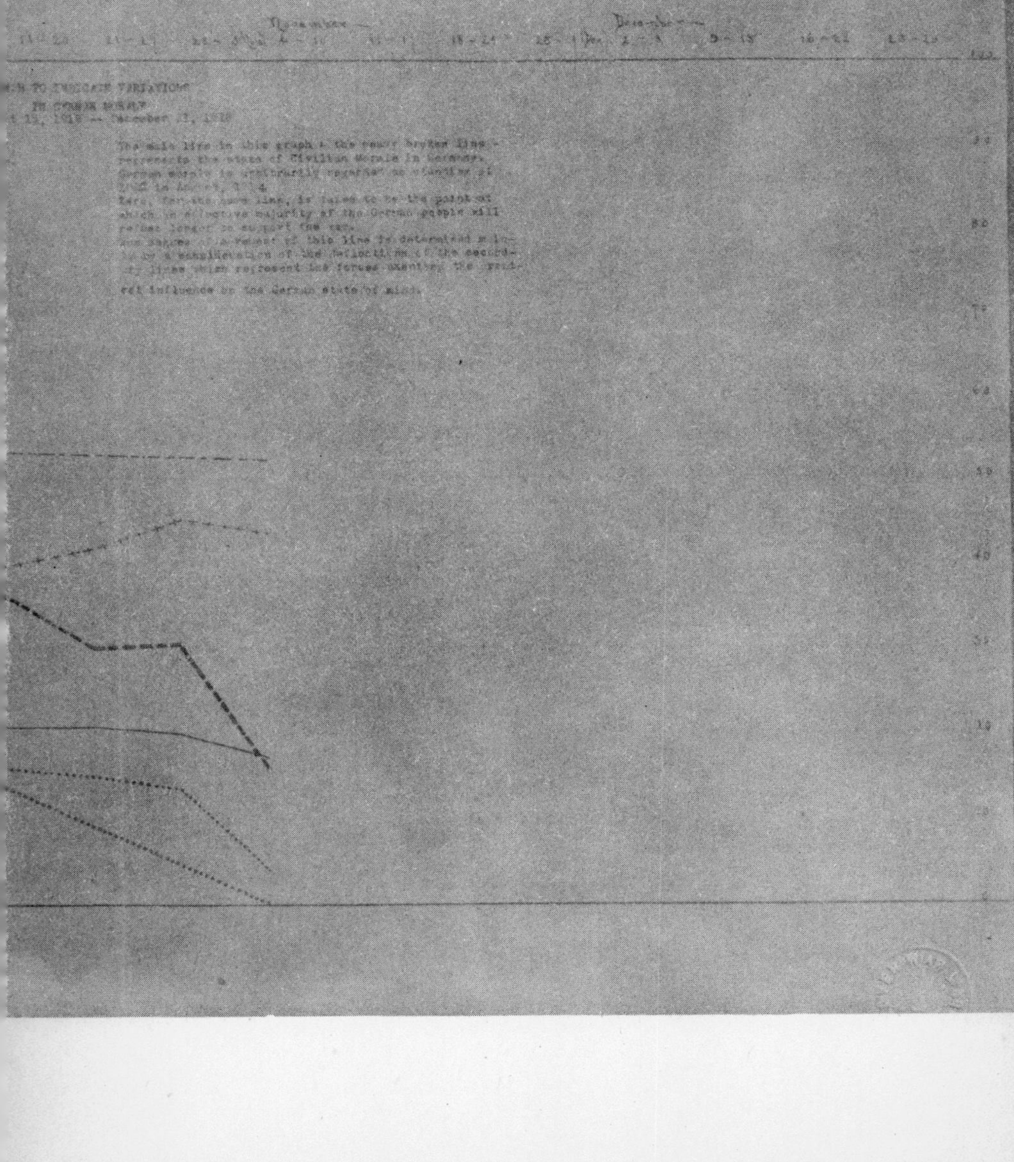

...H TO INDICATE VARIATIONS
IN GERMAN MORALE
...t 11, 1918 -- December [illegible], 1918

The main line in this graph - the heavy broken line - represents the state of Civilian Morale in Germany. German morale is arbitrarily regarded as standing at 100 in August, 1914.
Zero, for the same line, is taken to be the point at which an effective majority of the German people will refuse longer to support the war.
The degree of movement of this line is determined mainly by a consideration of the deflections of the secondary lines which represent the forces exerting the greatest influence on the German state of mind.

November — December —

[illegible]

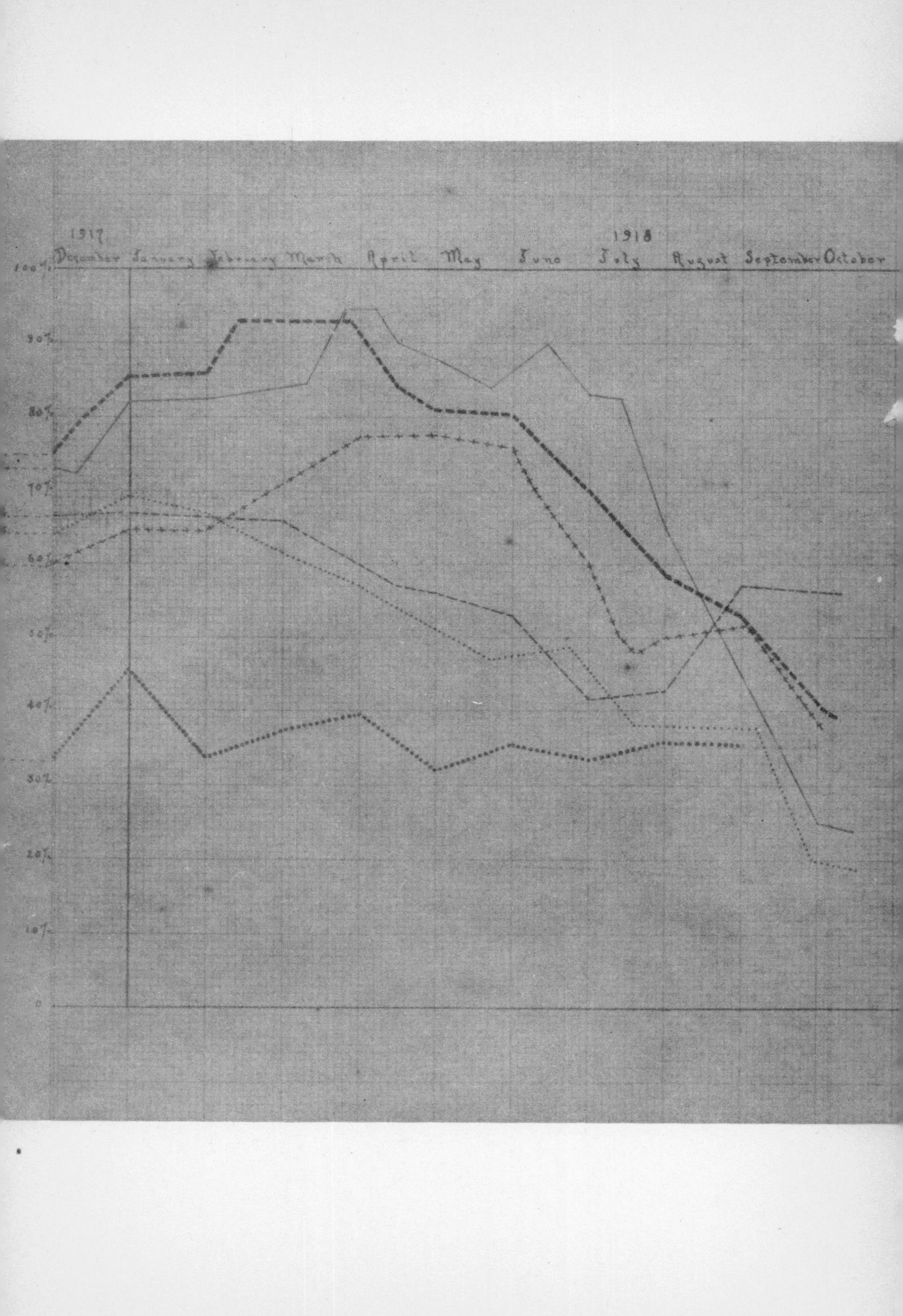
1917
1918
December January February March April May June July August September October
100%
90%
80%
70%
60%
50%
40%
30%
20%
10%
0

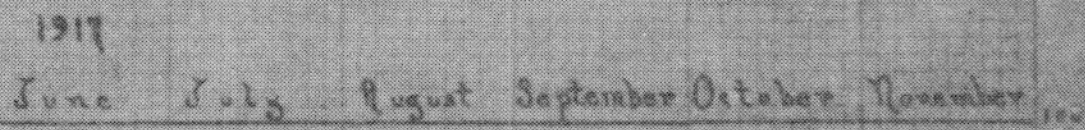

6.

6.

…D INDICATE VARIATIONS
…F GERMAN MORALE
…914 — October 1918.
…April 1916 - November 1917

The main line in this graph - the heavy broken line - represents the state of Civilian Morale in Germany.
German morale is arbitrarily regarded as standing at 100% in August 1914.
Zero, for the same line, is taken to be the point at which an effective majority of the German people will refuse longer to support the war.
The degree of movement of this line is determined mainly by a consideration of the deflections of the secondary lines which represent the forces exerting the greatest influence on the German state of mind.

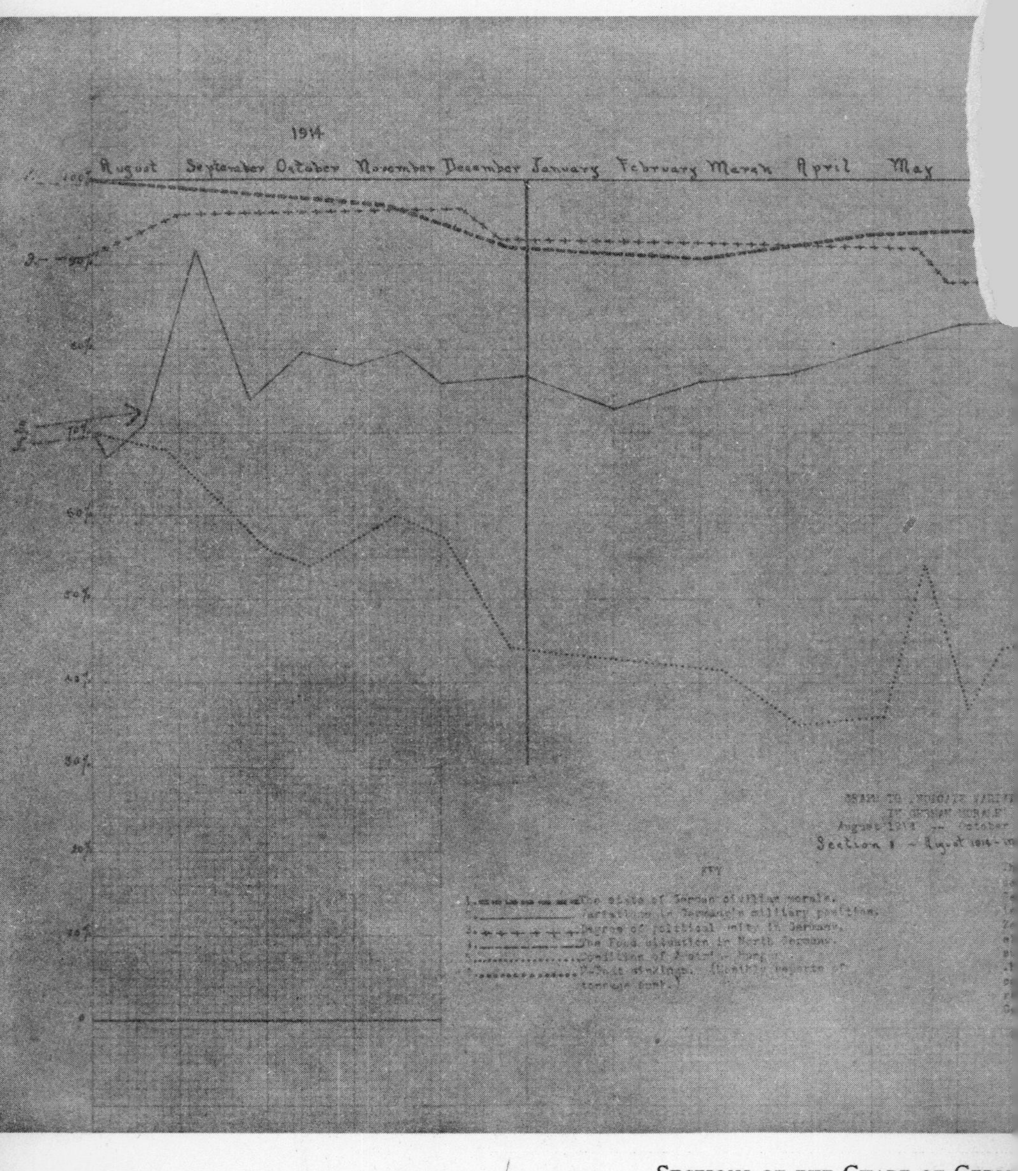

SECTIONS OF THE CHART OF GERM

Reprints of photostat copies of sections of the Cha
sent to the writer by the United States War Departn
Division. The chart came in four sections, which were
into two sections. The chart shows not only the ups a
the food situation in North Germany, the political unit
and the variations in Germany's military position fron
1918. Greatly reduced.

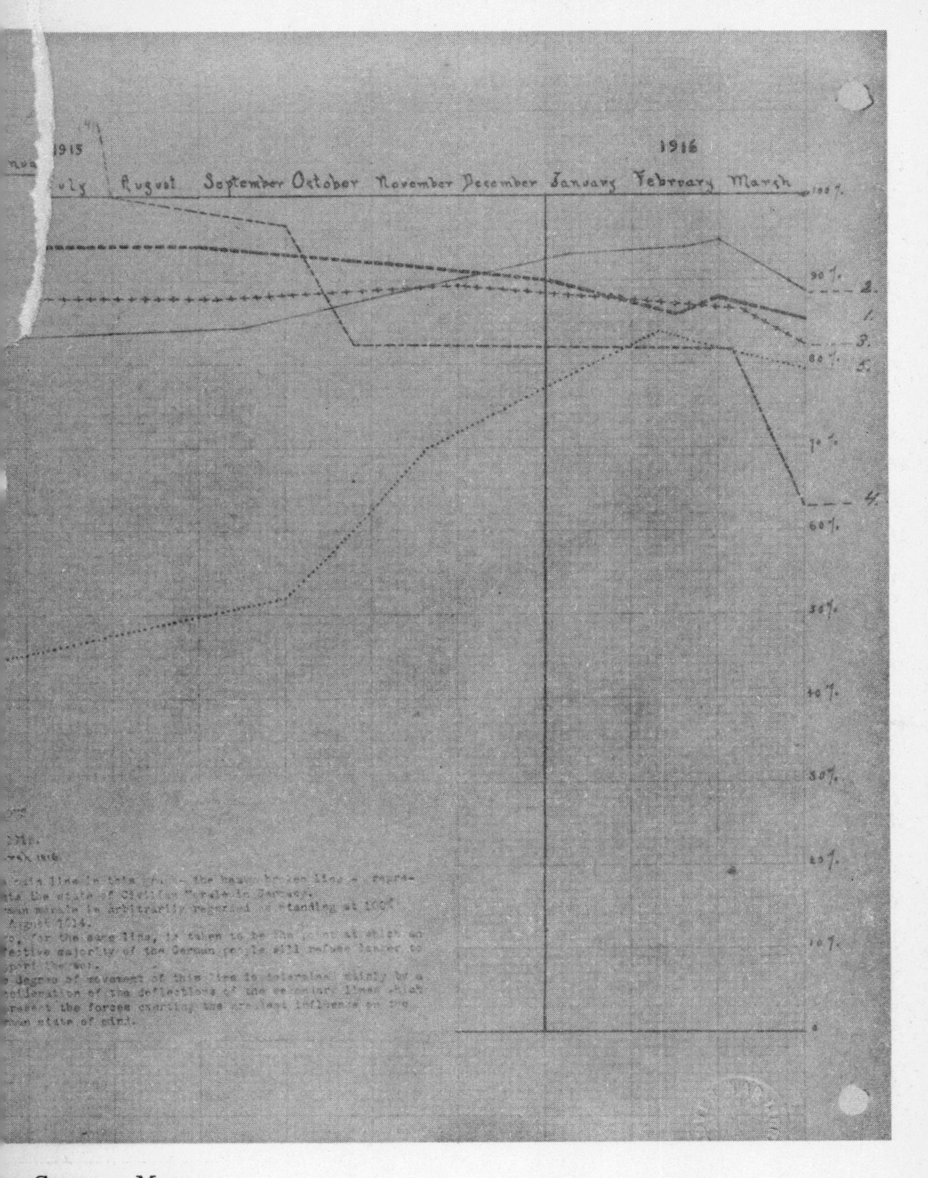

ᴀɴ Civilian Morale

t of German Civilian Morale which were
ent, General Staff, Military Intelligence
combined, for the purpose of this work,
d downs of the German morale but also
of the Empire, the submarine sinkings,
the beginning of the war to November

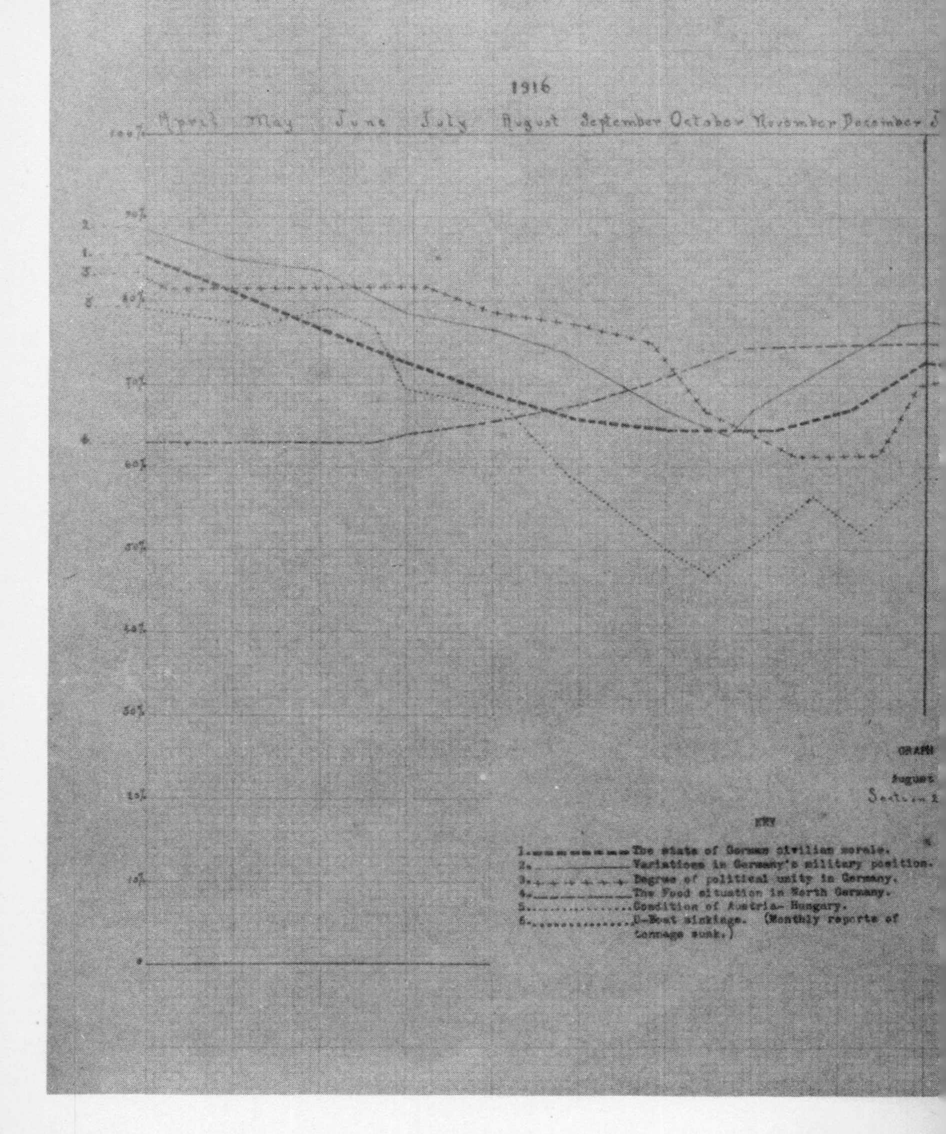
1916
April
May
June
July
August
September
October
November
December
100%
90%
80%
70%
60%
50%
40%
30%
20%
10%
0
GRAPH
August
KEY
1. The state of German civilian morale.
2. Variations in Germany's military position.
3. Degree of political unity in Germany.
4. The Food situation in North Germany.
5. Condition of Austria- Hungary.
6. U-Boat sinkings. (Monthly reports of tonnage sunk.)

November December

GRAPH TO INDICATE VARIATIONS
IN GERMAN MORALE
August 1914 - October 1918
Section 3 – December 1917 – October 1918
KEY

1. ▬▬▬▬▬ The state of German civilian morale.

2. ________ Variations in Germany's military position.

3. + + + + + + Degree of political unity in Germany.

4. — — — — — The Food situation in North Germany.

5. . . . . Condition of Austria-Hungary.

6. . . . . U-Boat sinkings. (Monthly reports of tonnage sunk.)

- - - - - - - - - - - - - - - - - -

The main line in this graph - the heavy broken line - represents the state of civilian morale in Germany.

German morale is arbitrarily regarded as standing at 100% in August 1914.

Zero, for the same line, is taken to be the point at which an effective majority of the German people will refuse longer to support the war.

The degree of movement of this line is determined mainly by a consideration of the deflections of the companion lines which represent the forces exerting the greatest influence on the German state of mind.

August – September – October
12 – 18 | 19 – 25 | 26 – 1 Sept | 2 – 8 | 9 – 15 | 16 – 22 | 23 – 29 | 30 – 6 Oct | 7 – 13

KEY:

1. The state of German civilian morale.
2. Variations in Germany's military positi
3. Degree of political unity in Germany.
4. The food situation in North Germany.
5. Condition of Austria-Hungary.
6. U-Boat sinkings. (Monthly reports of tonnage sunk.)

100
90
80
70
60
50
40
30
20
10
0

of superior forces, could be seen."[17] This is borne out by the official report from Headquarters of the 461st Infantry Regiment, October 21, 1918, which stated in part:

> In the sector of the Army Corps the troops have recently again shown a marked tendency to request a barrage by light signals as soon as they perceive the enemy in the advance zone. This practice not only shows the enemy how much the infantry is frightened by his approach, but it also indicates that the infantry lacks confidence in its own means of defense. This idea is apparently becoming fixed in the companies.[18]

On July 24, 1918, the *Tribune de Genève* reported that information from a good source revealed that discontent was spreading in the German Army:

> Many acts of indiscipline are known and the High Command has not succeeded in stopping them. A regiment which was to go into rest quarters has been sent to the West front. When these troops realized that they were going to the West front they mutinied and threw their rifles and packs out of the window, stopped the train and fled across the fields.[19]

Checking up on the initial propaganda campaign in the spring and early summer of 1918, the Intelligence Section found that German commanders were reporting lowered morale in the ranks of their troops. The German soldiers had become uneasy and were rapidly losing faith in their officers by reason of the information scattered from the air.[20] In the *Kölnische Zeitung* for October 31, 1918, a "High Officer on the West Front," analyzing the military reverses, wrote:

> What caused the most damage was the paper war waged by our enemies who daily flooded us with hundreds of thousands of leaflets, extraordinarily well arranged and edited.[21]

[17] *Summary of Information,* Second Section, General Staff, General Headquarters, A.E.F., Chaumont?, 1917–1919, Vol. III, No. 227, November 14, 1918, p. 1450. [18] *Ibid.*

[19] *Press Review,* Second Section, General Staff, General Headquarters, A.E.F., printed by the 29th Engineers 1917–1919, No. 212, August 14, 1918; hereafter cited as *Press Review.*

[20] Lieutenant C. H. Ball, *New York Times,* April 20, 1919, Section 7, p. 4.

[21] *Kölnische Zeitung,* October 31, 1918.

In an American Divisional Summary of January 28, 1919, is found the following, from the interrogation of S——, an infantryman:

> One of the things that made a great impression on the German soldiers, and which S—— believes helped to shorten the war, was the propaganda dropped by American planes. . . . . Despite orders the soldiers continued to obtain the papers. Many sent them home to their families.[22]

GERMAN EFFORTS AT COUNTER-PROPAGANDA

From the very beginning of the war, Germany, like all of the warring nations, conducted a campaign of patriotic propaganda at home to keep up the morale of the German people and the troops. This work had been put into the hands of the Kriegspresseamt, which had also the task of issuing war news to the German press. This double duty resulted in a failure to organize an effective propaganda system in the Fatherland, since the Kriegspresseamt concentrated its efforts mainly on the war news. This deficiency was not noticed during the first few years of the war, but when the Allied organizations began to hammer at the German front with *Flugblätter* the Germans became aware of their weakness. Even then the military leaders failed to act, since the majority of these leaders did not understand the psychology of the war.[23] As for the Minister of War, he was a soldier with military duties and therefore more interested in the conduct of the war from a military standpoint than from a morale standpoint.[24]

By the spring of 1917, however, even the War Minister had come to recognize the need for greater attention to counter-

[22] Heber Blankenhorn, "War of Morale," *Harpers' Magazine,* CXXXIX (1919), 524.

[23] Matthias Erzberger, *Erlebnisse im Weltkrieg* (Stuttgart and Berlin, 1919), p. 7.

[24] General der Artillerie z.D. von Stein, *Erlebnisse und Betrachtungen aus der Zeit des Weltkrieges,* p. 102; hereafter cited as *Erlebnisse und Betrachtungen.*

propaganda. In the latter part of May he called a meeting in which the Imperial Chancellor, the Secretary for Foreign Affairs, the Minister of the Interior, the Prussian Minister of the Interior, the Minister of Education, and a number of military officials took part. The confidential report of this meeting, issued by the War Ministry, throws some light on the propaganda activities of the Allies:

Z No. 4240/17. g. A. 1
WAR MINISTRY
Strictly Confidential

Report of the sitting of 25 May 1917 regarding the enemy anti-Monarchistic activities and discussion of steps to be taken. . . . .

The enemy endeavors to bring about anti-monarchical feeling among the fighting forces and the people have taken on a wider field recently and are supported by highly suspicious material spread in a most vigorous manner. For the most part the enemy is concentrating on leaflets in word and picture, which are being dropped from the air, or come in from the outside and are disseminated here. It is high time that this strong undermining work of the enemy be countered with similar propaganda in even more active manner.[25]

Then follows a discussion of the steps to be taken to fight the demoralizing activities of the Allied propagandists. In the Foreign Office there was to be set up a central agency for the collection of propaganda, and close co-operation between this and the press was to be established. Important people were to be enlisted to write articles for the press, or to give speeches in towns and villages all over Germany to combat enemy propaganda and harmful rumors. The government was to adopt a stronger internal policy. "Strong opposition to all propagandists —even Deputies—is in order." The churches, the schools, and the Military Hospitals were to be used as agencies for "enlightenment." Teachers and wounded officers were to conduct lectures on patriotic subjects in an effort to raise the morale of the mass of the people and the soldiers behind the front.

The co-operation of women was requested, and women's

[25] *U.D.Z.*, V, 180, Anlage XIII.

organizations were to sponsor patriotic meetings and lectures based on material sent by the Kriegspresseamt. The Kaiser was to be placed more in the public eye than heretofore. To gain the loyalty of the people he was to make more trips to the smaller towns and villages. He was especially asked to show his interest in the working people by visiting factories and working quarters. The press was to convey, in word and pictures, details of the Kaiser's activities, so that the people could see how hard their ruler was working for the welfare of his people. The Emperor was also to be given the credit for all governmental measures aimed at alleviating the food situation. The final point in the report dealt with the necessity of providing ready money for this internal propaganda.[26]

The Army officials also took steps to raise the morale of the men at the front. In a Memorandum drawn up and submitted by General Ludendorff to the Chief of the General Staff of the Field Army, under date of July 29, 1917, we read:

> Everything which is likely to prejudice the morale of the troops, e.g., leaflets sent down from the air by the enemy or sent out from home must be kept at a distance.[27]

By September 15, 1917, the "Vaterlandischen Unterricht unter den Truppen" was set up. With this it was hoped to raise the morale of the German soldiers. "Three years of the war," said the statement of purpose, "have naturally tired the soldiers and made them long for home, family, vocation. The more these desires press upon the troops the more it behooves us to impress upon them the realization of their duty and bring them to a stronger resolve to continue the fight."[28]

[26] See *U.D.Z.*, V, 130, Anlage XIII, for the complete report.

[27] General Erich von Ludendorff, *The General Staff and Its Problems: The History of the Relations between the High Command and the German Imperial Government as Revealed by Official Documents,* 2 vols., translated by F. A. Holt, O.B.E. (New York, 1920), II, 388.

[28] Walter Nicolai, *Nachrichtendienst Presse und Volksstimmung im Weltkrieg* (Berlin, 1920), pp. 119 ff.; hereafter cited as *Nachrichtendienst Presse und Volksstimmung.*

The Army High Command was to see to it that patriotic instruction took place among the troops, the method by which this was to be done being left for military leaders to decide.[29] The High Command asked for the co-operation of all officers. The needs of the troops and their thought and action were to be studied, and the necessary tact was to be used to impart the patriotic instruction to the greatest possible advantage. The officers were to keep from the troops all incendiary material such as enemy leaflets, and were to bend every effort to strengthen the will to victory among their men. The instructions continued:

> It is important to find out which problems are disturbing the troops, and to fit the instructions to the needs. The following are valuable in this instruction:
>
> *a*) Correspondence of the Kriegspresseamt.
> *b*) Pictures and placards suited to the understanding of the men.
> *c*) Leaflets.
>
> The Kriegspresseamt will send educational material and from this the material suited to the particular needs can be selected.[30]

The patriotic instruction was to be conveyed through lectures, films, field preaching, and army newspapers. It is significant that "no discussion during the instruction is to be permitted." The points to be stressed in this work were: (1) The causes of the war, reasons Germany entered, and results, especially to the German worker, if she lost; (2) the great strength of the German military machine, the victories of the U-boats, and the work of the great munitions factories; (3) the necessity and significance of the co-operation of all classes—

[29] On July 23, 1918, the French picked up documents which gave a prospectus of the organization for patriotic instruction in the German Army. According to these documents the purpose of the instruction was to instill a uniform "patriotism in all the soldiers, to intensify their resisting power and their common will to conquer." *Summary of Information,* Second Section, General Staff, A.E.F., Vol. II, No. 137, August 16, 1918, p. 949.

[30] Walter Nicolai, *Nachrichtendienst Presse und Volksstimmung,* p. 119. See also *Summary of Information,* Vol. III, No. 228, p. 1454.

military, governmental, industrial, and commercial—and the necessity for authority on the one side and obedience on the other. Faithfulness to the Kaiser was especially to be urged.[31]

One great weakness of this attempt at patriotic instruction was that it was left in the hands of the military leaders. These were too busy with military details to bother about the Vaterlandische Unterricht.[32] To be sure, a great deal of work along the line of patriotic instruction was done; but, as one German writer expressed it, "What good would it do to try to oppose the cry of the enemy for a struggle for freedom and justice against the militarists of Europe?"[33] Furthermore, the Kriegspresseamt was not capable of enlightening and arousing the people at home. To accomplish these a Reichspresseamt would have been necessary, but such an organization was never set up by the Germans.[34]

As soon as it became known that Lord Northcliffe was to be at the head of the British section on Propaganda for Enemy Countries, the Germans became alarmed. Ludendorff wrote to the Imperial Chancellor on March 20, 1918, suggesting that Germany's loose propaganda organization be centralized and made more effective. Commenting on Lieutenant-Colonel von Haeften's suggestion, Ludendorff said, "I agree entirely with the Lieutenant-Colonel's suggestion. His proposal for the creation of a kind of Imperial Ministry of Propaganda seems to me worthy of serious consideration."[35]

No effort was made, however, to set up an organization similar to that of Northcliffe's in England. The only evidence of a more spirited campaign against the Allied propagandists was the appearance in the early part of 1918 of the *Flugblätter*

[31] Nicolai, *Nachrichtendienst Presse und Volkstimmung,* p. 121.

[32] Ludwig Lewinsohn, in the Foreword to his *Revolution an der Westfront,* says that the Vaterlandische Unterricht, "which were conducted by young officers, were laughed at."

[33] Friedrich Stieve, *Gedanken über Deutschland* (Jena, 1920), p. 109.

[34] General der Artillerie von Stein, *Erlebnisse und Betrachtungen,* p. 102.

[35] Ludendorff, *The General Staff and Its Problems,* II, 405.

der deutschen Korrespondenz.[36] These were small pamphlets dealing with various phases of German life written by university professors or specialists in a particular field of German political, social, or economic life. In the foreword to the May 1918 pamphlet Dr. Martin Hobohm says:

> This pamphlet is one of a series of pamphlets and correspondence being put out by friends of the Fatherland to bring about a healthy political understanding among the people.[37]

The military leaders took steps to combat the increasing spirit of discontent among the troops in September 1918 when they attached an Information Officer to the staff of the G.H.Q. This "Offizier-Kriegsberichterstatter" was to be the head of a press bureau which was to furnish newspapers with "authorized war stories." The aim was to interest the public in the happenings at the front, thus strengthening the bond between the country and the army, with the result that the morale of both would be raised. The soldiers and officers were to furnish the Offizier-Kriegsberichterstatter with information of interest.

> When your division, your regiment, your company, when a group of men, when a single man distinguishes himself by any remarkable action, send me a brief account of it: a sort of *"tableau d'honneur"* where each hero will be cited (surname, other names, unit, civil occupation, birthplace, and place of residence, decorations). Send me at the same time a list of newspapers, both local and regional, in which each of those whose names have been inscribed on this *"tableau d'honneur"* would like to have it appear. I will take the necessary steps to have your "homefolks," your friends and acquaintances, know what you have done. You will receive specimen copies.[38]

Another effort to combat Allied propaganda was made through the *Nachrichtenblatt der 18 Armee,* which made its appearance in September 1918. This news sheet called on the

[36] Otto Baumgarten, *Vaterlandsdienst Flugblätter der deutschen Korrespondenz,* Nr. 6, May 1918.

[37] *Ibid.*

[38] *Summary of Information,* Second Section, G.H.Q., General Staff, A.E.F., Vol. III, No. 170, September 18, 1918, p. 1121.

troops to pay no attention to the lies in the *Flugblätter* of the Allies: "The enemy is trying to drive a wedge between our forces and separate them, to call on the people to strike. Fight against these temptations."[39]

Fighting the promises that the Allies were making to the German soldiers these leaflets said:

The enemy is not promising food or peace to the Kaiser, nor to the people nor the government, but to the few soldiers in the rifle pits, and to a future state of Germany which does not exist. . . .

Read them and you will find that the enemy is farther from peace now than ever and that it is determined to destroy us. . . . Comrades, the English propaganda minister is a crafty thief and knows all tricks, and never keeps his promise.[40]

Use was also made of letters from loyal German soldiers in the campaign against the defeatist spirit within Germany. The *Kölnische Volkszeitung* for October 31, 1918, printed the following from a soldier at the front.

One wants to fly in the air when one gets the inquiry from home: "Tell me, Fritz, is it true that the soldiers do not want to advance farther?" . . . .

The talkers and faultfinders in the hinterland ought to be ashamed to think that of us.

Have we not done enough for you by protecting you for so long? I am facing the enemy for the fifth time. I was wounded four times, as were many others also. And yet you question our loyalty and our love for the Fatherland. You talkers are not deserving of our sacrifice. You are to blame if the war is lost! Just continue as you are and you will soon find out what it means to have the enemy in the land.

The writer then goes on to say that the soldiers are being told to desert. The promise that such action on the part of the soldiers will lead to their speedy return to their homes is false. "Do you know what the English did to the Boers in Africa?" If the people in Alsace or East Prussia lose their spirit, there is some reason for it, he says; but for those "in the hinterland, who have not heard the aeroplanes humming above nor the

[39] *Nachrichtenblatt der 18 Armee,* No. 1.

[40] *Ibid.,* No. 3.

sound of bursting bombs, there is no excuse. Pull yourselves together and give yourselves and us a new spirit."[41]

But all of no avail. The Allies were better propagandists. The contrast between the British and the German propagandists is stated very well by Karl von Vetter when he says:

> In these days the Briton shot not only with thousands of cannons, tens of thousands of M.C. He not only shot from hundreds of airplanes; he not only rammed with thousands of tanks against us; but he flooded us with millions of leaflets. Comrades, you know them. You remember how it would often take one's breath, when he wanted to say—had to say—"That is swindle!" Our responsible officials knew nothing of the soldier in the field, what he wanted, asked, suffered, and feared. No! They did not want to know. The English knew and told it. . . . . And then the enemy told us everything that the criminal had got us into. . . . . Election scandals, the thousands of soldiers' grievances, compensation, and the food situation, the fanatical annexation idea—all were thrown to us in the midst of the battle. How could it help but have an effect on the used-up, half-starved, troops? . . . . The G.H.Q. put a high premium for the delivery of the leaflets. It did not receive many.[42]

The 21st number of the *Nachrichtenblatt der 18 Armee* admitted defeat in the field of propaganda.

> In the sphere of leaflet propaganda the enemy has defeated us. Shooting poison darts from a secure hiding place was never a German art. We realized, however, that this struggle is a life-and-death matter, and that one has to fight the enemy with his own weapons. Yet the spirit of the enemy leaflets skulks around and refuses to be killed.[43]

This issue of the *Nachrichtenblatt* also described how the Allied leaflets "took hold" of the German troops. At first the strong person laughed at them; but later, when be began to think over the contents, the "poison" started to work slowly. As for the weak person, "his heart pounds rapidly. He is staggered, begins to question, and finally becomes faint-hearted."

[41] *Kölnische Volkszeitung,* October 31, 1918.

[42] Karl von Vetter, *Der Zusammenbruch der Westfront. Ludendorff ist schuld! Die Anklage der Feldgrauen* (Berlin, 1919), p. 8.

[43] *Nachrichtenblatt der 18 Armee,* No. 21.

Nachrichtenblatt der 18. Armee.

Nr. 1. A. H. Qu., den 17. Sept. 1918

Den Starken zur Wehr,
Den Schwachen zur Stærkung,
Den Zweiflern zur Aufklærung.

Anregungen und Mitarbeit von Allen erbeten.

Kameraden!

Wiederum ist ein Durchbruch des Feindes an deutscher Tapferkeit, Ausdauer und Hingabe zerschellt.

Wiederum ist mit Gottes Segen und selbstloser Arbeit eine Ernte glücklich unter Dach, welche die Ernæhrung in der Heimat sicherstellt.

Das Schwert des Feindes und die wirtschaftliche Absperrung haben also wiederum versagt.

Nunmehr strebt der Feind danach, mit Lüge, Verleumdung und Verdrehungen die Einheit unserer inneren Front zu durchbrechen. In Tausenden von Flugblættern, gefælschten Zeitungen, Drucksachen usw. versucht der Feind das Vertrauen zu unseren Führern zu untergraben. Er will deutsche Soldaten zum Ueberlaufen verleiten, durch die verschiedensten Machenschaften fordert er im Namen „gutgesinnter Deutscher", die im Ausland sitzen sollen zum Generalstreik auf. In bodenloser Unverschæmtheit bezeichnen Wilson, Clemenceau und Lloyd George unter anderem die Herausgabe des linken Rheinufers als Kriegsziel der Entente! Zwietracht wollen sie sæen zwischen uns selbst, zwischen uns und unseren Bundesgenossen.

Der Feind rechnet also mit Schwachheit, Verzagtheit und schlechter Gesinnung in unseren Reihen, ein Ansinnen, das jedem Deutschen in berechtigtem, stolzen Selbstbewusstsein das Blut zu Kopfe treibt aus dem Gefuehl heraus, wie gering uns der Feind der ganzen Welt gegenueber einzuschætzen wagt!

Auf zum Kampf gegen diese empœrenden Versuche! Durch wahrheitsgetreue Widerlegungen wollen wir auch dieses hinterlistige Kampfverfahren des Gegners zerschlagen!

Eine Reihe von Flugblættern wird hierzu in næchster Zeit verteilt werden. Das ist der Zweck des

Nachrichtenblattes der 18. Armee:

Den Starken zur Wehr!
Den Schwachen zur Stærkung!
Den Zweiflern zur Aufklærung!

Einsendungen mit Feldpost an A. O. K. 18, Abt. V. U.

Weitergeben von Hand zu Hand.

German Counter-Propaganda

Calling on the German troops to disregard the "lies" of the Allies this *Nachrichtenblatt* aimed to combat the propaganda of the Allies. It was distributed to the men by their officers. The men were asked to pass it on to others.

Then the second and third leaflets flutter down: "The strong becomes weak, the weak becomes feeble and broken in spirit."

> The enemy has defeated us not as man against man in the field of battle, bayonet against bayonet. No, bad contents in poor printing on poor paper has made our arm lame.[44]

The propaganda of the Allies was supreme! We need only to look at the differences in the promises of the two opposing propaganda groups to discover the reason for this. The Allies promised a just peace, bread, home, liberation of the German people from Prussian "slavery," and the destruction of military autocracy. What had the Germans to promise their people? What bright future could they hold up to their troops?

> He who promises bread, should he not find believers among the hungry? He who promises peace should he not find believers?[45]

DESERTIONS AMONG THE TROOPS

Much of the propaganda of the Allies was intended to encourage desertions from the ranks. The German soldiers were informed not only that they would be well treated if they surrendered to the Allies but that by such action they would hasten the end of the war and the establishment of a republic in Germany. Furthermore, the mass of troops were told to turn their guns on their officers and thus free themselves from Prussian militarism. The officers were accused of keeping plenty of food for themselves and forcing the men to suffer hunger and privation. The soldiers were told that the odds were against them, that their cause was hopeless. Add to all this the news of the conditions at home where the wives, children, and parents were suffering untold hardships, and you have enough cause for discontent in any army. As General von Hindenburg said:

> Dangers and work in the field, complaints from home, were demoralizing to the troops, especially when they could see no end to it. The enemy said in his innumerable leaflets that he did not mean to be

[44] *Ibid.*

[45] *Nachrichtenblatt der 18 Armee,* No. 21.

harsh with us, that we should only be patient and renounce all that we have conquered, then all would be well. We could then again live in peace. New men and a new government would provide for peace within Germany. Further struggle and efforts were useless.

Such the soldiers read and discussed. The soldiers thought surely these could not all be lies, and permitted themselves to be poisoned and poisoned others.[46]

A decline in discipline among the troops was noted as early as August 1917, and from then it grew more and more serious. On June 13, 1918, a transport in Limberg had the following inscriptions:

Wir kämpfen nicht für Deutschlands Ehr'
Wir kämpfen für die Millionäre.[47]

After the retreat of the Marne in July 1918, Hindenburg and Ludendorff met with the Kaiser to discuss the situation. Ludendorff opened the conversation by admitting a great defeat and stated that the war spirit of a number of the divisions left much to be desired. He related that an attacking division of troops, while coming back from the front, were called "strike-breakers" and "war-prolongers."[48]

Official reports from the front also revealed the spirit among the troops. One of these, in telling about the defeat of August 1918, states:

41st. Inf. Div. Div. S.T. Qu.
den 14 Aug. 1918

DIVISIONAL ORDER

. . . . Many troops of the division however, did not fulfill their duty. All those who did not go to the front when the enemy no longer pressed them, those who, instead of looking for and holding the front line, made the front free for the enemy, and sought for . . . . some safe place, have shamefully violated their oath to defend the flag. . . . .

[46] Generalfeldmarschal von Hindenburg, *Aus meinem Leben* (Leipzig, 1920), p. 360.

[47] *U.D.Z.*, VI, 15.

[48] Alfred Niemann, *Revolution von Oben, Umsturz von Unden* (Berlin, 1927), p. 87.

But those who threw away their weapons in order to get away sooner, and not be led into the battle again, acted traitorously and absolutely without honor. . . . .

GEN. (NAME)
General-Major and Division Commander[49]

In General von Kuhl's Report to the *Untersuchungsausschusses* we read about "desertions en masse, countless hordes of men on furlough who returned to the front either very late or not at all," and the "voluntary surrender to the enemy of entire battalions and divisions."[50] And in the *Kölnische Volkszeitung* we read that in the spring of 1918 "it came to the point where many soldiers deserted from the front. This took such a great hold upon the men that a field court-martial had to be instituted."[51]

No accurate figures on the number of German soldiers who deserted to the Allies are available. The number is variously estimated at from 40,000 to 50,000. This may be too high and it may be too low. The Allied propagandists, of course, felt that they caused deserters to come over to the Allies in great numbers. Lieutenant C. H. Ball, for example, says:

. . . . Many a prisoner was brought in with a well-thumbed copy of a booklet which had been printed on the American side and presented to the Boches for "educational purposes." Toward the end of the war the number of prisoners thus equipped with reading matter grew so rapidly as to create a serious housing problem.[52]

The only record of desertions that we have is the record of those who deserted to Holland during the last two months of the war. According to a communication of the Institute Intermédiaire International there were, after the institution of the "Fremdenamt" on September 16, 1918, 4,009 German deserters registered in Holland.[53] If one allowed the same number for

[49] The complete report is printed in Philipp Scheidemann, *Der Zusammenbruch* (Berlin, 1921), pp. 185–86.

[50] *U.D.Z.*, III, 212; also Lutz, *The Causes of the German Collapse*, p. 85.

[51] *Kölnische Volkszeitung*, February 3, 1919.

[52] *New York Times*, April 20, 1919, Section 7, p. 4.

[53] *U.D.Z.*, VI, 171.

Switzerland and the Scandinavian countries, and then added a graduated percentage of the total thus obtained for deserters before September 16, 1918, and another percentage for desertions to the Allies, the total would probably run higher than 40,000.

The German High Command was feeling the effects of the loss of troops. On June 23, 1918, General Ludendorff issued a general order as follows:

GENERAL HEADQUARTERS OF THE ARMY IN THE FIELD. IA No. 8915

DESERTIONS

1. Every man going to the enemy will be punished with death on return to Germany.
2. All his property within the country will be seized.
3. He will lose his citizenship; his next of kin will not have the right to receive an allowance.
4. If a man is suspected of having betrayed his country, if only for having been admitted into a so-called privileged camp, action will be taken against him for treason to his country.
5. It is useless to reckon on escaping the penalty by remission or by lapse of time. . . . .

(*Signed*) LUDENDORFF[54]

However, even this threat of the officials did not stop desertions. The soldiers were tired of the war. Since Germany could promise them no relief, they accepted the invitation of the Allies to desert. In the Allied prison camps they could find relief. The feeling among the troops in this regard is well expressed in a letter of a German officer when he wrote on January 23, 1918:

> There are people who would rather desert, who would rather hang themselves, than carry on another year. And these are not only the lower but the higher level of the people.[55]

LETTERS OF GERMAN SOLDIERS

Nowhere are the suffering and hardships of the war more realistically described than in the letters of the soldiers. The

[54] *Summary of Information,* A.E.F. Second Section, General Staff, Vol. II, No. 127, August 6, 1918, p. 899.

[55] *U.D.Z.,* V, 184, Anlage I.

German Michel not only was concerned over the conditions in the army but was greatly disturbed over the situation behind the front. Complaints from home came frequently in the latter part of the war, while some came as early as the summer of 1916. A letter from a German soldier, dated July 15, 1916, lamented:

> Almost all of the letters from home are filled with complaints. The wife complains that she, for instance, has to stand in the street at night to get butter. Others fear the neglect of wife and children. Comrades who have been in the Army only a short while tell of their heroic deeds when they are home on furlough. What preparations are being made to get the returning men into their occupations again? They will in many cases find their positions taken. Many fears beset them; twice I even heard the word "revolution" in this connection.[56]

In many of the letters the capitalists were attacked as the greedy ones who had brought on the war and who were prolonging it for their own good. One letter dated May 25, 1916, exclaims:

> . . . . or do we small tradesmen and middle-class people have to dig our own graves here while the large landowners and big capitalists, who are profiteering, are being relieved by substitutes, and we and our families have to go to destruction.[57]

The ever growing breach between the men and the officers is illustrated by the entry that Joseph Merk made in his diary in June 1917:

> June [1917]. Again and again the crass difference between officers and men shows itself. Most of the officers eat and drink well and work hardly any at all. Behind in the resting places they almost tread on each other's feet. The average man and the General Staff carry the burden in the war. The sentiment among all the men is worse than bad. Only the officer is the fine man; the other fellow is—a slave.[58]

On September 18, 1918, Field Marshal Duke Albrecht of Württemberg was moved to issue an army order concerning the complaints that officers were given preference over other ranks in the distribution of food and canteen supplies. Officers were ordered to take steps "to prove that this kind of talk has no

[56] *U.D.Z.*, V, 183. [57] *Ibid.*, p. 266. [58] *U.D.Z.*, V, 271.

foundation." Another object of complaint, according to this order, was that the officers sent home large quantities of food which, it was said, they obtained from canteens at the expense of the men's share:

I draw attention once more to these two points and expect the strictest check to be exercised in this respect, especially at a time when everything must be done to combat the growing discontent and lowering morale at the front and at home.[59]

Impatient over the prolonged peace negotiations at Brest-Litovsk, the German soldiers showed evidence of the influence of the Russian propaganda. S. Ludwig Schröder wrote to his parents on January 20, 1918:

The peace is still not coming. It makes no difference to any of us whether or not we get Courland, if only peace comes. . . . . I came out as a great idealist; but I am greatly disillusioned. Do not think that we are going to keep quiet about all that we have seen and experienced. Things will and must change in Germany. The Prussian officer dare not be the man in the government.[60]

And in a letter of February 1, 1918, the same writer said in part:

And when the World War is ended then will come the World Revolution. As to that there is no longer any doubt among us. You men there in Germany behind the green tables, who sit on your money bags—beware! *"Weh, wenn sich in dem Schoss der Städte der Feuerzunder still gehäuft,"* says Schiller. Yes, the barrel full to the top with powder. A spark is enough.[61]

On July 15, 1918, another soldier, Carl Lawrenz, of the Landwehr-Infantry Regiment 2131, wrote to his aunt, Frau Bündiger, in Charlottenburg:

My dear Martha writes that they want to take her cow out of her stable. If that happens the war is over for me. The officers have so many cows here in pasture that they suffer no hardship, and the officials

[59] *Summary of Information,* Second Section, General Staff, A.E.F., Vol. III, No. 219, p. 1403, November 6, 1918.

[60] *U.D.Z.,* V, 271.

[61] *Ibid.,* p. 281.

would take the bread from the tables of our family. They are starting as they did in Russia. What the paper says is right. I have recently seen many things happen as they did in Russia. Officers go on leave every 6 months while we have to wait 12 months. . . . .[62]

By the summer of 1918 many of the soldiers felt that they were at the end of their strength. "At home the discontent grows and out here one is already past the scolding stage and is still. Not a good sign!"[63] From an entry in the War Diary of Dr. Croner we get the following:

August 9, 1918. But here is an example of the absolute lack of the fighting spirit among our troops. They don't want any more. . . . . From each soldier who comes from the front one hears, "We have had enough."[64]

Almost complete submission to the will of the Allied propagandists in certain sectors of the German Army is evinced from the following letter from Lieutenant Werner Stephen, of the Reserve Infantry Regiment, No. 69, 12th Company, to Fräulein Luise Stephen:

May 15, 1918

. . . . The Entente is right when it says that our endless-suffering home-folks, our soldiers used to the last man, will have to collapse sometime. . . . .

"Believe in the victory" is the criterion for one or the other opinion. At the front hardly a man of us believes in this any longer.[65]

ARMY ORDERS DEALING WITH PROPAGANDA

In the course of 1918 the attacks on the morale of the enemy became so numerous that the military officials sought means of defense against this onslaught. Army orders were issued which instructed the men to deliver immediately all propaganda materials that they found, or suffer severe punishment. Each German soldier received three marks for the first example of a leaflet turned in and thirty pfennigs for each additional

[62] *Ibid.*, p. 298.
[63] *U.D.Z.*, V, 184.
[64] *Ibid.*, p. 299.
[65] *Ibid.*, p. 294.

piece of propaganda literature. He received five marks for delivering a book.[66]

To check the growing number of desertions the German military authorities issued "Instructions and Rules of Guidance" for the conduct of German soldiers who were taken prisoners:

> Not to be taken into the front line. To be issued to the rank and file by companies for perusal, then collected again and filed by regimental staffs for occasional re-issue and collection.
>
> For a man to allow himself to be taken prisoner by the enemy without having defended himself to the utmost is a dishonorable act equivalent to treachery.

The document then continued by telling how the German prisoners were tortured by the Allies. It warned them emphatically not to talk and give away any military secrets.[67]

That German soldiers became recruits for the Allied propagandists in the last few months of the war is shown by the army order of August 12, 1918.

> 15TH INFANTRY DIVISION
>
> On the afternoon of August 9, propaganda tracts of a seditious character, probably dropped by hostile aviators, were distributed along the road from Bac D'Arblincourt to the canal by German soldiers . . . . to passing soldiers.
>
> Everyone will be strictly warned that all tracts, whether loose leaves or packets tied up with a string, dropped by hostile aeroplanes or found, will be immediately turned over to headquarters with a statement of the place where they were picked up. It should be explained to the men, by citing the above example, how much damage they may cause by thoughtlessly distributing these tracts, and that they are liable to severe punishment.

[66] Friedrich Felger, *Was wir vom Weltkrieg nicht wissen,* p. 502. The total number of leaflets that the German soldiers delivered during the three months from May to July 1918 was as follows: in May, 84,000; in June, 120,000; in July, 300,000 (*ibid.*). In September in ten armies more than 803,760 leaflets were given up. Estimating the total for the fourteen armies on the West Front we reach the total of 1,100,000 leaflets in September 1918 alone (Thimme, *Weltkrieg ohne Waffen,* p. 50).

[67] Great Britain, *General Staff* (*Intelligence*), translation of a German document, July 1918 (SS. 737).

Every man in whose hands such a tract has been placed is in duty bound to ascertain the name and unit of the distributor and report it.[68]

General von Hutier's order of August 29, 1918, gives us an idea of the extent of Allied propaganda, and it also tells us what the Germans thought of Lord Northcliffe:

XVIIITH ARMY August 29, 1918

ARMY ORDER

The enemy begins to realize that we cannot be crushed by blockade, superiority of numbers, or force of arms. He is, therefore trying a last resort: while engaging to the utmost his military force, he is racking his imagination for ruses, trickery and other methods, of which he is the past master, to induce, in the minds of the German people a doubt in their invincibility. He has founded for this purpose a special Ministry, "The Ministry for the Destruction of German Confidence," at the head of which he has put the most thoroughgoing scoundrel [*der geriebenste Schurke*] of all the Entente, Northcliffe. . . . . The letters of German prisoners are falsified in the most outrageous manner; tracts and pamphlets are concocted to which the names of German poets, writers and statesmen are forged. . . . . His thought and aim is that these forgeries . . . . may suggest a doubt even for a moment in the minds of those who do not think for themselves and that their confidence in their leaders, in their own strength and in the inexhaustible resources of Germany may be shattered. . . . .

Explain these infamous attempts to your young and inexperienced comrades. . . . .

Pick up the leaflets and pamphlets and give them to your commanders. . . . . You will thus help the Command and you will help to hasten the hour of victory.

VON HUTIER,
Infantry General and Army Commander[69]

The Division Order of September 1, 1918, No. 9688, in compliance with Army Order, IId, Section No. 85704 (secret) of August 24, 1918, pointed out the dangers caused by the ever increasing propaganda tracts of the Allies. It gave orders for the officials to refute the propaganda. A few of the points to which the order called attention follow:

[68] *Summary of Information,* Vol. III, No. 157, September 5, 1918, p. 1054.
[69] *Ibid.,* No. 171, September 19, 1918, p. 1126.

a) In every single case it must be admitted that the authorities do not know of the presence of tracts before they have been read and the troops have assimilated them. That is why the arguments of these tracts should be refuted by us by facts and persuasion.

b) Each officer may find himself under the necessity of refuting these tracts as is set forth in (*a*) and should be capable of so doing, relying in the main on facts as they exist. . . .

c) Explanation and reaction must be rapid. Chiefs of regiments and separate units are held responsible that they combat without delay and by every means the errors and sentiments which enemy tracts have instilled in the troops.

d) A man of a unit of the 239th Division recently found in a copy of the *Cologne Gazette,* which he had bought, a seditious tract. Another one of exactly the same nature which must surely have come from another newspaper was found in a camp at Kairschesch. . . . It has not been determined whether these tracts came from the press of the *Cologne Gazette* itself or whether they were shipped in with the papers after their arrival in the circulating field library. . . .

Report in detail, without fail, each new case of this kind.

(*Signed*) PASCHEN[70]

Wilson's peace proposals and his Fourteen Points had a decided effect on the morale of the soldiers. An army order of September 16, 1918, instructed the officers to counteract, with every possible means, the effect of Wilson's proposals.

119TH INF. DIV. Ia/II No. 4233. SECRET

DIVISIONAL ORDER

The latest peace manifesto carries with it the great danger of weakening the fighting determination of our troops. It is now the first duty of each and every officer to counteract this pernicious result by every means possible.

It is advisable, first of all to lay down the facts of the Peace Note as briefly as possible.

In spite of this, discussion as to the note is bound to arise amongst the rank and file. This will afford the best opportunity for officers to influence their men in an unconstrained manner. It will be advisable for this purpose to secure the support of the more intelligent and reliable men. . . .

[70] *Summary of Information,* Vol. III, No. 178, September 26, 1918, p. 1156.

The men must be influenced, in a serious but kindly manner to use their weapons in order to withstand the enemy's attack. . . . . It must never be allowed to happen that strong detachments should be captured by the enemy . . . . without noise of fighting being heard. . . . .

We must shoot and we must fight; then no enemy will be able to break through and peace will be with us sooner than many think possible.

This work of instructing the men and of winning them over is now the most important duty of all officers.

(*Signed*) HAGENBERG[71]

Many other army orders were of the same tone. Always the appeal was for the troops to disregard the leaflets or for the officers to take steps to counteract them. During the months of September and October German high officials appealed directly to the people and the troops to disregard the propaganda and to keep their fighting spirit. In the *Vossische Zeitung* for September 8, 1918, Freytag-Loringhoven pleaded for a new spirit in the face of difficulties. He asked his readers to remember the spirit of the Prussian people in 1811 when they faced Napoleon, and pleaded for this same spirit to the end.[72]

On September 2, 1918, von Hindenburg issued his famous address to the German people which was printed on a large placard and posted throughout the Empire. In this he told of the attacks the enemy was making on the spirit of the German soldiers and people behind the lines.

[71] *Summary of Information,* Vol. III, No. 192, October 10, 1918, p. 1249. From an order of October 17 we learn that the Allies were making use of the radio to influence the German soldiers. "The messages," said the order, "contain unfavorable reports on our political, military, and economic situation." Immediate counteractive measures were enjoined. To this effect the following orders were issued:

"1. The receiving of German Communiqués and of German news service from now on is permitted to all Army radio stations.

"2. The receiving of communiqués, news service and propagandistic appeals of the enemy, often in German, clearly is forbidden."

Three stations only were to be allowed to receive this propaganda, and these were ordered to send it to the station commander "without allowing it to be seen by a third person" (*ibid.,* No. 226).

[72] *Vossische Zeitung,* September 8, 1918.

We are in a terrible struggle against our enemies. If numbers alone decided the war, Germany would have been defeated long since. The enemy knows, however, that Germany and her associates are not to be defeated by force of arms alone.

The enemy knows that the spirit, which prevails among our troops, is making us victorious. For that reason he has begun, besides the struggle against German military force, a struggle against the spirit of the Germans. He wants to poison the spirit of the Germans and believes that our military force will cease when the spirit is destroyed. We must not take this plan of the enemy too lightheartedly. . . . .

Therefore, German soldiers and people, if one of these poisonous pieces comes to you in the form of a leaflet, or a rumor, remember that it comes from the enemy. . . . .

Resist it, German people and soldiers!

(*Signed*) VON HINDENBURG
Generalfeldmarschal[73]

The Kaiser also sent out an appeal which was published in the 10th number of the *Nachrichtenblatt der 18 Armee:*

To the German Army and the German Navy. For months past the enemy has been storming our lines with immense efforts of strength and without any pause in the fighting. You have to endure and defy the numerically far superior enemy during weeks of struggle, often without rest. . . . .

Troops of all German tribes are doing their duty and defending the Fatherland heroically on foreign soil.

The position of my fleet, in asserting itself against the combined enemy naval forces and assisting the Army in its hard struggle of their untiring work, is a difficult one. . . . .

The hour is grave. However, in reliance on our strength and on God's gracious help, we feel ourselves strong enough to defend our beloved country.

GREAT HEADQUARTERS
October 4, 1918

WILHELM I. R.

Everyone's initiative and co-operation is being sought!

Communications via field-mail to A.O.K. 18, Division V.U.
(To be passed from hand to hand.)[74]

[73] See illustration on next page.

[74] *Nachrichtenblatt der 18 Armee,* No. 10; also Lutz, *The Fall of the German Empire,* I, 166–67.

Eine Kundgebung Hindenburgs an das deutsche Volk.

Wir stehen in schwerem Kampf mit unseren Feinden. Wenn zahlenmäßige Ueberlegenheit allein den Sieg verbürgte, läge Deutschland längst zerschmettert am Boden. Der Feind weiß aber, **daß Deutschland und seine Verbündeten mit den Waffen allein nicht zu besiegen sind.**

Der Feind weiß, daß der Geist, der unserer Truppe und unserem Volke innewohnt, uns unbesiegbar macht. Deshalb hat er neben dem Kampf gegen die deutschen Waffen den Kampf gegen den deutschen Geist aufgenommen, er will unseren Geist vergiften und glaubt, daß auch die deutschen Waffen stumpf werden, wenn der deutsche Geist zerfressen ist. Wir dürfen diesen Plan des Feindes nicht leichtnehmen.

Den Feldzug gegen unseren Geist führt der Feind mit verschiedenen Mitteln; überschüttet **unsere Front** nicht nur mit einem Trommelfeuer der Artillerie, sondern auch mit einem **Trommelfeuer von bedrucktem Papier.** Seine Flieger werfen neben Bomben, die den Leib töten, Flugblätter ab, die den Geist töten sollen. Unsere Feldgrauen lieferten an der Westfront von diesen feindlichen Flugblättern im Mai 84000, im Juni 120000 und im Juli 300000 ab. Eine gewaltige Steigerung. Im Juli 10000 Giftpfeile täglich. 10000 mal täglich der Versuch, dem Einzelnen und der Gesamtheit **den Glauben an die Gerechtigkeit unserer Sache und die Kraft und die Zuversicht zu dem Endsieg zu nehmen.** Dabei können wir damit rechnen, daß ein großer Teil der feindlichen Flugblätter von uns nicht aufgefunden wird.

Der Feind begnügt sich aber nicht nur damit, den Geist unserer Front anzugreifen. er will vor allen Dingen **auch den Geist in der Heimat vergiften.**

Er weiß, welche Quellen der Kraft für die Front in der Heimat ruhen. Seine Flugzeuge und Ballons tragen zwar die angehängten Flugschriften nicht weit in unsere Heimat; fern von ihr liegen die Linien, in denen der Feind vergebens am Waffensieg ringt. **Aber der Feind hofft, daß mancher Feldgraue das Blatt, daß so harmlos aus der Luft heruntergeflattert ist, nach Hause schickt.** Zu Hause wandert es dann von Hand zu Hand, am Biertisch wird es besprochen, in den Familien, in den Nähstuben, in den Fabriken, auf der Straße. Ahnungslos nehmen viele Tausende den Giftstoff in sich auf; Tausenden wird die Last, die der Krieg ihnen ohnehin bringt, dadurch vergrößert, **und der Wille und die Hoffnung auf den siegreichen Ausgang des Krieges genommen.**

All diese schreiben dann wieder von ihren Zweifeln an die Front, und Wilson, Lloyd George und Clemenceau reiben sich die Hände! Der Feind greift den Geist der Heimat auch sonst noch an. **Die unsinnigsten Gerüchte,** geeignet, unsere innere Widerstandskraft zu brechen, **werden in Umlauf gesetzt.** Wir stellen sie gleichzeitig in der Schweiz, in Holland und Dänemark fest. Von dort breiten sie sich wellenartig über ganz Deutschland aus. Oder aber sie tauchen gleichzeitig, in unsinnigen Einzelheiten übereinstimmend, in den entlegendsten Gegenden unserer Heimat auf, in Schlesien, Ostpreußen und im Rheinland, und nehmen von da aus ihren Weg über das übrige Heimatgebiet.

Auch dieses Gift wirkt auf Urlauber und fließt in Briefen zur Front.

Und wieder reiben sich die Feinde die Hände! Der Feind ist klug. Er weiß für jeden das Pülverchen zu mischen. Die Kämpfer an der Front lockt er. Ein Flugblatt lautet:

> „Deutsche Soldaten! Es ist eine schändliche Lüge, daß die Franzosen die deutschen Gefangenen mißhandeln. Wir sind keine Unmenschen, kommt nur getrost zu uns herüber! Hier findet ihr rücksichtsvolle Aufnahme, gute Verpflegung und friedliche Unterkunft."

Man frage hierzu die tapferen Männer, **denen es unter unsäglichen Mühen gelang, der feindlichen Gefangenschaft zu entrinnen.** Ausgeplündert bis auf das Letzte, im Drahtpferch ohne Obdach durch Hunger und Durst für verräterische Aussagen gefügig gemacht oder durch **Schläge und Bedrohung mit dem Tode** zum Verrat an den Kameraden gezwungen, auf dem Transport zur schweren Arbeit von der französischen Bevölkerung **bespien, mit Unrat beworfen: So sieht in Wahrheit das Paradies aus, das der Feind** vorgaukelt.

Auch nachgedruckte Originalbriefe von Gefangenen werden abgeworfen, in denen diese schildern, wie gut es ihnen gehe. Gottlob wird es in England und Frankreich auch noch anständige und menschliche Kommandanten von Gefangenenlagern geben; sie sind aber die Ausnahmen. Und die Briefe, die der Feind abwirft, sind nur drei verschiedene. Diese aber sendet er in vielen Tausenden von Exemplaren vervielfältigt.

Kleinmütige schüchtert der Feind ein:

„Euer Kampf ist aussichtslos. Amerika wird euch den Garaus machen. Eure U-Boote taugen nichts. Wir bauen mehr Schiffe, als sie versenken. Euer Handel ist vernichtet. Wir sperren euch nach dem Kriege die Rohstoffe ab; dann muß Deutschlands Industrie verhungern. Eure Kolonien seht ihr niemals wieder." So klingt es aus seinen Flugblättern, bald Lockung, bald Drohung.

Wie steht es in Wirklichkeit?

Wir haben im Osten den Frieden erzwungen und sind stark genug, es auch im Westen zu tun — trotz der Amerikaner. Aber stark und einig müssen wir sein!

Das ist es, wogegen der Feind mit seinen Zetteln und Gerüchten kämpft. Er will uns den Glauben und die Zuversicht, den Willen und die Kraft nehmen.

Warum sucht der Feind immer noch nach Bundesgenossen im Kampf gegen uns? Warum trachtet er die noch neutralen Völker zum Kampfe gegen uns zu pressen?

Weil wir ihm an Kraft gewachsen sind. Warum hetzt er schwarze und andere Farbige gegen deutsche Soldaten? Weil er uns vernichten will!

Wieder anderen sagt der Feind: „Ihr Deutschen, eure Regierungsform ist falsch! Kämpft gegen die Hohenzollern, gegen den Kapitalismus, helft uns — der Entente — euch eine besondere Staatsform zu geben!" Der Feind weiß genau, welche Stärke unserem Staat und unserem Kaiserreich innewohnt. Aber gerade eben deshalb bekämpft er sie.

Der Feind versucht auch, alte Wunden im deutschen Volkskörper aufzureißen. Mit seinen Flugblättern und durch Gerüchte versucht er Zwietracht und Mißtrauen unter den Bundesstaaten zu säen. Wir beschlagnahmten am Bodensee viele tausend Flugblätter, die nach Bayern geschafft werden und gegen die Norddeutschen aufreizen sollten. Was der jahrhundertelange Traum der Deutschen war und was unsere Väter uns erstritten, das Deutsche Kaiserreich, wollen sie zerstören und

Deutschland zur Machtlosigkeit des 30 jährigen Krieges verurteilen.

Auch unsere Bundestreue zu unseren Verbündeten will der Feind erschüttern. Er kennt nicht deutsche Art und deutsches Manneswort. Er selbst opfert seine Verbündeten. Wer Englands Verbündeter ist, stirbt daran.

Und schließlich versendet der Feind nicht den ungefährlichsten seiner in Druckerschwärze getauchten Giftpfeile, **wenn er Aeußerungen deutscher Männer und deutscher Zeitungen abwirft.** Die Aeußerungen deutscher Zeitungen sind aus dem Zusammenhang gerissen. Bei Aeußerungen Deutscher, die wiedergegeben werden, denkt daran, daß es Verräter am Vaterlande zu jeder Zeit gegeben hat, bewußte und unbewußte. Meist sitzen sie im neutralen Ausland, um nicht unseren Kampf und unsere Entbehrungen teilen zu müssen oder als Hochverräter gerichtet zu werden. Auch die Verfechter extremer Parteirichtungen dürfen nicht den Anspruch erheben, für die Allgemeinheit des deutschen Volkes zu sprechen.

Es ist unsere Stärke, aber auch unsere Schwäche, daß wir auch im Kriege jede Meinung ungehindert zu Worte kommen lassen. Wir dulden bisher auch den Abdruck der feindlichen Heeresberichte und der Reden der feindlichen Staatsmänner, die mit Angriffswaffen gegen den Geist des deutschen Heeres und Volkes sind, in unseren Zeitungen. Dies ist Stärke, weil es Kraftbewußtsein beweist. Es ist aber eine Schwäche, weil es duldet, daß des Feindes Gift bei uns Eingang findet.

Darum, deutsches Heer und deutsche Heimat: **Wenn dir einer dieser ausgeworfenen Giftbrocken in Form eines Flugblattes oder eines Gerüchtes** vor die Augen oder die **Ohren kommt,** so denke daran, daß er **vom Feinde stammt.** Denke daran, daß vom Feinde nichts kommt, was Deutschland frommt. Das muß sich jeder sagen, gleichgültig, welchem Stande oder welcher Partei er angehört. Triffst du einen, der zwar dem Namen und der Abstammung nach deutsch ist, der aber seinem Wesen nach im Feindeslager steht, so halte ihn dir fern und verachte ihn. Stelle ihn öffentlich an den Pranger, damit auch jeder andere wahre Deutsche ihn verachte.

Wehre dich, deutsches Heer und deutsche Heimat!

Großes Hauptquartier, 2. September 1918.

von Hindenburg

Generalfeldmarschall.

A MESSAGE FROM HINDENBURG

This message of September 2, 1918, was posted throughout Germany. The Fieldmarshal appeals to the German people to remain loyal and to pay no attention to the propaganda of the enemy and the revolutionists within Germany.

But neither Hindenburg's nor the Kaiser's appeals were heeded in some quarters. The *Leipziger Volkszeitung* gives us an idea of how they were received when it says in the issue of November 2, 1918:

> For the Crown of Wilhelm II; to uphold the military apparatus and the power of Hindenburg the people are being goaded on to continue the fight. No more war! Immediate peace! Full political freedom! Down with militarism! . . . . Long live the Socialist Republic![75]

The people behind the lines and the soldiers had been "swamped by enemy propaganda."[76] The morale of the troops had dropped to the lowest possible level. Ludendorff wired to Berlin to request an immediate armistice of the Allies. On October 3 Hindenburg and a major of the General Staff appeared before Prince Max of Baden and told of the precarious condition of the Army. Von Kühlman recognized the impossibility of a victory for Germany in view of the state of mind of the army and the home front. Germany had been "hypnotized by the enemy propaganda as a rabbit is by a snake."[77]

Thus, even though, as the French Deputy Favry stated in the French Chamber on February 25, 1920, the Allies "saw the German army, at the end of the war, as well equipped as is possible," there was something lacking. He explains what that something was when he says that the German Army "did not have behind it the support of the home front and the will of everyone to give the sacrifices necessary for war, and to continue the war. It has been demonstrated by this war that a strong army is doomed to failure if it does not have behind it the whole-hearted support of the people."[78]

[75] *Leipziger Volkszeitung,* November 2, 1918.

[76] Ludendorff, *My War Memories,* II, 642.

[77] *Ibid.,* I, 361.

[78] France, Assemblée Nationale, *Annales de la Chambre des Députés,* Débats parlementaires, Session ordinaire de 1920 (Paris, 1920), Tome I, p. 235.

CONCLUSION

> The highest aim of enemy propaganda—the revolutionizing of Germany—has come to pass.—MAX SCHWARTE, *Der Grosse Krieg,* III, 494

An accurate estimate of the relative importance of the part played by propaganda in bringing about the collapse of the German Empire is impossible. It is impossible to give the exact percentages of victory due to any arm of the service. Who would say, for instance, that to the air service should be given 42 per cent of the credit for Germany's defeat and to the artillery 30 per cent? Or who would even venture to apportion the credit between the different Allied armies? How much more difficult it is then to weigh imponderables—states of army morale and the ideas which influence them! As between the effects of leaflets and shells it must be remembered that shell-fire worked in plainer view, and that it is difficult to put a yardstick to results produced by leaflets picked up unobserved, pondered unobserved, and, even when acted upon, probably denied by the German who surrendered.

We have seen throughout this study, and particularly in the last chapter, the important part that propaganda played in the war against Germany. We have seen how it reached the soldiers in the trenches and the people behind the lines. We have seen how it educated them to the war aims of the Allies and showed them weaknesses of the German forces in comparison with the Allied strength. We have seen further how the propaganda aimed to destroy the hope of a German victory and how it sought to give the enemy a new hope of a "better life," and how finally the "paper bullets" encouraged them to overthrow their government, rid themselves of the militarists and Junkers, and thereby bring Germany back into the society of nations.

Allied propaganda, therefore, sought to work not only negatively but positively as well. It not only aimed at the destruction of the Empire but also gave promise of a new nation and a new day. It sought to awaken a new spirit of freedom and a new nationalism in the hearts of the German people. While attacking the autocratic system, it praised democracy and showed the superiority of a democratic government over an autocratic government. And, finally, it set a premium upon the overthrow of the Hohenzollern dynasty in the form of promises of mild peace terms and aid in restoring the economic life of the new Germany.

These promises could not help but have an effect upon a war-weary German people and the battle-scarred German troops. In the army the effect was shown by the decline in discipline directly traceable to propaganda. General Marwitz stated in in an army order in June 1918: "The discipline, which is the keystone of our army is seriously shaken."[1] The Second Guard Division, which was one of the best divisions in the German army, "lost over 1450 prisoners in the fighting near Péronne in August." The prisoners of this division taken near Epéhy even exhibited "every sign of pleasure at being captured. Each fresh batch of prisoners brought into the cage was greeted with delight at our success."[2]

Behind the lines among the German people the effect was shown by bitterness and despondency that were all too prevalent during the last few months of the war. Siegfried Heckscher, head of the publicity department of the Hamburg-America Lines and a member of the Reichstag, summarized this feeling when he wrote in the *Vossische Zeitung* on July 7, 1918:

> Hundreds of thousands of Germans, when they have read a pronouncement by the President of the United States, ask themselves in despondency and bitterness what the German government says. So

[1] Great Britain, *General Staff* (*Intelligence*), General Headquarters, June 1918 (SS. 753).

[2] Great Britain, *General Staff* (*Intelligence*), General Headquarters, September 1918 (SS. 753).

there is formed a cloud of discontent and dull doubt which, in a great part, thanks to this Northcliffe propaganda, spreads itself more and more over the German people. . . . .

We try to shut our country off from the enemy espionage and from the work of agents and rascals but with open eyes we leave it defenseless while a stream of poisonous speeches pours over our people. . . . .

I repeat today what I have said for years, that Reuter and the English news propaganda are mightier than the English fleet and more dangerous than the English army.[3]

However, it must be remembered that propaganda was only one of the many weapons used in the war to combat the enemy and that it could not have been successful without the aid of the military forces and the conditions within Germany. After all, the odds were against Germany. The British blockade had such an effect upon Germany that by the spring of 1918 many people were actually on the verge of starvation.[4] This situation reacted unfavorably upon the spirit of the people, for empty or unsatisfied stomachs prejudice all higher impulses and tend to make people indifferent. As one German authority expressed it: "The people lived not only bodily but spiritually from hand to mouth."[5]

The German soldier lived under a continual strain, for he was facing great difficulties. He groped for a last straw. This last straw, this last ray of hope, was given him by the propagandists.

Without the British blockade and the help of America the propagandists would have made little headway in their attacks upon the morale of the enemy. America, by her entrance into the war, opened up new resources and gave a new spirit to the Allies, while the blockade was paralyzing the material resources of Germany and having a depressing effect upon the spirit of her people. "Dark tidings flowed in upon Great Headquarters"; and, as Winston Churchill expressed it,

The German nation had begun to despair and the soldiers became conscious of their mood. Ugly incidents occurred. Desertions increased,

[3] *Vossische Zeitung,* July 7, 1918. [4] *U.D.Z.,* I, 340. [5] *Ibid.,* VI, 49.

and the leave men were reluctant to return. The German prisoners liberated from Russia by the Treaty of Brest-Litovsk returned infected with the Lenin virus. In large number they refused to go again to the front. A campaign of unmerited reproach was set on foot against the German officer class. Their painstaking and thorough routine which had enabled them on all fronts to exact two Ally lives for every German, was no protection from the charge that they did not share the privations of the troops.[6]

Lieutenant General Altrock describes the situation in the following words:

> Our people gave the best. It struggled and suffered, hungered and bled, until finally the ground was prepared for the propagandists of the enemy, in union with the enemies within our country who were desirous of our downfall, to accomplish their end.[7]

Perhaps the best picture of the gradual disappearance of the morale of the German troops is given by L. G. Knesebeck, when he says that in the first year of the war the soldiers spoke of "death in the field of honor"; in the second year they spoke of "giving our lives for the Fatherland"; in the third year they spoke of "falling in a foreign land in the fulfillment of our duty"; and in the fourth year they spoke of "dying as a further offering to this terrible war."[8]

Thus it cannot be denied that the propaganda of the Allies was effective. Allied authorities were generally agreed that, sooner or later, Germany would be defeated; but even the most authoritative people thought that this defeat could not be accomplished before August 1919. Thus propaganda probably helped to hasten the end of the war. Speaking of this fact the London *Times* stated:

> Good propaganda probably saved a year of war, and this meant the saving of thousands of millions of money and probably at least a million lives.[9]

[6] Winston Churchill, *The World Crisis 1916–1918* (New York, 1927), II, 218.

[7] Lieutenant General von Altrock, *Deutschlands Niederbruch,* p. 18.

[8] L. G. Knesebeck, *Die Wahrheit über den Propaganda Feldzug und Deutschlands Zusammenbruch* (Munich, 1927), p. 117.

[9] *The Times* (London), October 31, 1918.

On November 10, 1918, the day before the Armistice, Lord Northcliffe was entertained in Paris at a *déjeuner d'honneur* by the *Continental Daily Mail.* In the course of his speech on the war situation he summarized the work of the propagandists as follows:

> We have conducted our propaganda through many channels and in increasing volume, and our leaflets and other publications have amounted to many millions of copies every week.
>
> If we have to some extent hastened the end, it is due to the fact that we are a company of experts and enthusiasts, and from the outset there has been a concentration of purpose born of complete unity. . . . .
>
> Ours has been a bloodless campaign and a costless one. I wish that we had embarked upon it at an earlier stage of the war.[10]

Dr. Philipp stated before the Committee of Inquiry that, while it was difficult to measure the influence of enemy propaganda, "I do not believe that without its successful help the German downfall could have succeeded as it did."[11]

When, therefore, all allowances have been made and all extravagant estimates pared to the bone, "the fact remains, propaganda is one of the most powerful instrumentalities in the modern world."[12] And, as history has shown, the highest aim of enemy propaganda—the revolutionizing of Germany—came to pass.

Thus, propaganda was an important instrument of warfare during the world conflict, and without a study of the part it played no historian can come to a real conclusion as to the causes of the collapse of the German Empire in 1918.

[10] *Ibid.,* November 11, 1918.

[11] *U.D.Z.,* V, 167.

[12] Harold D. Lasswell, *Propaganda Technique in the World War,* p. 220.

BIBLIOGRAPHY

GOVERNMENT DOCUMENTS

FRANCE

ASSEMBLÉE NATIONALE. *Annales de la Chambre des Députés.* Sessions ordinaires et extraordinaires de 1914. Tome II. Paris, 1915.

ASSEMBLÉE NATIONALE. *Annales de la Chambre des Députés.* Session ordinaire de 1920. Tome I. Paris, 1920.

ASSEMBLÉE NATIONALE. *Annales de la Chambre des Députés. Documents parlementaires.* Tome LXXXXI, Session ordinaire de 1917. Deuxième partie. Paris, 1918.

MINISTÈRE DE LA GUERRE ET DES AFFAIRES ÉTRANGÈRES. *Bulletin quotidien de la presse Étrangère,* 1917–1918.

GERMANY

Deutsche National Versammlung, Stenographisches Bericht 15 Sitzung, Februar 1919.

REICHSTAG. *Verhandlungen des Reichstags,* Band 313.

REICHSTAG. *Untersuchungsausschuss über die Weltkriegsverantwortlichkeit. 4. Unterausschuss, Die Ursachen des deutschen Zusammenbruches im Jahre 1918.* . . . . Dr. Albrecht Philipp. Berlin, 1925–1929. 12 vols. in 15.

BAYERN. *Verhandlungen der Kammer der abgeordneten des Bayerischen Landtags,* XII Band 242.

Preliminary History of the Armstice; Official documents, published by the German National Chancellery by order of the Ministry of State. Translated by the Carnegie Endowment for International Peace, Division of International Law. New York, etc., 1924.

GREAT BRITAIN

HANSARD. *Parliamentary Debates,* 5th Series, CIII.

————. *Parliamentary Debates,* 5th Series, CIV.

————. *Parliamentary Debates,* 5th Series, CIX.

Parliamentary Papers, 1919, XXX, "The War Cabinet Report of the Year 1918." London, 1919.

Parliamentary Papers, 1918, IV, "Sixth Report of the Select Committee on National Expenditures." London, 1918.

Report of the Central Committee for National Patriotic Organizations. London, 1916.

GREAT BRITAIN. *General Staff,* War Office.

Daily Review of the Foreign Press, series 2, March 1916 to August 1919. London, 1916–1919.

Supplement to the Daily Review of the Foreign Press, May 1916 to August 1917. London, 1916–1917.

Confidential Supplement to the Daily Review of the Foreign Press. London, 1916–1917.

Enemy Press Supplement to the Daily Review of the Foreign Press. 6 vols. London, 1916–1919.

Daily Review of the Foreign Press, Press and Propaganda supplement. London, 1917.

Intelligence, "Change in the discipline and morale of the German Army, January to September 1918."

Intelligence, "Translation of a German Document, July 1918." (SS. 737.)

THE UNITED STATES

Complete Report of the Chairman of the Committee on Public Information. Government Printing Office, Washington, D.C., 1920.

UNITED STATES ARMY, *General Staff,* A.E.F., 1917–1920.

Histories of Two-Hundred Fifty-one Divisions of the German Army Which Participated in the War, 1914–1918, compiled from records of the Intelligence Section of the General Staff, A.E.F., at General Headquarters, Chaumont, France, 1919. Government Printing Office, Washington, D.C., 1920.

Press Review, Second Section, General Staff, General Headquarters, A.E.F., December 1917 to June 1919. Nos. 1–477. n.p. Printed by the 29th Engineers, 1917–1919.

Summary of Air Information, Second Section, General Staff, General Headquarters, A.E.F., March–May and October–November 1918. Chaumont (?), 1918.

Summary of Information, Second Section, General Staff, General Headquarters, A.E.F., October–November 1917; December 1917–January 1919. Nos. 1–250. Chaumont (?), 1917–1919.

Summary of Intelligence, Second Section, General Staff, General Headquarters, A.E.F., January–February and October–November 1918. Nos. 1–286. Chaumont (?), 1918.

PROPAGANDA MATERIALS

Air Post Leaflets. Propaganda collection in the Hoover War Library, Stanford University.

Miscellaneous Collection of Fliegerabwürfe, Hoover War Library, Stanford University.

Alliance Française, *Bulletin* (Deutsche Ausgabe), Nos. 13–75 and 77–91.

BAUDRILLART, ALFRED, ed. *The German War and Catholicism.* Published under the Distinguished Patronage of the Catholic Committee of French Propaganda. Paris, 1915.

Kaiser und Krieg oder Republik und Frieden.

SIEGER, HEINRICH. *Bayern und der Frieden, München, n.d.* in Pamphlets, *Germany Revolution,* Vol III, Bavaria.

MILITARY JOURNALS

Nachrichtenblatt der 18 Armee, Nos. 1–21 (several numbers missing).

MANUSCRIPT MATERIAL

"Herron Papers," Vol. I. Hoover War Library.

EDITED AND COLLECTED WORKS

BALL, HUGO, ed. *Almanach der Freien Zeitung 1917–1918.* Collection of the most important articles of the *Freie Zeitung.* Bern, 1918.

ELTZBACHER, PAUL, ed. *Germany's Food, Can It Last?* English version edited by S. Russell Wells, London, 1927.

GOLDER, FRANK ALFRED, ed. *Documents of Russian History 1914–1917.* Translated by E. ARONSBERG. New York and London, 1927.

LUTZ, RALPH HASWELL, ed. *The Causes of the German Collapse in 1918;* sections of the officially authorized report of the commission of the German constituent assembly and of the German Reichstag, 1919–1928, the selection and translation officially approved by the commission. Translated by W. L. CAMPBELL. Stanford University and London, 1934.

———, ed. *The Fall of the German Empire, 1914–1918.* Documents of the German Revolution. Translations by DAVID G. REMPEL and GERTRUDE RENDTORFF. 2 vols. Stanford University and London, 1932.

MEYER, ERNST, ed. *Spartakus im Kriege,* die illegalen Flugblätter des Spartakus Bundes im Kriege. Berlin, 1927.

———, ed. *Dokumente des Kommunismus,* No. 2. Spartakusbriefe, II Band.

PURLITZ, DR. FRIEDRICH, ed. *Deutscher Geschichtskalendar,* 34 Jahrgang, I Band, I hälfte, Januar–März 1918. Leipzig and Vienna, 1918.

SEYMOUR, CHARLES, ed. *The Intimate Papers of Colonel House.* Boston and New York, 1928, Vol. III.

Woodrow Wilson's State Papers and Addresses. New York, 1924.

BIOGRAPHIES AND MEMOIRS

ADLER, DR. MAX. *Karl Liebknecht und Rosa Luxemburg.* Vienna, 1919.

BAUER, MAX. *Der Grosse Krieg in Feld und Heimat;* Erinnerungen und Betrachtungen. Tubingen, Osiander, 1921.

BROWNRIGG, REAR-ADMIRAL SIR DOUGLAS, BT. *Indiscretions of the Naval Censor.* London and New York, 1920.

DENIKIN, GENERAL ANTON I. *The Russian Turmoil,* Memoirs: Military, Social and Political. London, 1922.

ERZBERGER, MATTHIAS. *Erlebnisse im Weltkrieg.* Stuttgart and Berlin, 1919.

FYFE, HAMILTON. *Northcliffe.* An intimate biography. London, 1930.

HALL, J. NORMAN, and NORDHOFF, CHARLES B. *The Lafayette Flying Corps.* 2 vols. Boston and New York, 1920.

HARTSMANN, MORITZ. *Revolutionäre Erinnerungen.* Leipzig, 1919.

HINDENBURG, GENERALFELDMARSCHAL VON. *Aus meinem Leben.* Leipzig, 1920.

KRAUSS, GENERAL D. INF. A. D. ALFRED. *Die Ursachen unserer Niederlage;* Erinnerungen und Urteile aus dem Weltkrieg. Munich, 1921.

LUDENDORFF, GENERAL ERICH. *Meine Kriegserinnerungen, 1914–1918.* Berlin, 1919.

Ludendorff, The General Staff and Its Problems. The history of the relations between the High Command and the German Imperial Government as revealed by official documents. 2 vols. Translated by F. A. HOLT, O.B.E. New York, 1920.

RHEINBABEN, BARON ROCHUS A. K. VON. *Stresemann, the Man and the Statesman.* Translated from the German by CYRUS BROOK and HANS HERZL. New York and London, 1929.

STEED, HENRY WICKHAM. *Through Thirty Years.* A personal narrative. Garden City, New York, 1921.

STEIN, GENERAL DER ARTILLERIE z.D., VON. *Erlebnisse und Betrachtungen aus der Zeit des Weltkrieges.* Berlin and Leipzig, 1919.

TUMULTY, JOSEPH P. *Woodrow Wilson as I Knew Him.* Garden City, New York, 1921.

WELLMAN, WILLIAM AUGUSTUS. *Go Get 'Em!* The true adventures of an American aviator of the Lafayette flying corps who was the only Yankee flyer fighting over General Pershing's boys of the Rainbow Division in Lorraine when they first went "over the top." Boston, 1918.

WHITEHOUSE, VIRA B. *A Year as Government Agent.* New York and London, 1920.

BOOKS

ALTROCK, WALTER FERDINAND KONSTANTIN VON. *Deutschlands Niederbruch, Ursachen und Wirkungen.* Berlin, 1919.

ANTON, REINOLD. *Aus der Lügenwerkstatt der Lügenfeldzug unserer Feinde.* Leipzig, 1916.

BECKER, DR. OTTO. *Deutschlands Zusammenbruch und Auferstehung.* Berlin, 1921.

BECKMANN, EWALD. *Der Dolchstoss Prozess in München vom 19 Oktober bis 20 November 1925.* Munich, 1925.

BERGMANN, THEODOR. *Die Kriegssammlung Theodor Bergmann in Fürth,* 1920.

BERNSTEIN, EDUARD. *Die deutsche Revolution; ihr Ursprung, ihr Verlauf und ihr Werk.* Berlin, 1921.

BLANKENHORN, HEBER. *Adventures in Propaganda.* Letters from an Intelligence Officer in France. Boston and New York, 1919.

BLÜCHER, PRINCESS EVELYN MARY VON WAHLSTALT. *An English Wife in Berlin.* London, 1921.

BOUTON, STEPHEN MILES. *And the Kaiser Abdicates.* The story of the death of the German Empire and the birth of the Republic told by an eye-witness. New Haven, Yale University Press, [etc, etc.] 1920.

BREITHAUPT, WOLFGANG. *Volksvergiftung 1914–1918.* Berlin and Leipzig, 1925.

BRUCE, STEUART E. *The War Guilt and the Peace Crimes of the Entente.* New York, 1920.

CHURCHILL, WINSTON. *The World Crisis 1916–1918.* New York, 1927. Vol. I.

CLASS, HEINRICH (EINHARD). *Das deutsche Volk im Weltkrieg.* Leipzig, 1920.

CREEL, GEORGE. *How We Advertised America.* First telling of the amazing story of the Committee on Public Information that carried the gospel of America to every corner of the globe. New York and London, 1920.

CUTLACK, FREDRIC MORLEY. *The Australian Flying Corps in the Western and Eastern Theatres of War 1914–1918.* Sidney, 1923.

DEMARTIAL, GEORGES. *La Guerre de 1914; comment on mobilisa les consciences.* Rome, Paris, [etc.], 1922.

DRAHN, ERNST, and LEONHARD, SUSANNE. *Unterirdisches Literatur im revolutionären Deutschland während des Weltkrieges.* Berlin, 1920.

ELTZBACHER, PAUL. *Die Presse als Werkzeug der auswärtigen Politik.* Jena, 1918.

ERNST, WILHELM. *Die antideutsche Propaganda durch das Schweizer Gebiet im Weltkrieg, speziell die Propaganda im Bayern.* Munich, 1933.

FELGER, FRIEDRICH, ed. *Was wir vom Weltkrieg nicht wissen.* Berlin and Leipzig, 1929.

HANSI and TONNELAT, *A Travers les lignes ennemies, Trois années d'offensive contre le moral Allemand.* Paris, 1922.

HENTIG, HANS VON. *Psychologische Strategie des grossen Krieges.* Heidelberg, 1927, Vol. IV.

Hinter der Kulissen des französischen Journalismus, von einem Pariser Chefredakteur. Berlin, 1925.

HUBER, DR. GEORGE. *Die französische Propaganda im Weltkrieg gegen Deutschland 1914 bis 1918.* Munich, 1928.

KNESEBECK, LUDOLF GOTTSCHALK VON DEM. *Die Wahrheit über den Propaganda Feldzug und Deutschlands Zusammenbruch; der Kampf der Publizistik im Weltkrieg.* Munich, 1927.

KUHL, HERMANN VON. *Enstehung, Durchführung und Zusammenbruch der Offensive von 1918.* Berlin, 1927.

LAMBACH, WALTHER. *Ursachen des Zusammenbruchs.* Hamburg, 1919.

LASSWELL, HAROLD D. *Propaganda Technique in the World War.* London and New York, 1927.

LEWINSOHN, LUDWIG. *Die Revolution an der Westfront.* Charlottenburg, 1919.

LIDDELL HART, BASIL HENRY. *The Real War 1914–1918.* London, 1930.

MOLTER, BENNETT A. *Knights of the Air.* New York and London, 1918.

MOSER, DR. OTTO VON. *Kurzen strategischen Überblick über den Weltkrieg 1914–1918.* Berlin, 1923.

MUEHLON, WILLIAM. *The Vandal of Europe.* Translated from the German by W. L. MCPHERSON. New York, 1918.

MÜHSAM, DR. KURT. *Wie wir belogen wurden.* Munich, 1918.

MÜLLER, OSCAR. *Warum musten wir nach Versailles?* Kriegspresseamt publications, No. 1.

MÜLLER, RICHARD. *Vom Kaiserreich zur Republik.* Vienna, 1924. 2 vols.

NETTER, EUGENE. *Der seelische Zusammenbruch der deutschen Kampffront.* Munich, 1925.

NICOLAI, WALTER. *Nachrichtendienst Presse und Volksstimmung.* Berlin, 1920.

———. *The German Secret Service.* Translated with an additional chapter by GEORGE RENWICK. London, 1924.

NIEMANN, ALFRED. *Revolution von Oben, Umsturz von Unden.* Berlin, 1927.

———. *Reichsniedergang.* Munich, 1919.

PIERREFEU, JEAN DE. *French Headquarters 1915–1918.* Translated from the French by MAJOR C. J. C. STREET, O.B.E., M.C. London, 1927.

POWELL, E. ALEXANDER. *The Army Behind the Army.* New York, 1919.

RECHBERG, ARNOLD VON. *Reichsniedergang.* Munich, 1919.

REED, JOHN. *Ten Days That Shook the World.* New York, 1919.

ROSENBERG, ARTHUR. *The Birth of the German Republic.* Translated from the German by IAN F. D. MORROW. London, 1931.

RUNKEL, DR. FERDINAND. *Die Deutsche Revolution.* Leipzig, 1919.

SCHEIDEMANN, PHILIPP. *Der Zusammenbruch.* Berlin, 1921.

SCHWERTFEGER, OBERST. *Ursachen des Zusammenbruchs.* Berlin, 1923.

SPAIGHT, J. M. *Air Power and War Rights.* London and New York, 1924.

STERN-RUBARTH, DR. EDGAR. *Die Propaganda als politisches Instrument.* Berlin, 1921.

STIEVE, FRIEDRICH. *Gedanken über Deutschland.* Jena, 1920.

STUART, SIR CAMPBELL. *Secrets of Crewe House.* London and New York, 1920.

THIMME, HANS. *Weltkrieg ohne Waffen.* Die Propaganda der Westmächte gegen Deutschland, ihre Wirkung und ihre Abwehr. Stuttgart and Berlin, 1932.

UNGEWITTER, RICHARD. *Deutschlands Wiedergeburt durch Blut und Eisen.* Stuttgart, 1919.

VETTER, KARL VON. *Der Zusammenbruch der Westfront. Ludendorff ist schuld! Die Anklage der Feldgrauen.* Berlin, 1919.

VIERECK, GEORGE SYLVESTER. *Spreading Germs of Hate.* New York, 1930.

WOLF, PROFESSOR DR. HEINRICH. *Angewandte Geschichte.* Band 4, *Weltgeschichte der Lüge.* Leipzig, 1925.

WRIGHT, QUINCY, ed. *Public Opinion and World Affairs.* Chicago, 1933.

WRISBERG, ERNST. *Der Weg zur Revolution 1914–1918.* Leipzig, 1921.

YOUNG, GEORGE. *The New Germany.* London, 1920.

PAMPHLETS

(No attempt is here made to list all of the pamphlet material used in this research. In order that this bibliography may not be too lengthy, only the most important pamphlets are listed.)

ADLER, VICTOR. *Die Arbeit Bewegung im Kampfe gegen den alten Klassenstaat.* Socialistische Bucherei. Heft 10. Wiener Volksbuchhandlung, 1919.

ALTROCK, GENERALLEUTNANT. *Militärische-politische Zeit und Streitfragen.* Heft 3. Berlin, 1919.

BAUDRILLART, ALFRED. *Notre propagande.* Edition Speciale de la *Revue Hebdomadaire.* Paris, 1918.

BAUMGARTEN, FRIEDRICH. *Das Landwehr-Infanterie Regiment.* Nr. 25. Erinnerungsblätter Deutsche Regimenter.

BAUMGARTEN, OTTO. *Die Schuld am deutschen Zusammenbruch.* Tagebuchblätter eines höheren preussischen Verwaltungsbeamter. Tübingen, 1918.

————. *Vaterlandsdienst Flugblätter der deutschen Korrespondenz.* Nr. 6. Flugblätter series.

BEER, DR. MAX. *Der demokratische Gedanke im Kriegführenden Deutschland.* Bern, 1918.

BINDER, H. *Was wir als Kriegsberichterstätter nicht sagen durften.* (Private print of the author.) Munich, 1919.

Der "Dolchstoss"; Warum das deutsche Heer Zusammenbruch (von einem Soldat von der Front). Berlin, 1920.

GOTHEIN, GEORG. *Warum verloren wir den Krieg?* Stuttgart and Berlin, 1919.

HAENGGI, KARL. *Die deutsche Propaganda und die Schweizer Presse.* Bern, 1918.

KANTOROWICZ, HERMANN. *Der Offiziershass im deutschen Heer.* Freiburg im Breisgau, 1919.

KOESTER, DR. ADOLF. *Fort mit der Dolchstoss Legende! Warum wir 1918 nicht weiter kämpfen konnten.* Berlin, 1922.

LEHMANN, RUSSBÜLDT. *Warum erfolgte der Zusammenbruch an der Westfront? Flugerabwürftes des bundes Neues Vaterlandes,* Nr. 3. Berlin, 1919.

Northcliffe, die Geschichte des englischen Propagandafeldzuges. Berlin, 1921.

PLENGE, JOHANN. *Durch Umsturz zum Aufbau.* Münster *i. Westf.* 1918.

RAWITZ, PROF. DR. BERHARD. *Deutschlands Zusammenbruch und Wiederaufrichtung.* Gegenwärtsfragen II Reihe. Berlin, n.d.

STADTLER, DR. E. *Der Bolshewismus und seine Überwindung*. Revolutions Streitfragen, 6 Heft, Berlin, 1919.

WERNSDORF, JULIUS. *Dies Buch gehört dem Bundesrat*. Eine Studie die "deutschen Republikaner in der Schweiz" während des Weltkrieges. Zurich, 1918.

ZIMMERMAN, BODO. *Der Zusammenbruch*. Berlin, 1919.

ZWEHL, GENERAL HANS VON. *Der Dolchstoss in den Rücken des Siegreichen Heeres*. Berlin, 1921.

MAGAZINE ARTICLES

"Allied Propaganda," *Bellman*, Vol. XXV, October 26, 1918.

ASTON, SIR GEORGE, "Propaganda and the Father of It," *Cornhill Magazine*, XXXXVIII, pp. 233–44.

"Bernstorff Explains Why Germany Lost," *Current Opinion*, LXIX, August 1920.

BLANKENHORN, HEBER, "War of Morale; How America Shelled the German Lines with Paper," *Harpers' Magazine*, CXXXIX, 1919.

CLARK, V. S., "The German Press and the War," *Historical Outlook*, Vol. X, November 1919.

CREEL, GEORGE, "America's Fight for World Opinion," *Everybody's Magazine*, Vol. XL, February 1919.

"Der Grosse Betrug," *Süddeutsche Monatshefte*, July 1921.

"Fashions in Propaganda," *New Republic*, Vol. 19, July 2, 1919.

FORD, G. STANTON, "The Committee of Public Information," *Historical Outlook*, Vol. XI, March 1920.

"Government Propaganda," *Nation*, Vol. CVIII, March 1, 1919.

"Government and Propaganda," *Nineteenth Century*, Vol. LXXXV, January 1919.

HERRICK, R., "Paper War," *Dial*, Vol. LXVI, February 8, 1919.

HILTEBRANDT, PHILIPP, "Propaganda und Kriegsziele," *Deutsche Rundschau*, Vol. CLXXVI.

IRWIN, WILL, "Age of Lies: How the Propagandists Attack the Foundation of Public Opinion," *Sunset*, XLIII, December 1919.

LAUTERPRACHT, H., "Propaganda by Governments," Transactions of *Grotius Society*, Vol. XIII.

LORINGHOVEN, FREYTAG, "Heersverfassung und Volksmoral," *Deutsche Rundschau*, Vol. CLXXIX, April 1919.

"Ludendorff Realizes Defeat in 1918," *Current History*, Vol. X, Part 2, July 1919.

LUDWIG, EMIL, "The Great Revolt at Kiel," *Living Age*, Vol. CCC, March 29, 1919.

MEINECKE, FREDERICH, "Die geschichtliche Ursachen der deutschen Revolution," *Deutsche Rundschau,* Vol. CLXXIX, May 1919.

"Moral Breakdown of Germany," *Public,* Vol. XXI, August 31, 1918.

"Our Publicity Offensive," *Literary Digest,* Vol. LX, February 8, 1919.

"Propaganda Poison," *American Law Review,* Vol. LIII, January 1919.

SLOSSON, E. E., "Propaganda and Projectiles," *Independent,* Vol. XCIII, March 30, 1918.

STREET, C. J. C., "Behind the Enemy Lines," *Cornhill Magazine,* XXXXVII (1919).

"Success of Allied Propaganda," *Literary Digest,* Vol. LIX, October 5, 1918.

Süddeutsche Monatshefte, Jahrgang 21, 1923–24 (April and May 1924).

VENCESI, ERNESTO, "The Roman Congress of Oppressed Nationalities," *New Europe,* May 2, 1918.

NEWSPAPERS

Berliner Tageblatt, 1917–1918. (Berlin).

Kölnische Volkszeitung, November 1915—November 1918. (Cologne).

Kölnische Zeitung, 1918. (Cologne).

Labor Leader, May 1918 to November 1918. (London).

The Times (London) (see index for 1917–1919).

Müncher-Augsburger Abendzeitung, September 1918. (Munich).

Norddeutsche Allgemeine Zeitung, 1918. (Berlin).

Stars and Stripes, official newspaper of the A.E.F. in France. Vols. I–II, February 8, 1918, to June 13, 1919. Paris, 1918–1919.

Vorwärts, 1917–1918. (Berlin).

Vossische Zeitung, 1918. (Berlin).

MISCELLANEOUS

Almanach Catholique française pour 1920. Pub. sous le patronage du Comité Catholique de propagande française à l'étranger. Paris, 1920.

Times History of the War. (London) Vol. XXI. "British Propaganda in Enemy Countries." Printed and published by *The Times,* London, 1920.

DEARLE, N. B. *Dictionary of Official War-Time Organizations.* London, 1928.

VIC, JEAN. *La Littérature de Guerre.* Manuel méthodique et critique des publications de langue française (Août 1914—11 Novembre 1918). Ouvrage couronné par l'Académie française. 5 vols. Paris, 1923.

APPENDIX A

LETTER from the director of the Bavarian Archives verifying the citations in Ernst, *Die antideutsche Propaganda durch das schweizer Gebiet im Weltkrieg, speziell die Propaganda in Bayern.*

22. August 1935
An Herrn GEORGE G. BRUNTZ
136 Loma Alta Ave.
Los Gatos
California, U.S.A.

Zu Ihrem Schreiben von 8. Juli 1935.
An den Generaldirektor der Staatl. Archive Bayerns.

Die gewünschte Nachprüfung der Broschüre Ernst hat ergeben, das die erwänten Zitate in den Akten des ehem. bayer. Kriegsministeriums einwandfrei belegt und wörtlich genau wiedergegeben sind.

Der Verfasser der Broschüre ist Überdies rem bayer. Kriegsarchiv als gewissenhafter Wissenschaftler wohlbekant.

J. A.
(*Signed*) SCHAD

APPENDIX B

Correspondence regarding the names of the six Swiss journalists who came to America in 1918 to view the preparations America had made for the war. The first letters to Mr. George Creel and Mrs. Vira Whitehouse are not included because they were merely letters of inquiry.

1. Reply of Mr. George Creel to the inquiry from the writer regarding the names of the Swiss journalists who, he states in his official Report of the work of the C.P.I., were brought over here for propaganda purposes.

September 23, 1935

My dear Mr. Bruntz:

I did not receive your first letter, hence my failure to answer it.

I am sorry not to be able to give you the information you request but it would require a visit to the Congressional Library, and possibly days of research, and I simply have not the time.

Mrs. Whitehouse wrote a book, and you may be able to find it in one of your libraries out there.

Sincerely,

(*Signed*) George Creel

2. Letter from Mrs. Vira B. Whitehouse in reply to one from the writer requesting the names of the six Swiss journalists who came to America under the auspices of the American C.P.I.

October 15, 1935

My dear Mr. Bruntz:

I trust that you will pardon my delay in answering yours of Sept. 30th but I have been away and very busy. It seems ridiculous that I can not tell you off hand the names of the Swiss journalists who came to the United States for the Committee of Public Information in 1918, but 17 very busy years is a long time! I am no longer young but I do not yet sit in an arm chair and think over old times.

There was, I know, a Monsieur Martin (one of the troublesome prima donnas) from the *Journal de Genève* and a Herr Oeuri or Uri from the *Basler Nachrichten.* If you should write to either one of them, if they are alive, they could tell you of the others.

You ask also what German newspapers used the stories these journalists wrote. Their own Swiss papers, of course, used their stories and they were commented upon in German papers as the Swiss neutral papers were closely studied in Germany. The office of the Committee of Public Information in Bern had of course a clipping bureau but I do not know what happened to its records. . . . . I should think all records must have been destroyed. . . . .

Yours sincerely,

(*Signed*) Vira B. Whitehouse

3. Letter sent to Herr Oeri of the *Basler Nachrichten.*

Cher Monsieur,

Je suis en train d'écrire ma dissertation pour mon doctorat à la Hoover War Library de l'Université de Stanford, et je traite le sujet "Allied Propaganda and the Collapse of the German Empire in 1918." Une partie de cette recherche concerne le travail du American Committee on Public Information. En 1918, Madame Vira Whitehouse était l'agent américaine du comité, et elle a persuadé un groupe de journalistes suisses à venir aux Etats-Unis. Elle m'avise que vous étiez un de ceux qui vinrent aux Etats-Unis pour vous rendre compte de la préparation militaire et industrielle de ce pays pour la guerre.

Madame Whitehouse ne peut me donner la liste des autres journalistes, en conséquence, je me demande si vous pourriez me la fournir. De plus, connaîtreriez-vous quelques journaux qui ont publié les comptes-rendus de ces journalistes pendant leur séjour aux Etats-Unis?

Je vous serais infiniment reconnaissant des renseignements qu'il vous sera possible de me fournir, et dans l'attente du plaisir de vous lire, je vous prie de croire, Cher Monsieur, à l'expression de mes sentiments distingués.

George G. Bruntz

P.S. Repondez en allemand si cela vous est plus facile.

4. Reply of Herr Oeri of the *Basler Nachrichten,* to the preceding.

Sehr geehrter Herr,

In Beantwortung Ihrer geschatzten Zeilen vom 8 Dezember teile ich Ihnen mit, dass die Swiss press Delegation von 1918 aus folgenden Herren bestand:

1. †Dr. Ed. Feuter, *Neue Zuricher Zeitung,* Zurich.
2. †Dr. William Martin, *Journal de Genève,* Genève.
3. J. Elie David, *Gazette de Lausanne,* Lausanne.
4. *Ernst Schurch, *Bund,* Bern.

5. *Dr. Edwin Strub, *National-Zeitung,* Basel.
6. *Dr. Albert Oeri, *Basler Nachrichten,* Basel.

Die mit † bezeichneten Herren sind unterdessen gestorben. Die mit * bezeichneten Herren haben ihre Zeitungsartikel in Broschuren zusammengefasst, die ich als Druchsache separat habe an Sie abgehen lassen. Ob Zeitungsnummern mit den Artikeln der Herren Feuter, Martin und David noch zu haben sind, weiss ich nicht. Sie erkundigen sich am besten direkt bei den betreffenden Redaktionen.

Unsere Einladung nach U.S.A. durch das Committee on Public Information des Herrn Creel hatte den Zweck, durch die Schweizerpresse, die während des Kriegs auch in Deutschland viel gelesen wurde, den Deutschen den richtigen Begriff vom Rustungs und kriegswillen der Amerikaner beizubringen, an den sie immer noch nicht recht glauben wollten. Dadurch, dass der Waffenstillstand während unserer Heimreise geschlossen wurde, viel naturlich dieser Zweck dahin. Aber für uns Alle war die Reise doch ein wichtiges Erlenis voll unvergesslicher Belehrung, und wir waren voll Dank für deren Ermoglichung.

Ich selbst bin als Gast der Carnegie-Friedensstiftung 1930 noch einmal in U.S.A. gewesen und bin damalsauch nach Californien gekommen und konnte allerdings leider während der Ferien—die Stanford Universität besuchen. Mit besonderer Bewunderung erinnere ich mich an deren Bibliothek. Meine Reise-erinnerungen von 1930 habe ich den erwahnten Heften beigelegt. . . . .

Mit vollkommener Hochachtung als Ihr ergebener.

(*Signed*) Dr. A. Oeri

APPENDIX C

CORRESPONDENCE regarding the location of the "Chart of German Civilian Morale." Major E. Alexander Powell discusses the chart in his book *The Army Behind the Army.* In an effort to locate it and to get photostat copies of it, the writer sent a letter of inquiry to Mr. Powell. The letters below are some of the replies received.

1. Letter from Major E. Alexander Powell

MAITLAND, FLORIDA
13 February 1936

MY DEAR MR. BRUNTZ:

Your letter of January 25th, addressed to me at Chevy Chase, has just overtaken me. I am sorry that it did not reach me more promptly.

I have no idea what has become of the Chart of Civilian Morale which hung on the wall of Secretary Baker's office, and I doubt if he knows either, though you might write to him at Cleveland. I think it would be better, however, to address an inquiry to General Malin Craig, Chief of the General Staff, in Washington, who will see that your letter reaches the proper hands.

Regretting that I can not help you in this matter, but wishing you all success with your thesis, I am

Very sincerely
(*Signed*) E. ALEXANDER POWELL

P. S. Mr. Baker's private secretary was Ralph Hayes, a very intelligent young man. If you can find his address in Who's Who why don't you write him?

2. Reply to a letter sent to Mr. Newton D. Baker

MY DEAR MR. BRUNTZ:

I have received your letter of January 25. I am sorry to say that I do not remember the particular chart to which Major Powell refers, but it is true that the General Staff made continuous studies both of the enemy morale and of all other information procurable about the situation in enemy countries. No doubt these studies are all in the custody of the Army War College, which is under the presidency of Colonel

W. S. Grant and is located in Washington. I would advise that you write Colonel Grant for any information you desire.

Very truly yours
(*Signed*) NEWTON D. BAKER

3. Letter from the Army War College

February 24, 1936

DEAR SIR:

I am in receipt of your letter of the 11th instant relative to a chart showing the morale of the German civilian population, said to have been kept in Secretary Baker's office during the last months of the World War.

The preparation of such a chart and the keeping of it up to date would not have devolved upon this institution, but in an effort to find out what I could about it, the office of the Chief of Staff, which would have been charged with such a function, was contacted. That office informs me that it could find no record of it, and two employees in the Secretary of War's office, who were also there during the World War, and who were in a position to have known of the chart, had there been any such, contributed the information that they never saw it. These facts coupled with Secretary Baker's statement in his letter to you that he did not recall it, lead me to believe that it never existed.

I regret my inability to give you a more satisfactory reply.

Very truly yours,
(*Signed*) W. S. GRANT
Colonel, Cavalry
Acting Commandant

4. Letter from the War Department General Staff, Military Intelligence Division

March 23, 1936

DEAR SIR:

With reference to your request of March 3, 1936, addressed to the Chief of Staff, which was referred to this Division for attention, there are enclosed photostat copies of sections of "Graph to Indicate Variations in German Morale" which evidently furnishes the information you desire.

Very truly yours,
For the A. C. of S., G-2:
(*Signed*) C. K. NULSEN,
Lieut. Colonel, General Staff,
Executive Officer, G-2

INDEX